PALESTINE MAPPED

THOMAS SUÁREZ

PALESTINE MAPPED

FROM THE RIVER TO THE SEA IN EARLY GEOGRAPHIC THOUGHT

INTERLINK FOUNDATION
In association with Interlink Publishing
Northampton, Massachusetts, USA

FIRST PUBLISHED IN 2025 BY INTERLINK FOUNDATION
IN ASSOCIATION WITH INTERLINK PUBLISHING
46 CROSBY STREET, NORTHAMPTON, MASSACHUSETTS 01060
WWW.INTERLINKFOUNDATION.ORG
WWW.INTERLINKBOOKS.COM

LIBRARY OF CONGRESS CATALOGING-IN-PUBLICATION DATA AVAILABLE
ISBN-13: 978-1-62371-615-8

PRINTED AND BOUND IN MALAYSIA
10 9 8 7 6 5 4 3 2 1

PRAISE FOR SUÁREZ'S PREVIOUS BOOKS ON THE HISTORY OF CARTOGRAPHY:

"His commitment to the study of the work of the early European cartographers of Southeast Asia is apparent everywhere, and he gives few footholds for the critics of minutiae ... this is a stimulating work ... fresh and revealing ... I thoroughly recommend it to discerning readers."
— Andrew S. Cook, India Office Records, The British Library, in *Imago Mundi* 53

"A book that is a model for the treatment of the history of the cartography of a particular region."
— Kenneth Nebenzahl, founder of cartography lecture series, Newberry Library

"Exceeded all my expectations ... a truly valuable book."
— Fred Musto, Map Librarian, Yale University

"An intriguing book ... intellectually rich, hugely informative, and lucidly written ... At last the mapping of this important and fascinating area [SE Asia] has the author and the book it deserves."
— International Map Collectors' Society Journal, Summer 2000

PRAISE FOR SUÁREZ'S PREVIOUS BOOKS ON PALESTINE:

"The book [I recommend to read about Palestine] is Thomas Suárez, *Palestine Hijacked*, a damning story, heavily documented, will be sent to oblivion, far too revealing to be tolerated."
— Noam Chomsky

"A tour de force, based on diligent archival research ... the first comprehensive and structured analysis of the violence and terror employed by the Zionist movement and later the state of Israel against the people of Palestine."
— Ilan Pappé

"[Suárez] seeks to pierce the fog of time, in which lies can become myths, the disappearance of a people can seem inevitable, and calculated crimes can look like fated tragedies—so much so that later, ongoing crimes somehow are sheltered by the past crimes."
— Steve France, *Mondoweiss*

"A unique resource ... Anyone who wants to fully fathom the history of Israel's founding needs to read this book."
—*Washington Report on Middle East Affairs*

PREVIOUS BOOKS ON THE HISTORY OF CARTOGRAPHY

- *Early Mapping of the Pacific* [Charles E. Tuttle, 2004]
- *Early Mapping of Southeast Asia* [Charles E. Tuttle, 1999]
- *Shedding the Veil: Mapping the European Discovery of America and the World* [World Scientific, 1992]

CONTRIBUTING AUTHOR

- *En el archipiélago de la Especiería. España y Molucas en los siglos XVI y XVII* [Desperta Ferro Ediciones, 2021]
- *"Cartography and the Making of the Philippines from Antiquity to Now,"* in Carlos P. Quirino's *Philippine Cartography 1320-1899 [Vibal, 2018]*
- *"Early Portuguese Mapping of Siam,"* in *500 Years of Thai-Portuguese Relations* [Thai Ministry of Foreign Affairs, 2011]
- *"Genesis of the American West: The Cortes Map," in Mapping the West: America's Westward Movement 1524-1890* [Rizzoli, 2002]

In memory of all those in Gaza who were
slaughtered, maimed, orphaned, or condemned to engineered starvation
as this book was written.

CONTENTS

FIG. 1: "A native school, Palestine". Stereograph, gelatin silver. C.H. Graves, publisher, Philadelphia, c1903. (The two images of a stereograph joined by the author into a single image.) [Library of Congress Prints and Photographs Division, LOT 13738-1, no. 94]

ACKNOWLEDGEMENTS

Four friends generously assisted in the writing of this book. Lama Alhelou helped solve a mystery requiring contact in Gaza. Richard Casten kindly read the draft with his meticulous scientist eyes and shared his suggestions for clarity and precision. Dr. Ghada Karmi was, as always, invaluable for insights and perspective. I am particularly indebted to author Rawan Yaghi who patiently translated Arabic place-names and inscriptions, some of which date back more than a millennium and were no small challenge.

Of the various institutions that preserve and make available artifacts of our collective past, I would like especially to acknowledge those who generously waived fees in consideration of the book's academic nature. This book as such would otherwise have been impossible. My great thanks to the Art Institute of Chicago; Bayerische Staatsbibliothek; Catherine Hubbard of the Bibliothèque Municipale de Rouen; Nadège Danet, Bibliothèque Nationale de France; the Bodleian Library; US Library of Congress; National Library of Finland; Huntington Library; Nasser D. Khalili Collection of Islamic Art; Trinity College, Cambridge; Ger Potze, University Library Vrije Universiteit Amsterdam; and the Walters Art Gallery. My thanks to Andrew Gaudio, Library of Congress Rare Book and Special Collections Division, who kindly photographed two details for me to accurately decipher the chronology in fig. 100.

The Madaba map, a mosaic map of the Levant that once formed the floor of a Byzantine church in Jordan, presented unique image problems. Lucinda Curzon and Shaker Khanfar, on the scene, fulfilled my request for a photograph of the entire map from above. Their visit fortuitously coincided with restoration to the church built over the map, so that the extant sections of the mosaic are exposed free of the modern floor and church furnishings, resulting in the extraordinary photograph in fig. 13. The Embassy of the Hashemite Kingdom of Jordan to the UK generously supplied the high resolution, eye-level image of the map in fig. 16.

I could not imagine a better colleague in this project than Interlink Publishing. Interlink's fearlessness, imagination, always with an eye toward the betterment of the human condition, are what publishing should be about. My great thanks to the entire staff, in particular Michel Moushabeck, Interlink founder; Harrison Williams, book design; David Klein, copy editing; Pam Fontes-May, production; Greta Morgenstern, proofreading; and Hannah Moushabeck, publicity.

My partner, Nancy Elan, was an invaluable source of critical feedback, guiding me out of impasses and on to where my thoughts logically should have known to go. My great thanks to her for helping me do the best I can.

A closing word: This book is in a sense a meeting of the twists and turns of my life. My original "life," music, plays no visible role in this book, yet it was because of music that my life broadened and that my relationship to Palestine grew from observer to active participant. Neither this book, nor my previous *Palestine Hijacked*, would otherwise exist. In the spirit of that larger debt to a life of opportunity and possibility, I want to express my gratitude to my family for their ever-constant support and wisdom: my sister Gina, my brother John, my amazing daughter Sainatee, and my parents, who taught us all to navigate an unjust world with critical eyes.

FIG. 2: The Mediterranean, northern Africa, and western Asia, from a nautical map of the world by the Genoese cartographer Nicolo di Caverio, c1506. The dominant feature is the massive vignette representing Jerusalem. The inset at the bottom is a north polar map of the world. [National Library of France; image the Library of Congress, Control Number 2021668721]

INTRODUCTION

The mapping of Palestine—the land between the Jordan River and the Mediterranean Sea—is as much about the societies doing the surveying as it is about this gem of the earth they charted. Both blessed and cursed by forming a pivotal crossroad of continents and peoples, Greek, Roman, and Arabic mapmakers all included Palestine in their world view, and the land had already been home to millennia of civilizations when it begot the Abrahamic faiths that have charted its place in the human landscape ever since.

Maps are subjective creatures. All maps are products of their makers' worldview, their assumptions, culture, and what, even subliminally, they want the map to do. There is no such animal as a "neutral" map, and examining maps' inner souls is especially important in the case of Palestine. The vast majority of surviving early maps of Palestine are of European origin, especially once we reach the age of the printed book. Yet in retrospect, throughout the centuries that European civilization has been mapping Palestine, Palestine has all the while been charting European civilization's collective unconscious.

Palestine is at the core of a schism in the West's self-identity, and its mapping of the land simultaneously reflects, and furthers, that schism. The "West" touts itself as the flagship of an enlightened, secular, law-based world order, the torch-bearer of human rights, while brutally inflicting precisely the opposite vision on Palestine. On the surface, this hardly seems remarkable—but the West's Palestine schism is not the routine hypocrisy of nations. It is not the familiar sabotaging of democracy and human rights in South America, Africa, or Asia in the pursuit of neoliberal economics, natural resources, and empire. Geopolitical interests alone do not explain the West's behavior in Palestine.

The Palestine it sees at the heart of the medieval world map does.

When those of us from a European cultural background look at medieval *mappaemundi* centered on Palestine, or the centuries of "Holy Land"-themed maps that typify European cartography of the region to this day, we see ourselves in their reflection. Throughout European scientific advancement and

FIG. 3: Genesis, from the Furtmeyr Bible, a German bible containing the Old Testament from Genesis to Ruth, by the artist Berthold Furtmeyr, 1465-1470. [Bavarian State Library; image the Library of Congress, Control Number 2021667755]

secularization of the past half millennium, Palestine has remained a place apart in the Western psyche, and thus in its maps, a realm where cultural hardwiring supersedes sextant and chronometer. Maps are an active participant in what is known in political parlance as the "Palestine exception."

That "exception" is today's determination to bring the medieval *mappamundi's* imagery to life. This obsession, with roots in the Reformation, took active form in the nineteenth century as messianic Christian groups moved to Palestine to await the return of Christ—which required the return of "the Jews" (in quotes because of the pejorative tribal connotation) as well. The Zionist movement appeared to be that "ingathering."

The early mapping of Palestine is almost entirely the mapping of outsiders, not Palestinians. There is no way to know to what extent the absence of Palestinian maps reflects the limits of any indigenous mapmaking tradition, versus maps being swallowed whole by time. Two thousand years ago, Palestine was a largely polytheist, or animist ("pagan") civilization, but it was from its Judeo-Christian civilization that the surviving early cartographic record comes. Palestine's place in the larger worldview mattered far more to outsiders—pilgrims, adventurers, merchants, would-be conquerors—than to the land's people, and navigating the internal geography of Palestine did not require maps as durable artifacts.

In describing the medieval period, I have used the terms "Latin" and "Arabic" (not "Arab") to identify the two large mapping traditions invariably referred to in the existing literature as "European" and "Islamic." Identifying one group by continent and the other by religion is more than inconsistent—it is outright ironic, because "European" mapmaking of the period typically had to do with Christianity, whereas "Islamic" mapmaking rarely had to do with Islam. Moreover, some "Islamic" mapmakers were European. The single binding element of the two traditions was language, not religion, not place.[1] However unintendedly, the traditional terms have been a gear in the subliminal "othering" of the Arabic world.

After about 1500, "Latin" loses usefulness as those mapmakers began using their vernacular, and so I turn to the convenient shorthand "Western," a term that is useful in the very way that it is problematic. The term's implied "east-west" dichotomy fairly represents that group's view of itself, a view that remains key to its geographic psychology through to the present. Similarly, I use the Eurocentric shorthand "Middle East" when appropriate.

The word "map" itself merits definition. Modern scholarship has expanded the meaning all the way to the metaphysical, but our needs are simpler: for the purposes of this book, a map is any spatial representation of geography or geographic concept, regardless of the medium in which it is executed or stored. *Mappamundi* (plural *mappaemundi*) is used to refer to early world maps not based on any projection, that is, created with no attempt to translate the sphere to a flat surface, even if its creator understood the earth to be a sphere.

Finally, the question: Why this book? What justifies writing a book on maps in a time of genocide? It is in fact my long awareness of the power of maps, both outright and, most potently, subliminal, that led to this book. At the core of the Israeli state's power is nomenclature: its self-identity as the *Israel* cited in the Biblical Genesis, placing it apart from the realm of all other earthly nations and securing wide Christian devotion. Maps, typically under the "mapping of the Holy Land" narrative, are exploited to reinforce that psychosis. This book does not seek to invert that cartographic weapon into a counternarrative, as to do so would be to remain trapped in its paradigm. Rather, this book strives simply to treat it as what it is: one particular strand in Palestine's complex cartographic history.

—Tom Suárez, June, 2025

FIG. 4: A Roman silver coin ("denarius") of 32-31 BCE, depicting a galley with rowers. [Art Institute of Chicago, 1920.743]

CHAPTER 1

ECHOES OF AN INDISTINCT PAST

Any journey back to the early mapping of Palestine begins the way it must begin for any region: with the admissions that we know nothing until very recent times in human history, that the earliest traces of cartographic thought survive only in copied and recopied form, and that what does remain is doubtfully representative. What survives is skewed by a minefield of variables: the material from which the map was made, or indeed whether it existed in physical form at all; the intention or ability of its creators to preserve it; the ravages of climate, wars, natural disaster, social upheaval, political bickering, and censorship; the need to reuse scarce media; and its destruction as part of the deliberate destruction of memory and identity—this last motive a likely, if partial, explanation for the lack of any known survivors of the many manuscript maps of Palestinian villages we know were made by Zionist scouts in the 1940s.

A map's chance of survival increased dramatically if it was part of a book, rather than a loose-sheet, and the advent of printing vastly increased the survival rate, the identical map existing in many copies. Examples of most maps that appeared in European printed books since 1472 (the first such map, fig. 23) survive, sometimes in numerous quantities. As a result, the vast majority of maps of Palestine produced in the past five hundred years were composed through a "Western" Judeo-Christian lens, and the majority a Protestant, proto-Zionist lens.

The fifteenth through eighteenth centuries will likely emerge as the golden age of map survival. The advent of wood pulp paper in the nineteenth century does not bode well for future historians studying material after about 1850, and our era may be dimmer still as we enter an age in which maps, particularly those of everyday life, typically exist in nonphysical form. Future generations will face hurdles to see our digital maps: the media must survive intact, its ones and zeros must still be readable, and a device to read them must be available, along with software that knows how to piece together its data into an image. Future historians may well know more about the fifteenth and sixteenth centuries, rich with artifacts on remarkably durable rag paper or vellum, than they do about the twenty-first century.

Posterity has been kinder to Palestine than it has to most geographic areas. By about 800 BCE, the Assyrians wrote of the *Philistia* (Philistines), a confederation extending from Gaza to Jaffa, and the well-traveled Greek historian and geographer Herodotus (ca. 484–425 BCE), a native of what is now Bodrum on the southwest coast of Asia Minor (Turkey), already leaves us reference to Palestine by its modern name. In his *Histories*, Herodotus speaks of the Scythians wanting to invade Egypt, but that

> When they had reached Palestine, the Egyptian king Psammetichus met them with gifts and prayers, and prevailed on them to advance no further.

Herodotus gives a geographical account of the tribute exacted from various regions by the Persian ruler Darius the Great (ca. 550–486 BCE), in which Palestine was in the same tax bracket as Cyprus and Phoenicia: three-hundred-and-fifty talents. Regarding its geography,

> Between Persia and Phoenicia lies a broad and ample tract of country, after which the region I am describing skirts our sea, stretching from Phoenicia along the coast of Palestine-Syria till it comes to Egypt, where it terminates.

Textual evidence suggests that Palestine would have been marked on Greek or Persian maps by Herodotus's time, but we have no sufficiently detailed descriptions of maps from the period. He speaks of a world map—"a bronze tablet, whereupon the whole circuit of the earth was engraved, with all its seas and rivers"—in the possession of Aristagoras, leader of the Ionian city of Miletus (western coast of Asia Minor) in the late-sixth-to-early-fifth century BCE. The pre-Socratic Greek philosopher Anaximander (ca. 610–ca. 546 BCE), a native of Miletus, is said by later Greek and Roman commentators to have made a world map, though only fragments of his writings survive. Similarly, in the second century BCE, Crates of Mallus is said to have made a globe sufficiently large to include a wealth of detail, and the Levant was familiar territory to all these geographers.

Another Mediterranean traveller who left record of Palestine was the Greek native of Asia Minor, Strabo (64 or 63 BCE–24 CE). In Book XVI of his *Geographia*, he writes that

> Beginning from Cilicia [southern Anatolia] and Mount Amanus [Nur Mountains], we set down as parts of Syria, Commagene, and the Seleucis of Syria, as it is called, then Cœle-Syria, lastly, on the coast, Phœnicia, and in the interior, Judæa. Some writers divide the whole of Syria into Cœlo-Syrians, Syrians, and Phœnicians, and say that there are intermixed with these four other nations, Jews, Idumæans, Gazæans, and Azotii, some of whom are husbandmen, as the Syrians and Cœlo-Syrians, and others merchants, as the Phœnicians.

The center of gravity shifted to Rome with Pomponius Mela, a native of Algeciras (near Cádiz), who in about 43 CE composed his sole surviving work, *De situ orbis libri III*. This treatise was enormously popular, and fourteen centuries later it became an early geographic work to be disseminated through the new medium of printing (Milan, 1471). Pomponius Mela expanded upon older Greek cosmological ideas of a balanced earth—southern land must exist to counter that in the north—

with the concept of an antipodes, with which contact is impossible due to a torrid equatorial ocean. Pomponius Mela introduces Palestine by first explaining that "Syria holds a broad expanse of the littoral, as well as lands that extend rather broadly into the interior, and it is designated by different names in different places."

> It is Palestine at the point where Syria abuts the Arabs, then Phoenicia, and then—where it reaches Cilicia [southeast Asia Minor]—Antiochia, which was powerful long ago and for a long time, but which was most powerful by far when Semiramis held it under her royal sway. Her works certainly have many distinctive characteristics. Two in particular stand out: Babylon was built as a city of amazing size, and the Euphrates and Tigris were diverted into once dry regions.

> In Palestine, however, is Gaza, a mighty and very well fortified city. This is why the Persians call it their treasury (and from that fact comes the name): when Cambyses headed for Egypt under arms, he had brought here both riches and the money for war. Ascalon is no less important a city. Jaffa was founded, as they tell it, before the flood, Jaffa is where the locals claim that Cepheus was king, based on the proof that particular old altars—altars with the greatest taboo—continue to bear an inscription of that man and his brother Phineus. What is more, they even point out the huge bones of the sea-monster as a clear reminder of the event celebrated in song and legend, and as a clear reminder of Andromeda, who was saved by Perseus [see p75].

Of mapmaking in Palestine at this time, we know nothing. Our cultural bias has it that "to map is human," and maybe it is to the extent that mapping in some form could be integral to society and survival, and to the extent that mapping can blur into the human instinct of art. The principal surviving early Levantine map of Palestine, the Madaba mosaic, certainly suggests a larger mapmaking tradition, as such a map did not appear in a vacuum. Yet there was no record of this monumental work until its modern discovery, demonstrating that the absence of any record of cartographic traditions of everyday life, which would have been in ephemeral media, does nothing to prove that there were no such maps.

In that purely hypothetical spirit, let's create an imaginary morning in a Palestinian household several thousand years ago. A woman instructs her son on how to visit his uncle, who has just moved to his wife's village. If the route is not complicated, she might map his way in nonphysical form: a memorized itinerary based on orientation with recognizable features and measured by time more than distance—what we'd now call "giving directions," or hearing them from our phone. Her map might have taken physical but transient form: pebbles arranged on the dirt, lines scratched onto the earth. More durable media remained short-lived: a schematic scratched with a stick onto a large leaf or piece of bark, a portable map supplanting reliance on memory.

Official, cadastral, scholarly, or commercial mapping might have benefitted from more durable media and archival intent. Egyptian influence brought papyrus to Palestine as an option for written documents, but these too rarely survived centuries of heat and moisture. The only long-lived media available to everyone was rock—and it is rock in which an early example of local Levantine mapmaking survives.

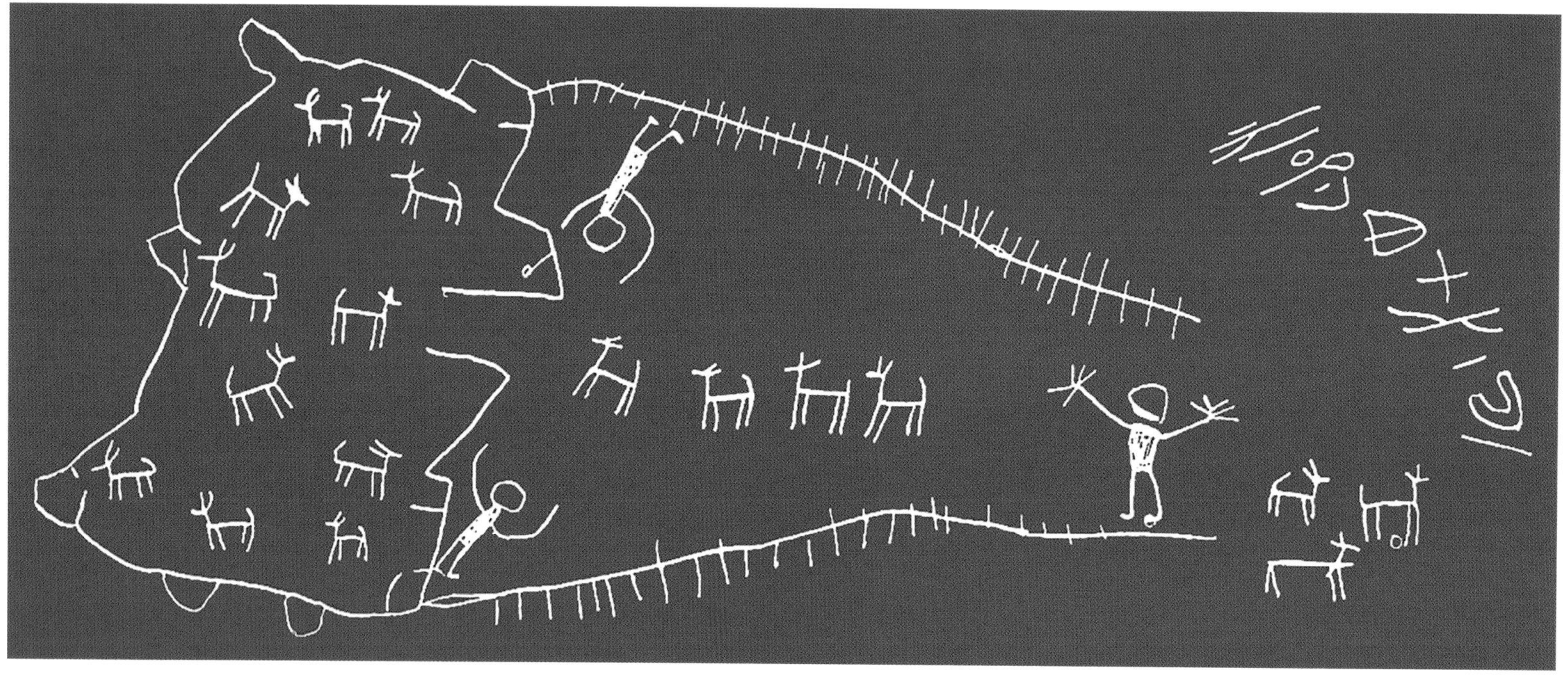

FIG 5: Drawing of a rock plan of a Levantine animal enclosure, early Christian era. [Image reworked from G. Lankester Harding, "The Cairn of Hani," *Annual of the Department of Antiquities of Jordan 2* (1953), 8–56.]

A plan of an animal enclosure of the type known as "desert kites" was discovered in the mid-twentieth century, etched on rock in Jordan (fig. 5). Dated to the early Christian era, its accompanying text is Safaitic, a Semitic script used in southern Syria and northern Jordan in the Ḥarrah region. It has been translated as:

> By Mani'at, and he built for Hani'. And he drew a picture of the pen [or enclosure] and the animals pasturing by themselves.[2]

The plan depicts animals being herded towards the enclosure by a person with arms raised. Outside the walls, a few animals appear to have escaped. To what extent the plan is typical of Levantine mapmaking at the time or earlier is unknown, but it does demonstrate the active idea of local geographic abstraction.

FIG 6: This mosaic zodiac with Greek iconography formed part of the floor of a synagogue at Hammath in the Galilee, likely dating from the third century. It was excavated in the early 1960s. The twelve signs of the zodiac surround the sun, represented by Apollo, and in the corners, imagery of the seasons. This photograph dates from before the remnants of a later structure were fully removed; the section of the mosaic under the rocks did not survive. A Palestinian tradition of zodiac mosaics continued into Byzantine times.

PALESTINE IN THE ROMAN CIRCUIT

Two fourth-century Roman maps depicting Palestine survive in medieval copies: a road map of the Roman world known as the Peutinger map, and a "dux" map of greater Palestine, showing Rome's provincial garrisons.[3] These just post-date Emperor Constantine's 313 Edict of Milan "legalizing" Christianity, and represent existing Roman mapping traditions.

A copy of c1200 of a map likely dating from 335 to 366, the Peutinger is an illustrated cartographic itinerary extending from the British Isles, Iberia, and North Africa on the west, through to the Middle East, Persia, Indian subcontinent, and Sri Lanka on the east. The map testifies to active intercourse within the vast Roman Empire, and its inclusion of Herculaneum, Oplontis, and Pompeii, as well as the exclusion of certain major roads, suggest that the lost original was itself based on an older prototype.

Now cut into sections, it was a continuous parchment scroll, long and narrow—6.75 meters by 34 centimeters—and was originally even longer, as the left-most section(s) that mapped parts of the British Isles and easternmost Iberia /northern Africa are missing.

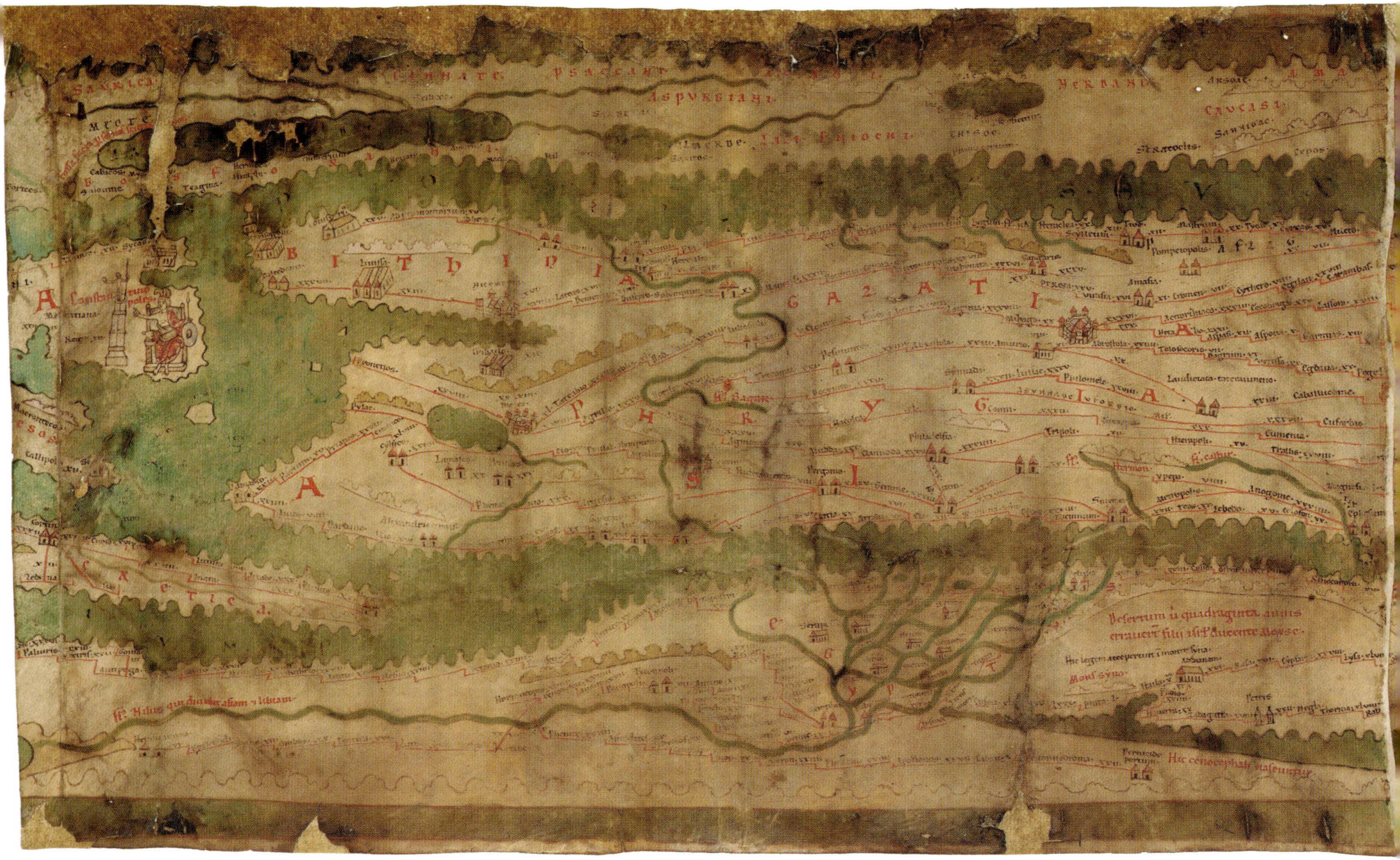

FIG 7 (top): The Peutinger map, the eleven sections into which the original scroll had been cut, here joined, plus a twelfth piece on the left (west) to account for a lost section(s) covering the British Isles and easternmost Iberia and Africa.

FIG 8 (bottom): Sections eight and nine of the Peutinger map, extending from Constantinople on the left to Antioch on the right, both represented by throned figures. Palestine is on the bottom strip of land, beginning to the right of center, at which point the map is oriented roughly west (i.e., north to the right). Note the Dead Sea just to the right of the break between the two sheets, fed by two rivers, the upper of which is the Jordan, flowing from the Sea of Galilee to the right. At the bottom, the long, narrow gulf is the Red Sea, whose small upward inlet is the Gulf of Aqaba, and the narrowing section to its left, nearly touching the Nile Delta, is the Gulf of Suez. See fig. 9 on the following page, an extract of the Ortelius engraving of the map from 1598, to see the features more clearly.

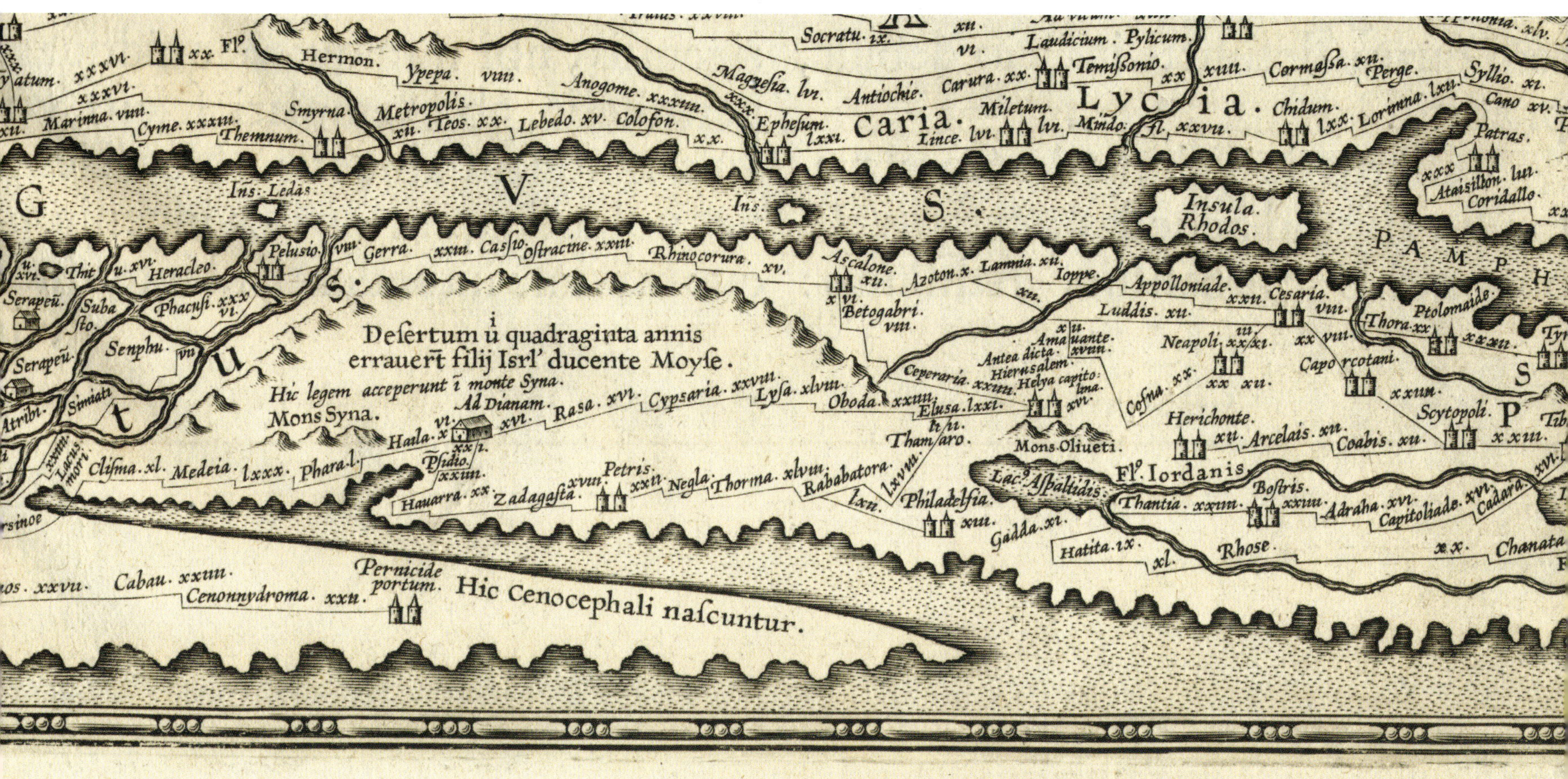

The map was discovered in 1494 in Germany by a scholar, Conrad Celtes, who bequeathed it to the antiquarian Konrad Peutinger. Its enormous significance was immediately understood, and the artifact itself became the subject of intrigue: first, rumors circulated (and remain) that Celtes had acquired it by theft, and then its whereabouts were unknown for part of the sixteenth century. It reappeared in time for the prolific Flemish mapmaker Abraham Ortelius (whom we will see again), an avid student of the history of cartography, to prepare a copper-engraved copy just before his death in 1598 (fig. 9, above).

The long, narrow scroll format had practical advantages, while sacrificing uniform scale and orientation. Geographic features are recorded when useful to its purpose: mountains, large rivers, forests, and the seas. Artificial features important to the traveler include Roman settlements and their connecting roads, staging posts (to rest, resupply, replace exhausted horses), the distances between them, and spas. Rome is represented by a throned goddess holding a lance, shield, and—symbolically—a globe. Constantinople and Antioch also merited throned figures. The unit of measure changed according to the region: most of the

FIG. 9: Sinai to Antioch, extracts of the lower part of sections six and seven (here joined) of the eight sections of Abraham Ortelius's 1598 engraved copy of the Peutinger map. The engraved copy is useful because the Peutinger itself has further deteriorated in the intervening centuries.

map is in Roman miles, while in Gaul it is in leagues, in the Persian lands parasangs, and in India what at least was understood to be Indian miles. Palestine is marked as a large region of the eastern Mediterranean.

Navigating to Palestine is the same for figs. 8 or 9, though features are easier to locate on fig 9. Italicized spellings refer to the Peutinger itself, fig. 8. Begin by finding the Nile delta, the wide river system on the lower left. Follow it to the right, through the Sinai. The first lake is the Dead Sea, with the Mount of Olives and Jerusalem (by that name and *Helya Capitolina*, the new Roman city) depicted above it, and Jericho (*Herichonte*) to the upper right. The smaller lake to the right is the Sea of Galilee, above which lie *Tyberias* (Tiberias), *Tyro* (Tyre), *Neapoli* (Nablus), and, to its left, *Luddis* (Lod). The letters *Palestina* begin to the upper left of Tiberias (on the Peutinger, in red). On the coast above lie *Ioppe* (Jaffa), *Azoton* (Ashdod), and, at the break, *Ascolone* (Ashkelon). In the lower left, Jordan: *Philadelphia* is Amman, *Gadda* is Gadara. In the Mediterranean Sea above Palestine, the small island is Rhodes, the large island Cyprus. Along the bottom is the southern tip of Sinai, with the Gulfs of Aqaba and Suez.

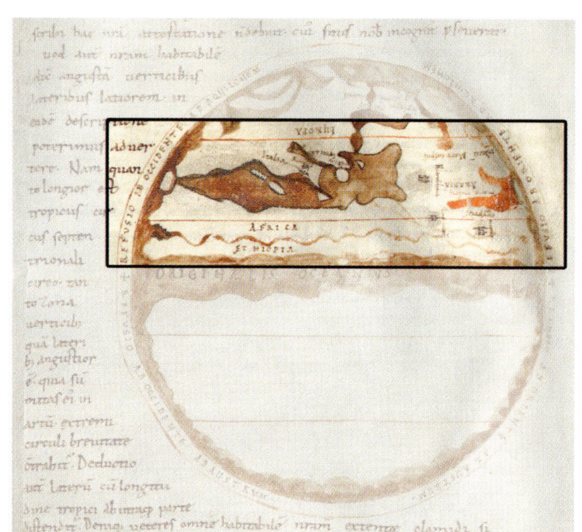

(Far right:) From the Macrobius *Dream of Scipio*, the circuits of the planets and the sun around the earth, surrounded by the zodiac.

(Right:) The Macrobius world map, with the area of the Peutinger map marked (see p25).

FIG 10: World map (north oriented) from Macrobius's Commentaries on Cicero's *Dream of Scipio*, this example ca. 1000. Crates divided the world into four roughly equal quadrants. These are separated by an equatorial ocean and a longitudinal ocean, and divided into five north-south climate zones. The equatorial ocean was believed impassable due to its extreme heat, and the subpolar zone of each quadrant was uninhabitable due to the extreme cold. [Bavarian State Library; image Library of Congress 2021668092]

If the extreme north-south compression makes the Peutinger map difficult to understand as a whole, another Roman world map from the early fifth century, typically found in manuscripts of Macrobius Ambrosius Theodosius's commentaries on Cicero's *Dream of Scipio* (51 BCE), puts it into better perspective (fig. 10).

Although the Macrobius mappamundi is a stark contrast to the Peutinger—it is rudimentary, covers the entire hemisphere, and makes no contribution to the practicalities of travel—they share a vastly truncated Africa as per common contemporary Roman thought, allowing us to see the Peutinger in context. Compare Macrobius's Africa (the landmass immediately above the equator, the midpoint) with the compressed landmass running along the bottom of the Peutinger, then stretch the Macrobius east-west, and the Peutinger will then make sense—notwithstanding that the road map had also to take exorbitant liberties with orientation.

Macrobius's work is rooted in a handful of earlier theorists, of which Crates of Mallus (ca. 168 BCE), who had been head of the library of Pergamum, is prominent. But this example of his map serves our topic as a transition from the Greco-Roman world, in which Palestine was a place as any other, to Christianized Europe: here *Hierosalema* is marked and accorded equal status with Rome.

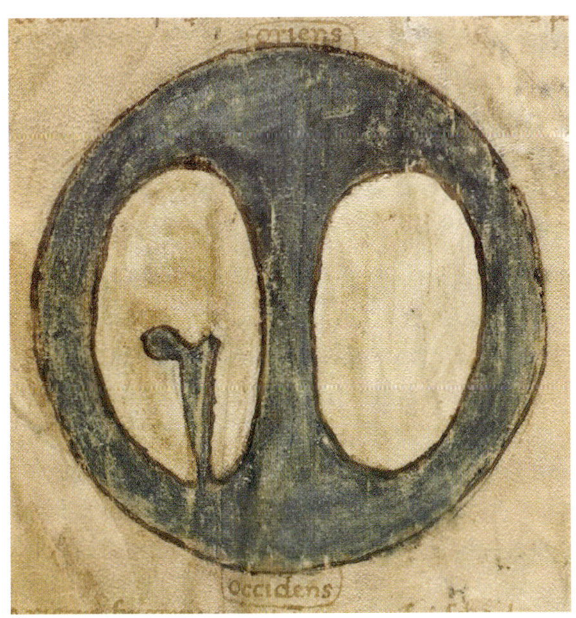

A world map in an early manuscript of Marco Polo's travels offers a variation of the same concept, a Mediterranean Sea defined on the south by a vastly truncated Africa (fig. 11). Oriented to the east, the antipodes is the right (southern) half, the known world the left. Of that known world, the entire upper half is Asia, the lower right Africa, the lower left Europe. The upper left bulge of the Mediterranean is the Black Sea, and the slight downward bulge at the top of the Mediterranean is Palestine.

FIG 11: World map from a manuscript of Marco Polo's travels, *Les voyages de Marco Polo de Venise,* ca. 1350 [National Library of Sweden, Shelfmark: M 304; Image Library of Congress]

FIG 12: *Dux Palestinae*, in *Notice des dignités*, a 15th century rendering of a fourth century Roman map. [Bibliothèque Nationale, Latin 9661]

Menoeis = Khirbet Ma'in (Hebron area)
Sabaia = vicinity of Apameia, Syria
Zodochata = Khirbet es-Sadaqa, Jordan
Hauare = Khirbet al-Khaldeh, Jordan
Robatha, Moabila = Qasr Mahalle, Jordan
Veterocania, Aila = Aqaba, Jordan
Birosaba = Beersheba
Zoara = Ghor es-Safi, south of Dead Sea
Chermula, Birsama = western Negev
Aelia = Jerusalem

(Next page) FIG 13: Mosaic map of Palestine, mid-sixth century, forming the floor of a church in Madaba, Jordan. [photo: Lucinda Curzon and Shaker Khanfar, 2025]

A map specifically of greater Palestine is among those in the Roman *Notitia Dignitatum*. Known only in medieval copies (fig. 12), it is a fourth- or fifth-century record of the provincial garrisons placed under the command of military leaders holding the title of *dux*. South is at the top. Highly stylized, the map's Jordan River boldly separates Jerusalem, Beersheba, and the western Negev from the rest on the east (left) bank.

Polytheist Rome considered Palestine to be an important part of its empire, but simply that; it did not look to Palestine as a special land on the earth, the heart of its spiritual identity. Christianized Europeans did. As the new Palestinian religion spread westward through Europe, it inspired converts to make their way eastward to what was now a holy land with holy sites. Judeo-Christianity's metaphysical linkage with Palestine was taking form.

Contemporary with these Roman maps, Saint Helena (Helena of Constantinople), the mother of Constantine I, put Christian pilgrimage to Palestine "on the map." Tradition has it that in Palestine ca. 325 she discovered the "true cross," the cross upon which Christ was crucified, solidifying not just relics but Palestine itself, as an object of veneration.

An unknown Christian pilgrim went to Palestine in 333-334 and left behind an itinerary "map" known as the *Itinerarium Burdigalense* (Bordeaux Itinerary) that survives in copies dating from ca. 800. Our unknown pilgrim recounts his journey from the city of Burdigala (now Bordeaux) in the Roman province of Gallia Aquitania, via Constantinople, Syria, and on to Jerusalem; then back by way of Greece, crossing the Adriatic to Italy, and onward home. It reads as a travel book, a mixture of successive place-names with distances, Biblical references, and superstition.

> From Jerusalem to Jericho is 17 miles ... From the city, about a mile and a half off, there is the fountain of the prophet Elisha ... Above the fountain is the house of the prostitute Rahab, to whom the explorers went and where she hid them. When Jericho was overturned, she alone escaped. There the city of Jericho, around whose walls the Israelites went with the Ark of the Covenant and the walls fell down ... From Jericho to the Dead Sea, nine miles. Its water is extremely bitter, where in the whole there is no kind of fish and no vessel of any kind, and if someone casts himself in so he might swim the very water turns him over. From there to the Jordan, where the Lord was baptized by John, is five miles ... From Jerusalem as you go to Bethlehem, four miles above the road on the right hand side is the tomb where Rachel, wife of Jacob, is buried. From there, two miles on the left-hand side, is Bethlehem, where the Lord Jesus Christ was born; there a basilica was made by Constantine's command ... the total of the route from Constantinople to Jerusalem is 1164 miles, 69 changes, and 58 rest stops.

ΚΟΡΕΟΥΣ
ΓΑΛΓΑΛΑ ΤΟ ΚΑΙ
ΔΩΔΕΚΑΛΙΘΟΝ
ΙΕΡΙΧΩ

ΙΟΥΔΑ
ΒΗΘΛΕΕΜ
ΕΦΡΑΘΑ
ΝΙΚΟΠΟΛΙC
CΑΦΙΘΑ
ΕΝΕΤΑΒΑ
ΡΟCΔΑΝ
ΚΛΗΡΟCCΥΜΕ

THE BYZANTINE PERIOD

Although they were heir to Greek and Roman civilization and the administrators of a large part of the Mediterranean region, the Byzantines did not leave behind a large cartographic legacy. Thanks to the durable medium of mosaic, one that does survive in part is an extraordinary pictorial map of greater Palestine that formed the floor of a church in Madaba, Jordan. Uncovered in the late nineteenth century, it dates from no earlier than 542 and not likely much later than 565. It is the earliest extant map of Palestine as the actual artifact rather than a later copy—indeed, it is the earliest surviving geographic map based on actual observation and of such detail to survive of any area. To set our bearings in the photograph in fig. 13, note the most conspicuous features of the surviving sections: the Jordan River in the upper left, emptying into the Dead Sea with two ships, and Jerusalem, the roughly oval city below it. But we need to start from home, Madaba, in part of the mosaic that did not survive the centuries. It would have been in the upper center of the photograph, above the north (left) end of the Dead Sea, probably in line with the city at the extreme upper right (southeast) of the extant map, likely Karak. Both cities were important for Christianity and trade. The map's loss of Madaba is particularly unfortunate, as the nature of the mapmakers' depiction of their own city might have revealed much about them and the intent of their map.

We leave imagined Madaba and head west (down) to the Jordan River. Nearing its east bank, a lion—

FIG 14: The southern surviving part of the Madaba map (extreme right of fig. 13). [photo: Lucinda Curzon and Shaker Khanfar, 2025]

what's left of it—chases after a gazelle. Only the lion's hind legs and tail remain, most of its original tesserae (mosaic pieces) having been replaced to expunge the image. The defacement is attributed to the anti-icon Iconoclast movements of the eighth or ninth century, and though this explanation leaves the unscathed gazelle an enigma, any pattern that might have explained the reasoning was lost with the missing bulk of the map.

Today, human exploitation of the Jordan has rendered it barely a trickle, but we are in the sixth century, when it was a major river. Peering into it, a fish faces upstream, away from the entrance to the Dead Sea, as if warning away the fish swimming toward the sea of its deadly water. A ferry takes us across to the western bank—not just any ferry, but a cable ferry, the mosaic clearly illustrating a rope secured to either bank with a device to guide the vessel back and forth. The Jordan ferry must have been a busy one in the sixth century.

Following the river north (left), the surviving map ends just where the Sea of Galilee had surely been. Far off to the left, by the church pillar, two solitary fragments are all that survive of Lebanon. The map likely extended as least as far north as Tyre and possibly as far as Sidon. Back to the main surviving section, Nablus lies obscured under the darkened area to the lower left. Jericho is easily identifiable above the damage, the city graced by palm trees.

Jerusalem is the largest city on the surviving map. The identities of some features are widely accepted, such as the Church of the Holy Sepulcher, colonnaded main streets, gates, walls, and a column erected by Hadrian, the Roman emperor from 117 to 138. In contrast, Bethlehem, correctly marked to the right (south) of the city, seems slighted and has no Church of the Nativity—possibly arguing against a dedicated religious function of the map, or reflecting the church's destruction during the very period the mosaic was made (it was then rebuilt by Byzantine Emperor Justinian I).

Most of the Mediterranean coast is lost. The only glimpse of blue sea that survives is at the very end of the left-most of the sections extending down to the bottom (west). The next extension to the right is Ashdod, and the fragment in line with the church pillar is Ashkelon. To go further south, we need to go to the right of the pillar, which is better seen in fig. 14. First is Gaza, and although the northern part is lost, enough is intact to see that it was a grand city graced by a Greek theater and columnated avenue. The northern Negev and Beersheba lie inland from Gaza, and the Nile Delta straddles the church wall.

That delta adds a twist to the question of the map's orientation. Assuming that the map is positioned as it was in the original church (and indeed that it was created for the church), the lettering places the map "right side up" to the church congregation, oriented to the east, facing the altar. But that would make the Nile east-west rather than north-south. Too much of the map is missing to judge whether that was an error (indeed one that European mapmakers would make more than a thousand years later) or whether orientation was not strict, the Nile deliberately shifted about 90° for practical use of space. The very concept of orientation loses some meaning with a map that one would walk over from any direction.

The surviving section of the map covers about 34.5 feet (10.5 meters) north-south (left-right), and about 16.5 feet (5 meters) east-west (top-bottom). Estimates of the original size, based on the surviving Lebanese fragments and extrapolating from some of the mosaic's legends, suggest that the original map was about 69 x 23 feet (21 x 7 meters).

FIG. 15: The town of Madaba, with the modern Greek church visible on the left, shortly after its construction over the sixth-century map. From the left half of a stereograph by the American Colony. Dated 1900-20 by the Library of Congress [LOC LC-M32- 1166 (P&P)], though the completed Church of the Beheading of John the Baptist at the center places the photo post ca. 1913.

FIG. 16: The interior of the Church of St. George today. [Photo courtesy of the Embassy of the Hashemite Kingdom of Jordan to the UK and the Jordan Tourism Board]

The making of the map was an extraordinary undertaking: the gathering of information, the cartography, sketching it out over a prepared surface, and the estimated two million colored tesserae that had to be planned, selected, shaped, and installed. What motivated the project? The main view is that the map's principal function was religious, whether to illustrate pilgrimage, Bible instruction, or both. Supporters of that view note Jerusalem's prominence and that many of the map's place names correspond to those in the *Onomasticon* of the early-fourth-century Palestinian bishop Eusebius of Caesarea.[4] Yet many of the other places marked are of no use for pilgrimage. Road stations shown outside of Jerusalem suggest that itinerary maps were consulted, and some of the icon symbols demonstrate common influence with the Peutinger or other Roman map.

Above all, what survives is only about a third of the original map, and our perspective is skewed because that third happens to include the most Christian-centric geography. We can't assume it is representative of the lost whole. Rather, the very question of a dedicated purpose is likely too restrictive for a map that people used to "walk" and "sail" their travels of the imagination, and even simply to see where things are.

In exchange for its somewhat cluttered look, the makers of the Madaba map included as much detail as the rough mosaic medium allowed. Historians of such maps must judge when a particular rudimentary, unnamed feature—a church, a road, a column—so resembles a historical feature as to be that feature, versus a generic motif. The Israeli state, instead, looks at all Levantine archaeology through the lens of its creation myth, usually to make the land and its history that of the "state." The Madaba map's iconography presented an additional, novel opportunity: to redirect from the bad press that Israel's occupation, ethnic cleansing, and

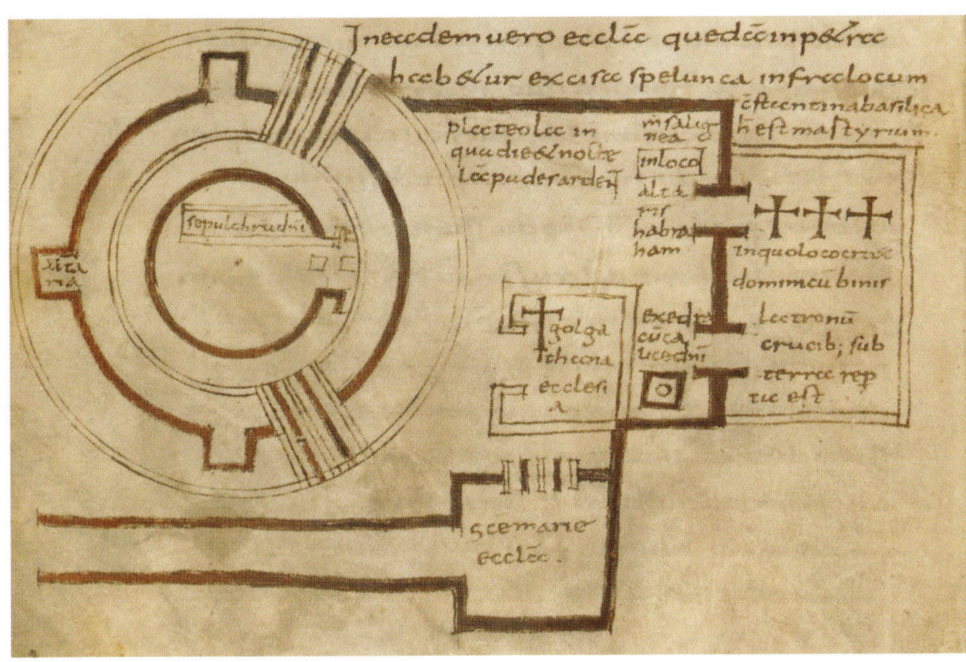

FIG. 17: Plan of the Holy Sepulchere, Bishop Arculf, ca. 670 (here ninth century, 836–859) [in a theological collected manuscript of various authors, Austrian National Library, Cod. 458]

- Concentric circles are the Church of the Holy Sepulchre, the sepulchre itself at the inner round cabin; indentations at 12, 6, 9 o'clock are altars.
- Three crosses on the right indicate where the crosses of Christ and the two thieves were discovered under the earth.
- Small brown box to their left, table where lamps are always lit.
- Larger brown box below it, where cup of the lord is kept.
- Yellow box to its left, Church of Golgotha.
- Large orange box, center bottom, Church of St. Mary.

excavation of East Jerusalem are all blatant breaches of international law, and that the illegal excavations threaten the integrity of historic structures inconvenient to its narrative. It exploited the Madaba map to move the story away from six decades of binding Security Council resolutions demanding that it stop.

In 2010 the Israel Antiquities Authority invoked the map, claiming that its image of a column in Jerusalem had been the reason for ongoing excavations deep below East Jerusalem's Old City. It announced that the map had led them to an astounding discovery, what excavation director Dr. Ofer Sion called "David Street" that once crossed Jerusalem in "the Land of Israel." This served not merely to distract from the ongoing crime, but to celebrate it. The news focus shifted to an uplifting, saleable story: *archaeologists follow enigmatic clues on an ancient map to an amazing discovery deep below Jerusalem's streets.*[5]

As the surveying tradition of the Romans died out, the final traces of its more empirical approach are visible in the earliest surviving maps of Palestine from Christian Europe, those of a Frankish bishop, Arculf, who visited Palestine in 670. Four Palestinian plans are associated with him: the Church of Jacob's Well in Nablus, the Ascension in Jerusalem, Mount Zion, and Jerusalem's Church of the Sepulchre (fig. 17). With Roman influence evident, they can be seen as forming a bridge between Late Antiquity and the Middle Ages.

We owe the account of his pilgrimage—and his maps—to the winds. En route back home to Gaul (then a region of Western Europe), Arculf's ship was blown far off course, instead landing in Iona, the island off western Scotland whose fabulous abbey welcomed him. The pilgrim dictated his account to the abbot of Iona Abbey and Nunnery, Adamnan, whose text survives in recopied form. Arculf is said to have etched his plans on wax tablets, though the earliest surviving manuscripts with maps date from the ninth century. "As to the situation of Jerusalem," Adamnan wrote, "we shall now write a few of the details that the sainted Arculf dictated to me," passing over "what is found in the books of others":

FIG. 18: Tripartite mappamundi, one of a few extant fifteenth century manuscripts, similar in approach, that use the T-O skeleton to "paint" the world. Jerusalem is marked at the center, and all three deltas of the "T" join the encircling Ocean Sea. From a manuscript of 1400-1425 of two works of the Roman author Sallust (86 BCE - 34 BCE), his *Bellum Catilinae* (concerning an internal Roman conspiracy) and *Bellum Iugurthinum* (a war between Rome and Numidia). [Beinecke Library, MS 358]

In the great circuit of its walls, Arculf counted eighty-four towers and twice three gates, which are placed in the following order in the circuit of the city: The Gate of David, on the west side of Mount Sion, is reckoned first; second, the Gate of the Place of the Fuller; third, the Gate of St. Stephen; fourth, the Gate of Benjamin; fifth, a portlet, that is a little gate, by which is the descent by steps to the Valley of Josaphat; sixth, the Gate Thecuitis.

FIG. 19: St. George slays the dragon on this portolan chart of the Mediterranean by Placido Oliva, ca. 1580. [Library of Congress, 2012586591]

It was Arculf who brought Europe its first reference to St. George, whose legends contributed not just to the exotification of Palestine, but the West as chauvinistic steward of the land. St. George was entirely Middle Eastern, born in Asia Minor in the second half of the third century to a Palestinian mother from Lydda (Lod), and it was in Lydda that he lived and was executed for practicing his Palestinian religion of Christianity. Yet England expropriated George and his legendary dragon-slaying—an embellishment that first appears in the twelfth century—as if England had sent its hero to defeat the dragon to its non-European would-be victims' eternal gratitude. Iconography of the esteemed saint made its way to a 1580 portolan chart by the Italian cartographer Placido Oliva (fig. 19), where George confronts the dragon by the Red Sea.

FIG. 20: Byzantine Jug, 578-636 CE, mass-produced for pilgrims by glass workshops outside Jerusalem's walls and probably filled with oil from holy sites. It is decorated with images of the cross alternating with diamond shapes. [Art Institute of Chicago, 1947.958]

CHAPTER 2

PALESTINE IN PARALLEL MEDIEVAL WORLDS

PART 1: THE CLOISTERED AND THE PILGRIM

Throughout the several centuries from the end of late antiquity to the early Renaissance, separate, parallel cartographic traditions treated Palestine in their own distinct ways.

Part 1: Palestine was a specific focus of two of these mapping lineages:

- The "T-O" motif: A three-part conception of the world that placed Palestine as the center of the earth by happenstance and, post-Christianization, by design; it ultimately became a map of Palestine itself.
- The pilgrim view: Christian pilgrimages yielded "true" maps of Palestine, especially following the First Crusade.

Part 2: Palestine evolved with, but was not the focus of, four others:

- Latin portolan (sea) charts
- Arabic mapping [6]
- Radical, hybrid world maps
- Ptolemy's *Geography*

When the scholar, theologian, and archbishop Isidore of Seville (Isidorus Hispalensis) was born in Cartagena, Spain, ca. 560 CE, the Western Roman Empire no longer existed as such, and classical civilization was in a state of decay. Isidore fought against this loss with his *Etymologiae*, an encyclopedic extract of books from antiquity. With his text, we see Palestine formally documented in a partly Christianized Europe.

FIG. 21: Tripartite (T-O) map of the world, from a ninth-century manuscript of an *opuscula* (short or minor work) of Isidorus. [Bibliothèque municipale de Rouen (Ms I-49, f° 74v)]

FIG. 22: Transitional T-O map in Arabic, in a Latin manuscript of Isidorus's *Etymologiae*, ca. 800. [National Library of Spain; image Library of Congress]

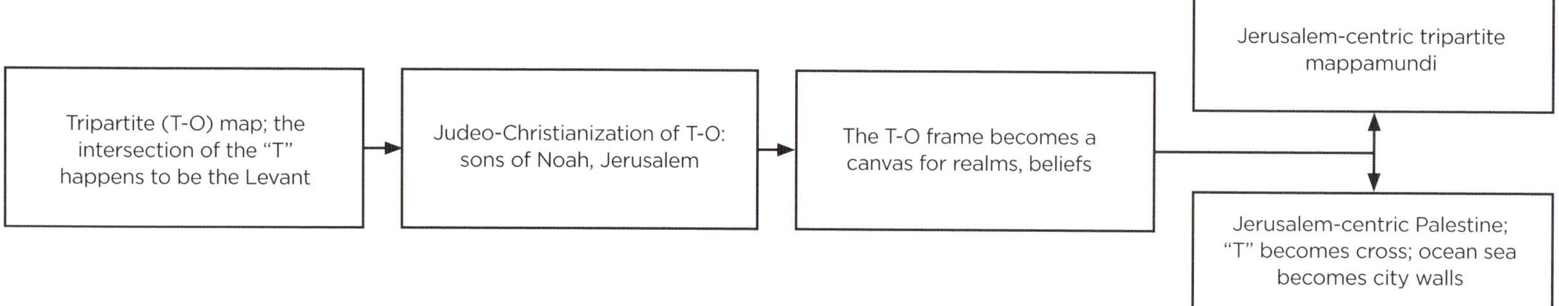

Manuscripts of the *Etymologiae* typically contain a simple tripartite map of the world, a "T" shape within a circle, hence commonly referred to as a T-O map—indeed the letters are sometimes construed literally, as representing *Orbis Terrarum* (i.e., the world). Its "O" frame is the earth and its encircling "ocean sea." With east at the top, the "T" divides the world in three, the upper half Asia, lower left quarter Europe, lower right quarter Africa. The vertical line of the "T" is the Mediterranean, the horizontal line the Nile (right) and

FIG. 23: T-O woodcut map set within a text leaf in the book *Etymologiae*, Isidorus Hispalensis, Augsburg, 1472.

FIG. 24: modified T-O map in the *Fasciculus temporum* of the Carthusian monk, Werner Rolewink, 1484. Woodcut. Numbers indicate the subdivisions of the three continents, the sum marked at the bottom.

waterways north (left). Since both the horizontal and vertical lines of the "T" are full diameter, ninety degrees apart, the point at which they meet, Palestine, occupies the precise center of the earth—literally when viewed as a flat earth, and conceptually when the same map was understood as a spherical earth.

This was happenstance, but flukey happenstance, because it coincided precisely with Christian belief placing Jerusalem at the center of the earth. Latin geographers looking to the Bible for guidance read in the Book of Ezekiel that God placed Jerusalem "in the center of the nations, with countries all around her," the Vulgate version referring to it as the "navel" of the earth. The Crusades brought the idea to the fore, and literature reinforced it. A variation is found in Dante, who placed Jerusalem at the center of the *inhabited* earth, and purgatory at the center of the antipodal hemisphere.

That the prevailing belief was of a geocentric cosmos makes Palestine's seemingly divinely ordained position all the more powerful. In the geocentric universe in fig. 25, we take a step further back and see that for the medieval viewer who assumed the earth to be the center of the universe, Palestine was the very center of creation.

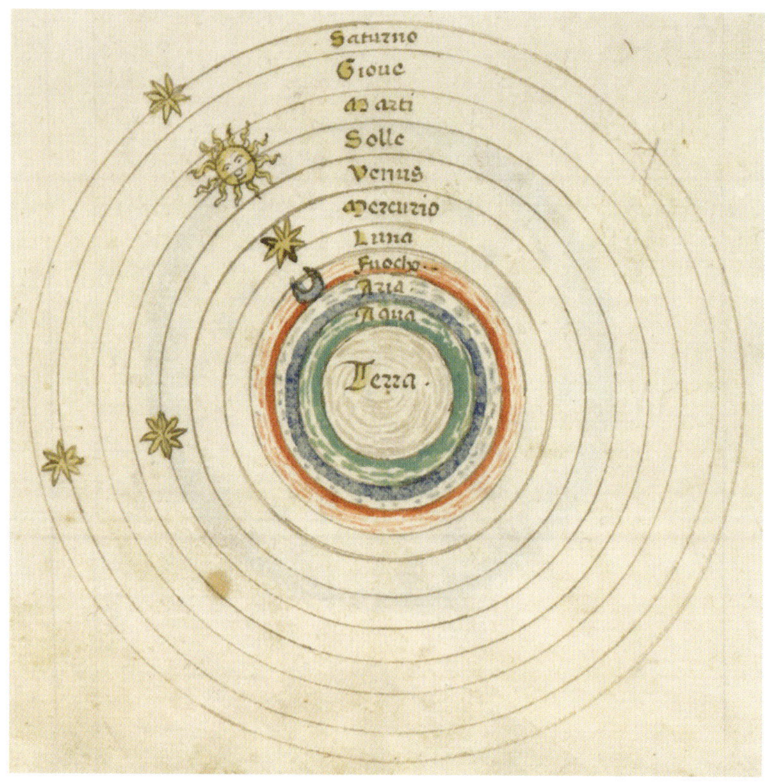

FIG. 25: The geocentric universe, in which Palestine would be the pivot point of the entire cosmos. The earth is surrounded first by the four elements, then the moon, Mercury, Venus, the sun, Mars, Jupiter, Saturn. From a leaf of *La Sfera*, Dati, Gregorio, fifteenth century. [National Library of Finland, Mscr. 1]

As this Greco-Roman tripartite world map became ubiquitous in an increasingly Christianized European society, it became a canvas through which Palestine emerged graphically as the central focus of "Western" identity. This evolution is illustrated in figs. 21-24 and the accompanying diagram.

- The first, fig. 21, is a pure T-O pattern, marking only the three continents.

- An unknown ninth-century Arabic emendator, likely in southern Spain, drew the T-O map in fig. 22, in which the T-O pattern moves from motif to the canvas upon which the earth is described. Much is still legible: in the upper half (Asia), the inscription states that the inhabitants are the Arabs, and that there is the Levant, the Hijaz [western Arabia], Mecca, Yathrib [Medina], Persia, Armenia, and Bahrain [literally, "the two seas"]. Europe (lower left quadrant) is the realm of the *Ajam* (non-Arabic speaking people), with mention of "the narrow sea" (Mediterranean), the Romans, and "Andalus until the two seas meet" (i.e., Strait of Gibraltar). The text in Africa remains only partially legible, with reference to the Berber, al-Zanj (Southeast Africa, Swahili Coast), the Sudan, and Morocco.

- In fig. 23, the T-O foundation becomes Judeo-Christianized, as the three continents now bear the names of their post-Deluge progenitor of humanity: Sem in Asia, Jafeth in Europe, Cham in Africa.

- The transition is complete in fig. 24. Palestine has carved out its own dedicated, autonomous space, the intersection of the "T" expressly modified to place Jerusalem as the center, the sole realm named on the earth other than the continents. In this particular example, keeping Jerusalem where the Bible placed it required some juggling. Had the mapmaker simply created Palestine's space from the existing horizontal of the "T," Palestine would have been slightly offset to the west (down). Instead, the horizontal line itself has been shoved up in order to keep Jerusalem at the precise center.

From here, the tripartite concept splits in two:

1. More commonly, it evolved directly into the full-fledged mappaemundi that place Palestine at the center.

2. Independently, the T-O zoomed in to its center, making the motif a map of Palestine itself.

PALESTINE AS THE CENTER OF THE WORLD

Encyclopedic, Palestine-centric mappaemundi filled in their canvases with realms both real and imagined, Biblical places and events in their respective locations and imagery from various medieval travel lore. The grandest surviving example, dating from ca. 1300 is now housed at the Hereford Cathedral. Its imposing size (about 64″ by 52″) allowed for rich Christian content, rooted in older sources such as the Roman priest Paulus Orosius, who went to Palestine in about 415, and the eighth-century theologian Beatus of Liébana. Some maps diverge from the circular, becoming oval or even rectangular while remaining rooted in the same Palestine-centric tradition, such as that by Ranulf Higden in fig. 32 (p51).

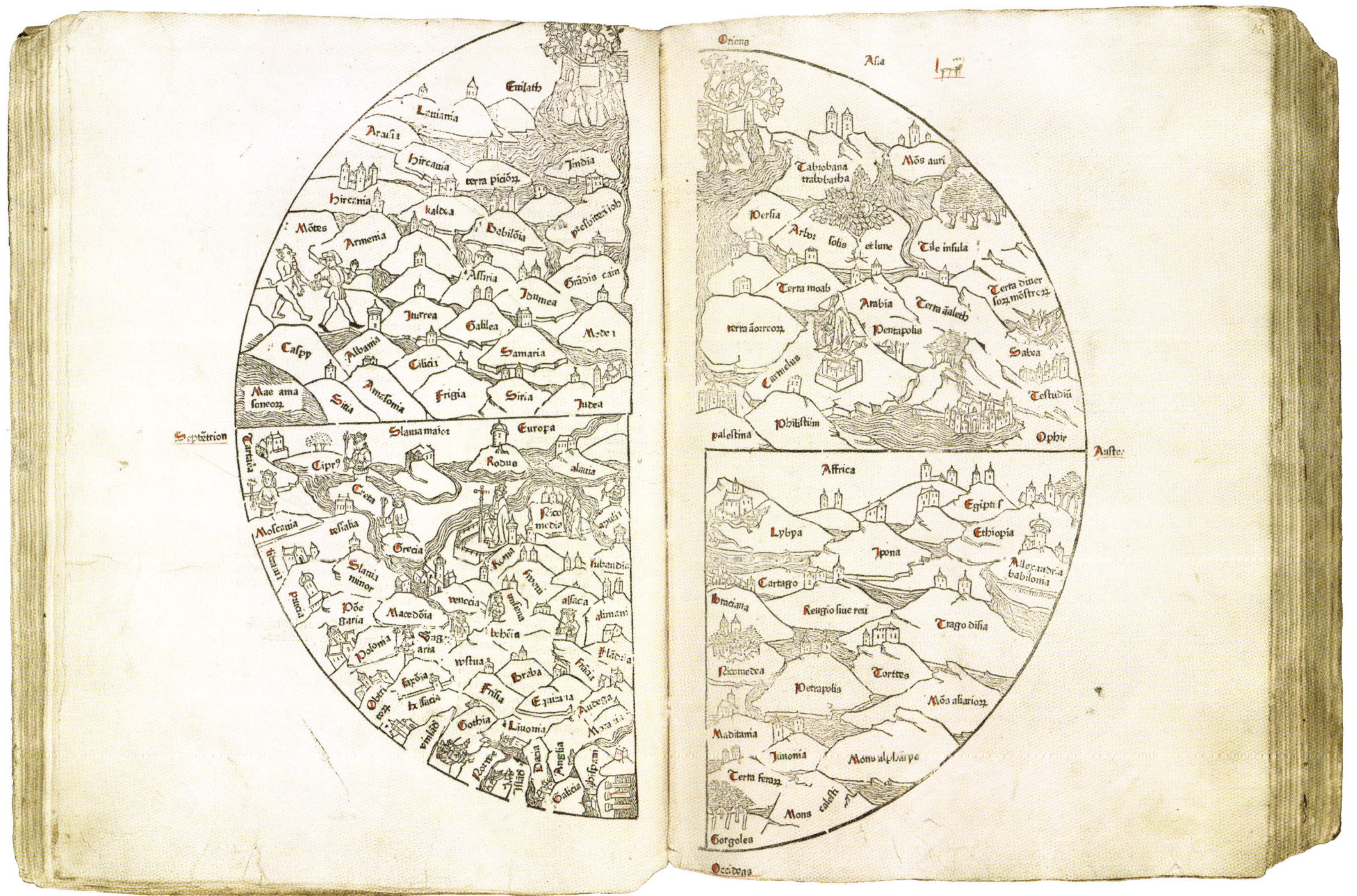

FIG. 26: World map, woodcut, on two sheets, in the *Rudimentum Novitiorum*, Lübeck (Germany), 1475. [Library of Congress, Incun. 1475 .R8]

The first detailed mappamundi to benefit from the medium of printing was a woodcut on two sheets in the work *Rudimentum Novitiorum*, printed in Lübeck in 1475 (fig. 26 & 27). Though this example comes from the end of the genre's lifespan, it is useful due to its relative simplicity. The *Rudimentum* cites the Bible as a geographic reference, and about half of the place-names in the map's Asia are derived from that book. It divides history into six "ages," beginning with the Biblical Creation, then Noah, Abraham, David, the destruction of Judea, and the birth of Christ. The third age contains a description of Palestine associated with the 1283 *Descriptio Terrae Sanctae* by Burchard of Monte Sion, of which we will see more.

Paradise occupies the extreme east (top) of the world map, following the description in Genesis, and is the source for its four rivers, the Ganges, Nile, Tigris, and Euphrates. One would have expected the two figures in Paradise to be Adam and Eve, but they are both male; they are likely Enoch and Elijah, two prophets whom God took straight to Paradise without their having to die first.

On the left is an enlarged detail of the center of the map (fig. 27). Starting at the top center, we see *presbiteri joh*, the mythical kingdom of Prester John, an opulent Christian stronghold that would welcome those of the faith who could reach it. The earliest known reference to the kingdom was a letter received by the Byzantine emperor Manuel I Komnenos in 1165, but whether this was the origin of the myth is not known. The legend may have been invented specifically to promote further Crusades by enticing participants with the belief that safety, and indeed luxury, awaited Christian soldiers fighting to regain the Holy Land. Whether or not that was its genesis, the myth helped achieve that end. As mapped here, Prester John was sufficiently close to Palestine to lure Crusaders. When all attempts to find it failed, later theories placed the kingdom in Africa.

Near Palestine, *Arbor solis et lune* in the upper right (for "et lune", fig. 26), the Tree of the Sun and Moon, derives from the *Alexander Romance*, myths about Alexander the Great. When the Sun Tree (masculine) and the Moon Tree (feminine) spoke to Alexander in an Indian language, he ordered the townsfolk to translate the trees' words, but they refused, for the trees had foretold Alexander's death. This oracular tree is also seen in a map associated with Jerome (fig. 33), in the upper right, to the left of the Red Sea. Below it on the *Rudimentum* map are *Terra Moab*, an ancient Levantine region on the east of the Dead Sea, and *terra amoreorum*, the Amorites, one of the seven tribes of Canaan. Familiar names follow, moving clockwise: *Carmelus* (Mt. Carmel), *Philistiim* (Philistines), *palestina*, *Judea*, *Siria*, *Sumaria*, *Galilea*. Moving further, *Assiria* and *Babil ia* are northern Mesopotamia (now Iraq), and *Idumea* is the ancient kingdom of Edom.

No attempt is made for consistent scale, and only modest concern given relative position. *Roma* is close by, in the lower left, and *Gr dis cain*, the Grand Khan, is just east of *Medea*. Various realms and places from medieval mythology are dispersed in haphazard fashion, mountains used to distinguish one from another.

Three years after the *Rudimentum*, ca. 1478, another work out of Lübeck, the *Prologus Arminensis in mappam Terrae sanctae*, contained two maps of Palestine entirely devoid of geographic outline. Instead, place-names were arranged in their perceived geographic relationship to each other. One map was oriented to the east and covered the wider Levant, while the other faced west and covered the Jerusalem environs.

Although two recut woodblocks of the *Rudimentum* mappamundi (1488, 1491, and their subsequent editions) brought its image to the mid sixteenth century, the depiction of Palestine as the center of the world as a serious concept had ended. Jerusalem did appear at the center of a woodcut world map in the 1581 *Itinerarium* of the theological commentator Heinrich Bünting, but this was purely emblematic. The map depicted Africa, Asia, and Europe in the form of a clover leaf (the arms of Bünting's native Hanover), with Jerusalem pictured in the large circle forming the leaves' pivot.

(Previous page) FIG. 27: Enlarged detail of the central section of the world map in fig. 26, in which the sheets have been mated and aligned for continuity.

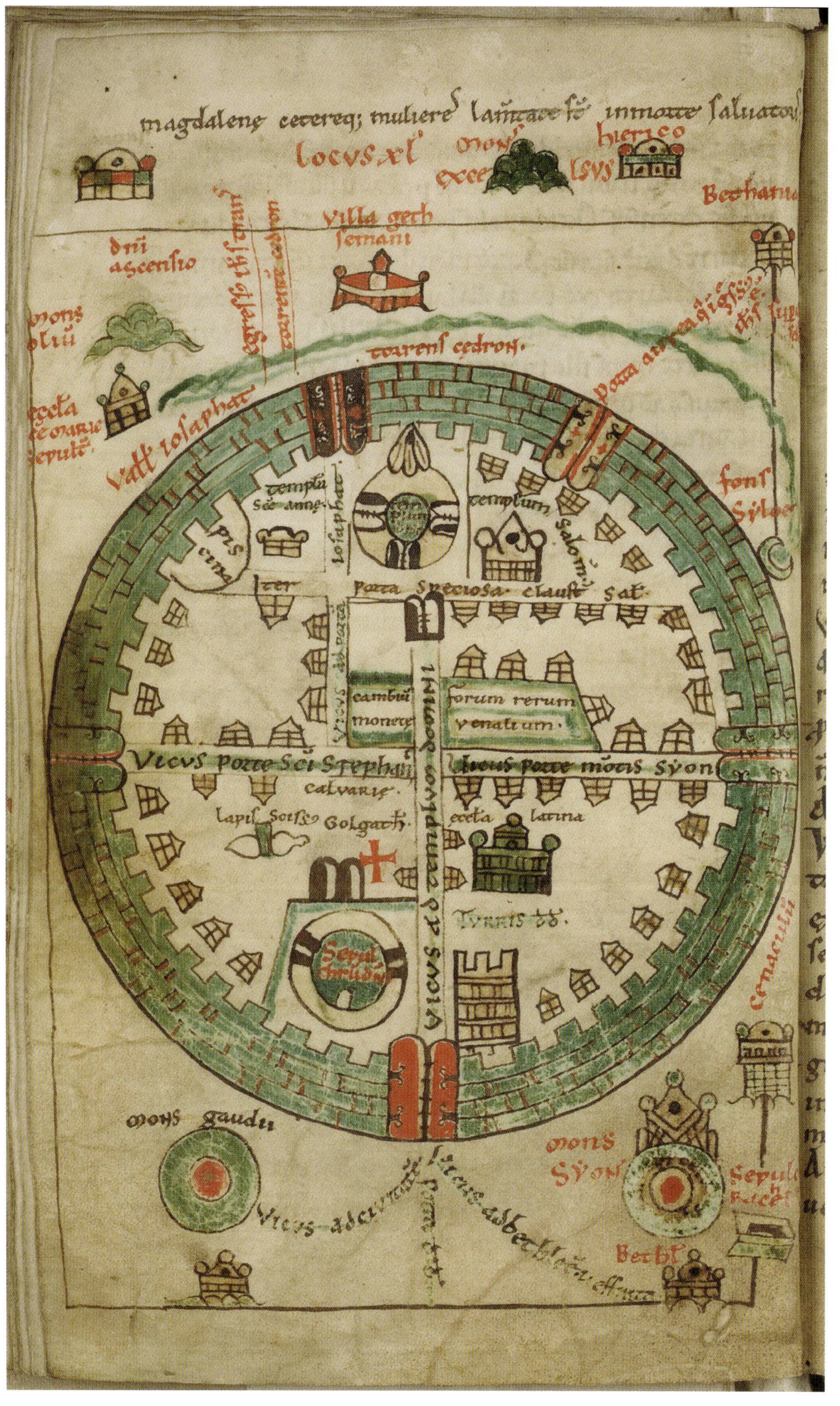

THE TRIPARTITE MAP "BECOMES" PALESTINE

The T-O motif's evolution into elaborate mappaemundi is half its story. In a parallel evolution found in pilgrimage guides inspired by the Crusades, the motif morphed into a map of Palestine itself.

As is visible in fig. 28, both the "T" and the "O" of the T-O skeleton have taken on new roles. The right half of the horizontal line of the "T," formerly the Nile, is now the way to Zion Gate, while the left half (waterways north) is now the way to St. Stephen's Gate. The vertical line of the "T," formerly the Mediterranean, now extends above the horizontal line, as it assumes dual roles as well. Below the horizontal, it is now a pilgrims' road instead of the Mediterranean, and the two pillars at its bottom are David's Gate instead of the Pillars of Hercules. The new extention above the horizontal is the path to the Lord's Temple.

FIG. 28: Jerusalem-centric map of Palestine, in a pilgrimage guide and chronicle of Foulcher de Chartres and the first Crusade (1096), *Gesta Francorum Iherusalem expugnatium*), 1106–09 [Abbey of Saint-Bertin, Saint-Omer, MS 776, fol. 50v].

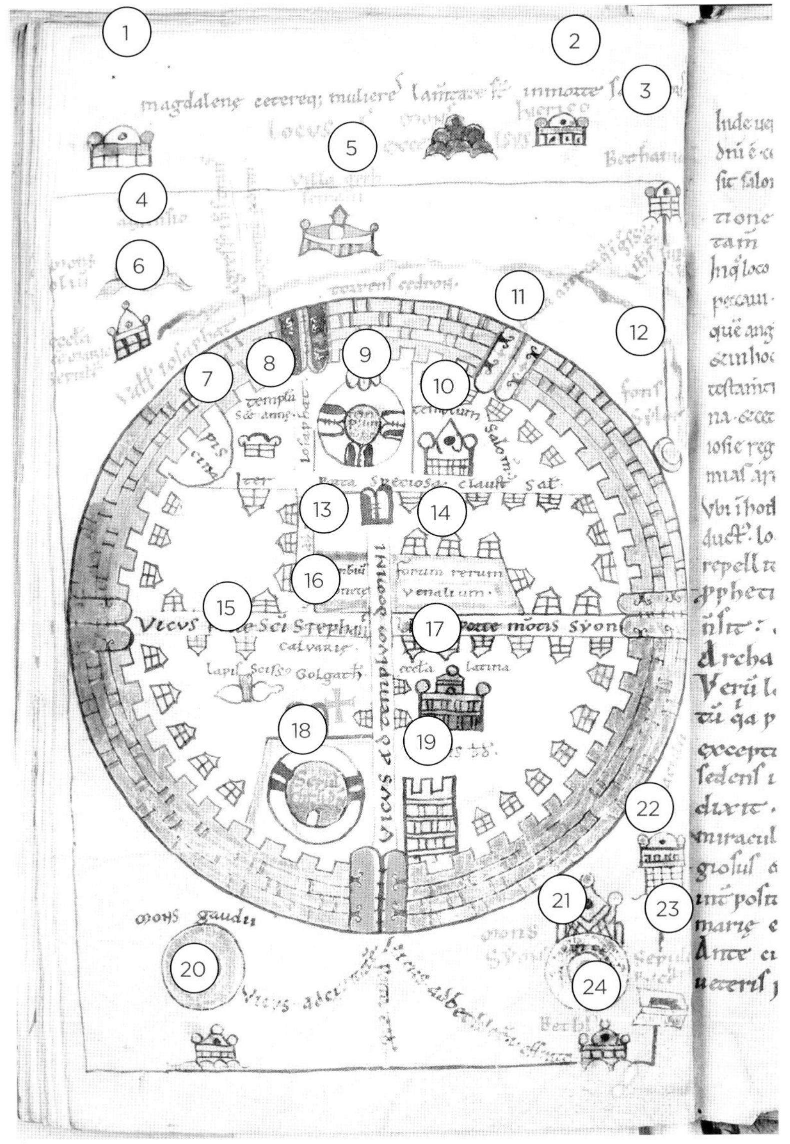

Key map for fig. 28:

1 Mary Magdalene;
2 Jericho;
3 Bethany;
4 Mount of Olives, with the ascension of Christ above;
5 Gethsemane (where Christ was arrested);
6 St. Mary's church;
7 pool (Solomon's?);
8 St. Anne's temple;
9 Lord's temple;
10 Solomon's temple;
11 golden gate (through which Christ entered);
12 Siloam pool (where Christ restored sight to a blind man);
13 a square for changing money;
14 a square for selling goods;
15 Rock of Calvary
(which split from the earthquake when Christ was crucified)
16 Calvary (Christ's crucifixion);
17 Latin church;
18 Christ's sepulchre;
19 tower of David;
20 Mountain of Joy (counterpart, opposite of, Mount Sinai);
21 Mt. Zion;
22 Cenacle (site of Last Supper);
23 Rachel's Tomb;
24 Bethlehem, with the road to it seen connecting to David's gate.

That path to the Lord's Temple accords the "T" the ultimate Christian symbolism. It extends just the right amount above the horizontal to transform the "T" itself into a Christian cross superimposed over the whole. The symbolism, also found on some mappaemundi, was an effective and efficient, if as here arguably subliminal, use of Christian iconography.

The final piece of the transformation of the T-O is the "O" itself. The earth's encircling ocean in the map's former life, it is now the massive encircling stone wall of the city. Beyond it, other places in Palestine branch out in the periphery.

THE PILGRIM VIEW

The evolution of the tripartite concept was largely a closed system that operated according to its own internal logic. Throughout the same centuries, the cartographic image of Palestine evolved independently in service to myriad concerns beyond the cloister walls: navigation, trade, the practicalities of everyday life, empire, and curiosity about the world for its own sake.

With the success of the First Crusade in wresting control of Jerusalem in 1099, Holy Land tourism became a going business in medieval Europe for those with the resources and drive. Despite the expense, danger of shipwreck, challenges of an unknown climate, and an

FIG. 29: Map of Palestine, Twelfth century. [Florence, Biblioteca Medicea Laurenziana, Ashb. 188]

often hostile reception, enough Europeans went that a commercial infrastructure arose to service them. Nor did the pilgrim-tourists stop coming after the fall of Acre in 1291, which ended European control in the region. The 1300s and 1400s brought determined adventurers, typically via Venice, sometimes via Puglia. Few wrote accounts of their trip, and fewer still left geographic descriptions or maps to illustrate it. But those who did initiated a new wave of Palestine mapping. Not until the sixteenth century, under the strain of European religious wars and Ottoman conquests, did the number of pilgrims markedly decline.

The mid-twelfth-century map of Palestine in fig. 29 is a rare survivor of the early post-Crusades period, before the coalescence of copied-and-recopied standardized models. Of an unknown hand and provenance, the map reflects firsthand experience and is striking for its unimpassioned approach. It is also an enigmatic map, not just for the mystery of who made it and why, but for its innovative, intriguingly individual method of representing cities: a gold square with double red parallel lines at ninety degrees, as if symbolizing city streets, an iconographic device unknown in other maps of the period. Left (north) to right along the coast, we see the "gold" cities of Beirut, Sidon, Tyre, Acre, Caesarea, Jaffa, Ascalon, and Gaza. Crusader castles and some smaller Palestinian towns are indicated with a red city icon.

A Syrian river system flows through the mountains to join Lebanon's, with a large gold square representing *Caesarea Philippi*, the Golan Heights. Exiting the Sea of Galilee, the river becomes the Jordan and ends at the Dead Sea, here named, as would be common, for Sodom, which along with Gomorrah was destroyed by God for their people's wickedness.

Throughout the map, Biblical references are clear but designed as annotations, not as the focus of the map. For example, below (west of) the Sea of Galilee, we see reference to the legend of the "five loaves" (*v panum*), which Christ multiplied so as to feed thousands.

In the mountains west of the Dead Sea is evidence of the map's post-Crusade infancy and its maker's relatively secular mindset: Marked with equal prominence as other gold cities, Jerusalem merited gold, but nothing more. Nearby Bethlehem is appropriately smaller, but also gold.

Moving farther south (right), we reach the map's most prominent feature, its conspicuously altered Red Sea. The original sea was rubbed from the vellum but is still visible, oriented north-south (i.e., horizontal) as was typical of the period, and was blue like the map's Mediterranean. In jarring contrast, the new, strangely shaped and densely colored Red Sea is NE-SW, an orientation for the sea virtually unknown in the day. The mountains to the north were extended over the original sea to nearly meet it, and adjoining details were added (presumably *reinstated*): the *Mare rubrum* label and the twelfth-century Crusader fort of *Helim* (Aqaba Fortress).

Reworking of such maps is not uncommon, but this replaced Red Sea's orientation and shape can not easily be explained as an evolutionary tweak or the result of cartographic precedent. We can be reasonably confident of only one clue: that the change was made by a different hand, because the parallel lines of the reinstated *Helim* icon curve to conform to the sea's bend, whereas on all the map's other iconographic town symbols, these lines are straight regardless of adjoining features.

As a whole, the (actual) Red Sea is oriented NW-SE, but at the top, the wedge-shaped Sinai splits the sea into the Gulf of Suez, which continues NW-SE, and the Gulf of Aqaba to the east, which is oriented NE-SW. At the apex of the Gulf of Aqaba lay the Crusader town of Ayla (Aqaba), the southern end of the Crusader fiefdom called Oultrejordain. We can speculate (though nothing more) that the map's new Red Sea is a bold "correction" based on reports describing Crusader exploits from Ayla south into the Gulf of Aqaba.[7]

The most likely candidate is the notoriously brutal Raynald of Châtillon, who in 1175 became lord of that fiefdom. In 1182, Raynald sailed the full length of the Gulf of Aqaba, reaching the bottom of the Sinai, and continuing to the west. Reports of Raynald's or other Crusader travels into the Gulf of Aqaba would have described a sea something like that of our map: oriented NE-SW, and with a pronounced "opening up" to the west (down) at its bottom. In other words, the Gulf of Aqaba was mapped as the Red Sea.

A small world map within a diagram of the elements in a fourteenth-century manuscript (fig. 30) boasts a Red Sea that is strikingly similar in orientation and shape, but this is likely an anomaly. More interesting is the Red Sea in the twelfth-century "Jerome" map (fig. 33): although the map's orientation is fluid, it primitively shows both gulfs and the opening up to the Egyptian side.

FIG. 30: East-oriented mappamundi, the Palestine-centric earth as the innermost of the four elements as per ancient Greek thought. The encircling "ocean sea" is water, then air, and the outermost element fire. Beyond it all lies the circuit of the moon. This east-oriented depiction of the earth itself shows the Mediterranean and Red Seas, the latter with the distinctive shape and orientation of the correction on the map in fig. 29. From a leaf of *La Sfera*, Dati, Gregorio, fifteenth century. [National Library of Finland, Mscr. 1]

FIG. 31: Jerusalem, mid-twelfth century. [Bibliotheque Municipale, Cambrai, MS. 466, fol. Ir]

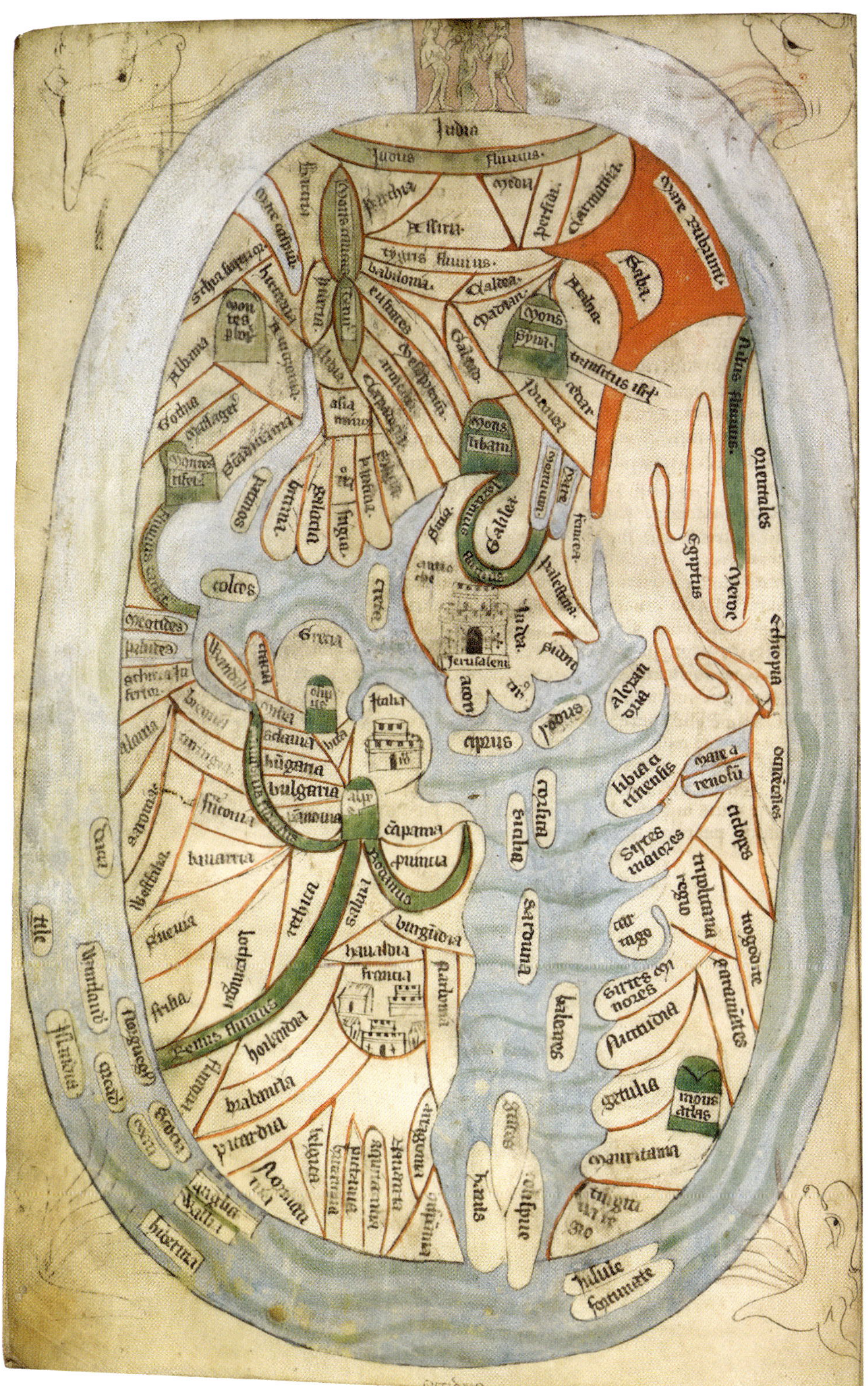

FIG. 32: Among the most popular of late medieval chronicles was the Polychronicon of the English Benedictine monk Ranulf Higden (c1280–1363-64), who resided at the monastery of St. Werburgh in Chester. Several copies of the manuscript survive with Higden's mappamundi, which share the same geographic approach despite wide variation in execution.

The most obvious characteristic of Higden's mapping of the eastern Mediterranean is its extreme longitudinal (i.e., here up-down) distortion. On the next page we will see how the "Jerome" map's (fig. 33) use of space placed the Palestinian coast and that of eastern Asia Minor in line with each other. Higden goes further, and as his is a world map, shows that he is shoving Palestine west—that is, psychologically, closer to Europe—rather than Asia Minor east. Acre (the left-most of the four Palestinian toe-like peninsulas) shares longitudinal space with Italy.

Paradise sits atop the top, with Adam and Eve and the Tree. His own England, along with other islands and non-islands such as Norway, sit in the encircling Ocean Sea. [Bodleian Library MS. Tanner 170]

One of the earliest extant plans of Jerusalem is in the same short-lived, more straightforward post-Crusade mindset, distinct from the idealized representations that followed (fig. 31). Drawn in about 1140, most of the buildings and streets depicted are identified, demonstrating the maker's intent to map only what was known through the report(s) consulted. The city walls are mapped as an irregular rectangle sitting on one corner, rather than the stylized circular imagery that we will see next.

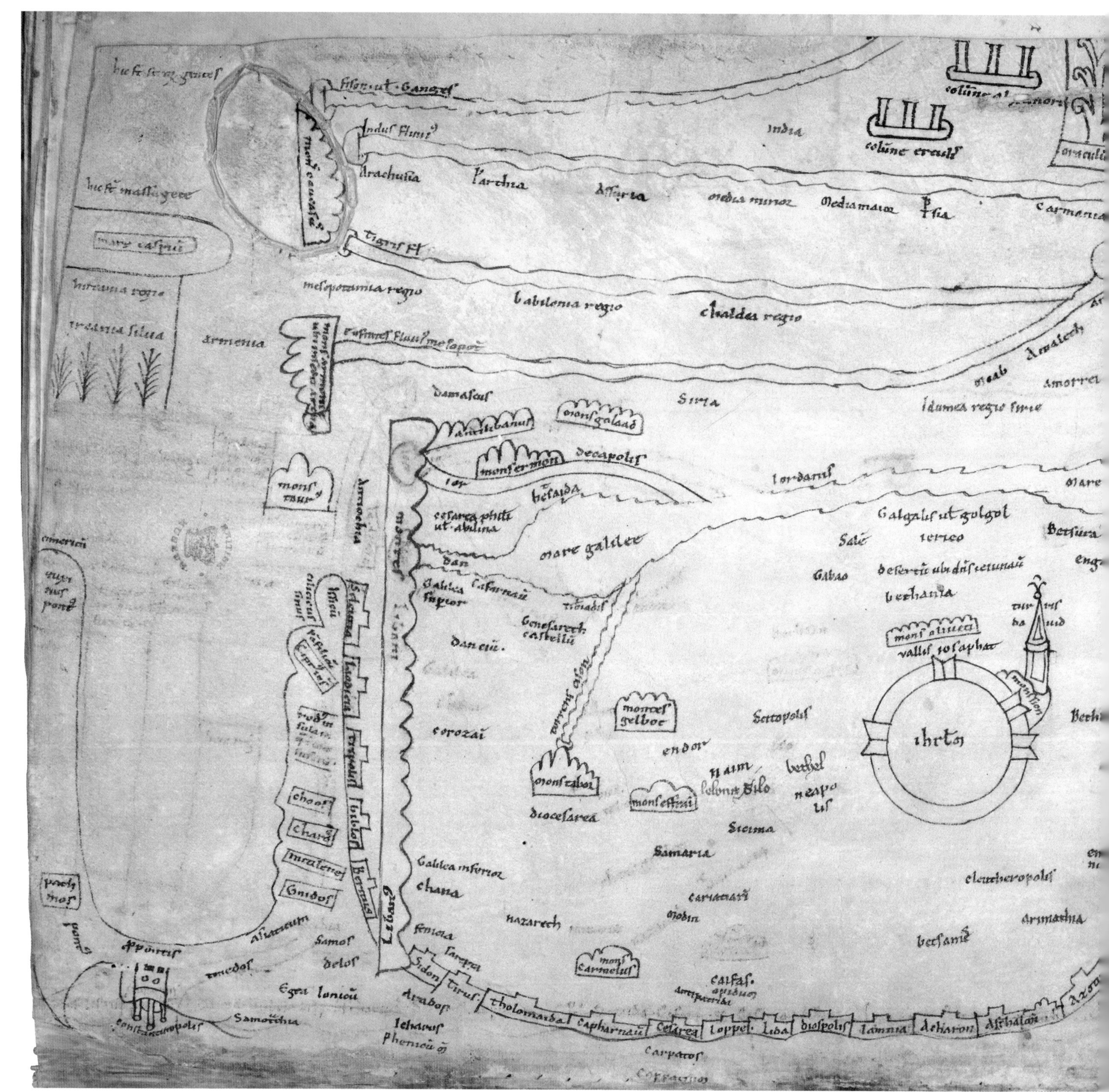

FIG. 33: Palestine, late twelfth century, in a manuscript of the works of Jerome and Eusebius. [British Library, Add. 10049, f.64v]

If the previous maps of Palestine and Jerusalem are the work of a fresh hand not yet encumbered by established patterns, a quite different map of Palestine drawn in Tournai (now Belgium) soon afterward demonstrates the labors of mapmakers amending their work as new information arrives or existing reports are reevaluated (fig. 33). The map is found in the writings of Jerome (d. 420), though it doubtfully had much to do with him—indeed the laborious reworking of the map demonstrates that it was not copied outright from an older model. What survives is at least a third attempt: vestiges of earlier drafts are visible under a map of Asia on the verso, and of another under the existing map of Palestine.[8]

Vellum was expensive—hence the laborious erasures rather than starting anew. This is especially apparent in the upper left, where a hole in the vellum has been mended by sewing in a new piece. On the map of Asia on the verso, the mapmaker took advantage of the repair to make it Crete, but no such artistic cover was possible for Palestine, where the replaced piece inelegantly contains one of the two mountain ranges from which the Biblical four rivers of Paradise emanate (Ganges, Indus, Tigris, and in the lower mountain, Euphrates).

Extravagant liberties with longitude were in part an accommodation to available space: None of the leaf was "wasted" on the Mediterranean. Asia Minor, the fat, down-facing peninsula in the lower left, is shoved so far to the east (up), that Constantinople, the upside down castle at its apex, is level with the Palestinian coast. This left the mapmaker no choice but to twist the Syrian and Lebanese coasts east-west. Orientation recovers at Sidon, remaining north-south for most of Palestine, then rounding eastward into an "Egyptian sea" at Gaza, to accommodate Alexandria.

Jerusalem is now given special honors appropriate for the map's function: large, double concentric circles depict the city walls with their four imposing gates. Immediately to the south is Bethlehem, where Jerome lived for many years.

FIG. 34: Palestine, Matthew Paris, working in St Albans, 1253–1259. This copy from his *Historia Anglorum*. [British Library, Royal 14 C. VII]

Matthew Paris, a Benedictine monk, was an indefatigable chronicler, an artist of illuminated manuscripts, and a mapmaker. Two dissimilar, important maps of Palestine by him survive: a unique map on a single leaf depicting the Crusader states, and the map on the left (fig. 34), a double-leaf focused on Acre that is known in three copies, none identical. They form the end of a road map taking the viewer on an imaginary trip from London, through France, on to Rome (which is as far as Paris got), south to Puglia, and from there by sea to Acre. Unlike road maps such as the Peutinger, Paris's is an itinerary, a specific trip—if only for the imagination, not the feet.

With Paris, we have the first explicit instance of a mapmaker who was heavily invested in both Palestine *and* the belief that the end of the world was imminent—the year 1250 was Paris's calculation. Storms, droughts, rivers flowing backwards, ships in the sky, earthquakes, eclipses, meteors, calendar calculations, and the 1238 Mongol advance on eastern Europe were all among his evidence.

Anti-Jewish aspects of Paris's text figure directly into his end-of-time beliefs, and thus Palestine's future. Jews were said to be in cahoots with the Mongols, and planned (among other deeds) to bring an end to Christendom using weapons smuggled in wine casks. He also invokes the story of the "Wandering Jew," which was popularized during the second quarter of the thirteenth century. Several variations flourished, but the essential myth is of a Jew who taunted Jesus on the way to the Crucifixion, for which he was condemned to walk the earth relentlessly until the Second Coming. While the myth easily adapts to the idea of a Jewish "return," it is not yet that.

When 1250 came and went, Paris likely deferred to the Joachimites, a movement that was well-known to him and that would later influence Protestant evangelicals. The Joachimites suggested 1260 as the end—but Paris died one year too soon to find out.

Matthew's map must be viewed in this end-of-time context. What was important to him to include? What "feel" did he want to impart in a map of the Holy Land composed on the eve of the end of the world? Perhaps counterintuitively, it is largely a practical map. He was less concerned with matching Biblical stories to their geographic spaces as he was with explaining Palestine. The large blocks of text that occupy much of the map are mainly geographic, economic, political, and demographic.

Acre dominates because there was much in the Christian stronghold he wanted to include, but liberties taken with scale do not contradict a regard for placing features in their generally correct position. The semi-island in the lower left corner is Tyre, and Damascus sits prominently at the top, to the left of the center. Moving to the right, we see the Jordan River and Dead Sea, followed by a misplaced Mt. Tabor. Below it lie Bethlehem, the Mount of Olives, the pool of Siloam, and, to the right, Cairo. Jerusalem is a square walled city. Imagery was relevant and informed: the camel illustrated to convey the active trade through Acre is correctly shown with two humps.

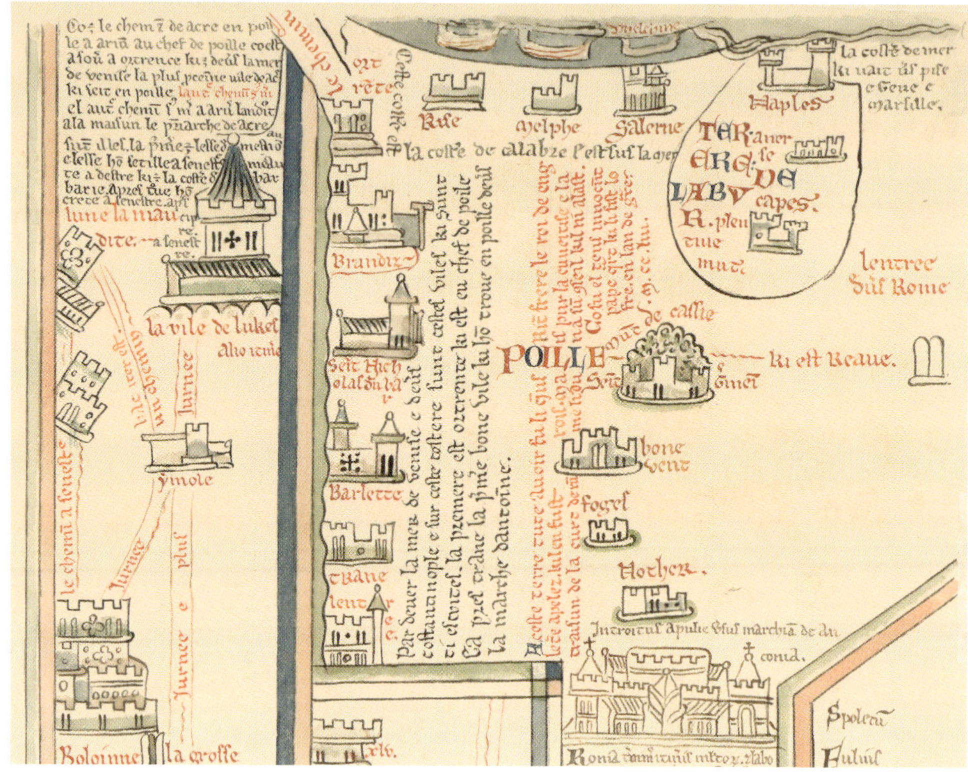

FIG. 35: Matthew Paris's London-to-Jerusalem itinerary map, detail showing the final European section before setting sail from southern Italy for Acre. Note Brindisi (Brandiz) to the upper left of center, a common point of departure. [*Itinéraire de Londres à Jérusalem*, Matthieu Paris, 1250, [Bibliothèque Nationale, GE DD-1985]

Matthew attached two flaps by a threadless hinge in which a strip of parchment is inserted through aligned slits. Although these relate to the manuscript's previous page, not our map, the entire London-to-Palestine itinerary should be seen as a single work. The upper flap has a map of Sicily on one side, and, on the side we see, upside down, a picture of Etna accompanied by a note describing Sicily's geography. The side we see of the lower flap has a historical summary of Rome.

Matthew Paris's slightly younger contemporary, the philosopher, scientist, and Franciscan friar Roger Bacon, was also keenly interested in Palestine, a topic that fit handsomely into his belief in empiricism—the concept that knowledge is based on observable and repeatable evidence, what we would now call science, and in which he was influenced by the Iraqi mathematician, astronomer, and physicist Ḥasan Ibn al-Haytham (ca. 965–ca. 1040). Bacon summarized Palestinian geography thus:

> Beginning with the coast, we find Gaza on the confines of Egypt and Palestine, then proceeding northward Ascalon, Joppa, Azotus, Caesarea, Acon, Tyre, Sarepta, Sidon, Barut, Gibeleth, Tortosa, Laodicea. From this last to Antioch is two days' journey. From Antioch to Tarsus in Cilicia three days' journey. Passing to the interior, we find Beer-sheba at the southern boundary. Twenty miles to the north is Hebron, the place of sepulture of the patriarchs. Near Hebron is Carmel, and a little to the east, the town and mountain of Ziph; fourteen miles to the north is Bethlehem, which is six miles to the south of Jerusalem. This city is twelve leagues from Joppa, and nine leagues to the east of it is Jericho. Tekoa, the country of Amos, is twelve miles to the south-east, and here we come to Pentapolis, the region of the Dead Sea, where nothing lives, where bodies that usually sink in water float, lumps of bitumen are found on the surface; here too are found the apples of Sodom.

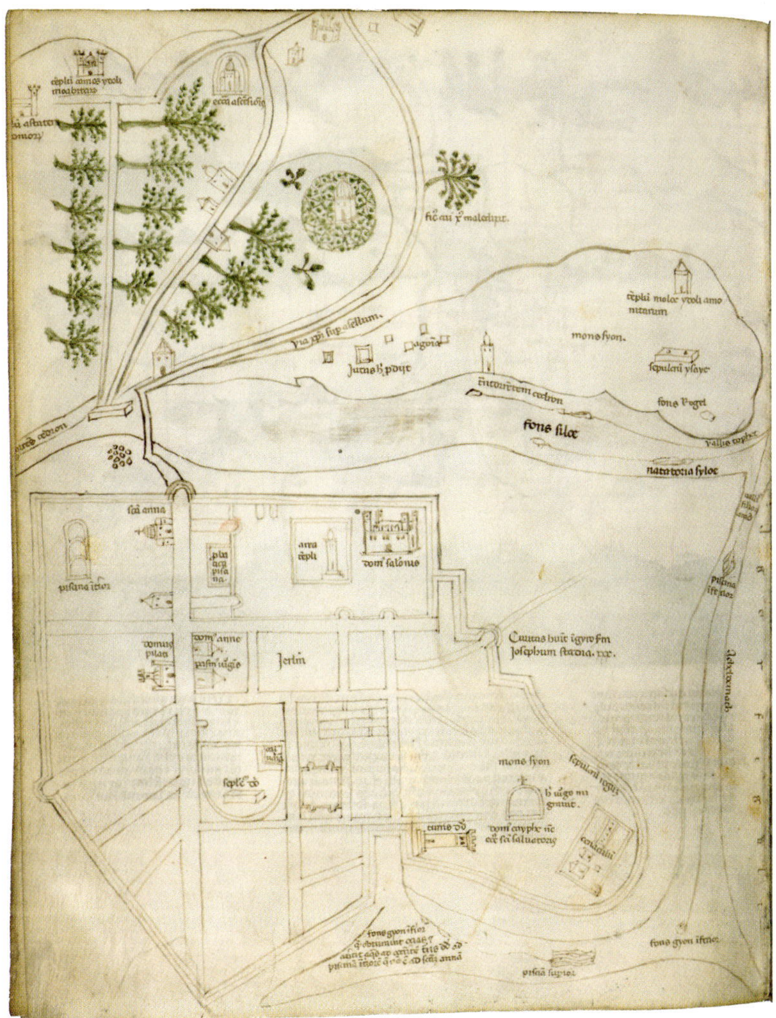

FIG. 36: Map of Jerusalem, from Marino Sanudo's *Liber secretorum fidelium crucis*. Mount of Olives is at the upper left. Within the city, the Temple Mount, Holy Sepulchre, Tower of David, and Mount Syon are illustrated and marked. The dominant feature is however the Kidron (Ceron) Valley flanking the top and right (east and south), of enormous Biblical significance, and associated with seasonal flooding. [Bodleian Library MS. Tanner 190]

> The Jordan flows into the Dead Sea. Its origin is by two branches from Lebanon, and it passes through the lakes of Gennesareth and Tiberias. North of Jericho is Scythopolis or Bethsan. Westward and to the north of Jerusalem is Anathoth, the birthplace of Jeremiah. Thence northward, twelve leagues from Jerusalem, is Samaria, now called Sebaste. North-eastward is the plain of Megiddo; north of this and east of Acon, at seven leagues' distance, is Nazareth.[9]

Bacon's interest in the scientific study of the geography of Palestine intersected with his spiritual theories:

> By geography, which is dependent on astronomy, we can determine the precise position and the physical conditions of the places named in Scripture. All these, apart from their literal importance, have a distinct spiritual significance. The river symbolizes the world; the Dead Sea, hell; Jericho, the flesh; the Mount of Olives, spiritual life; the valley of Jehoshaphat, humility; Jerusalem, the soul in the enjoyment of peace, or again the Church militant and triumphant. Minute research will reveal numberless intermediate meanings.

Among the several pilgrims to Palestine that influenced Latin mapmakers in the late medieval period, one stands out: Burchard of Mount Sion, who was in Palestine not for a quick sojourn, but for ten years between 1274 and 1284, and who wrote a detailed account of the land—one that proved all the more important to Christendom because of its loss of Acre seven years after he left.

The transmission of pilgrims' geographic data and its assemblage into cartographic form was rarely a straightforward matter of a traveler's original map being copied and recopied. Instead, names became associated with maps for reasons often having little to do with them, such as the manuscript in which it was included, as we saw in the case of the "Jerome" map. In the era of printed maps, they often assume the name of the publisher, engraver, or woodblock cutter, none of whom typically had any involvement in the map's geography. The case of Burchard illustrates another way: when mapmakers assign a particular traveler's nomenclature to maps conceived independently of the particular travels, so dissimilar maps may all carry that traveler's name. Such is the case with Burchard.

FIG. 37: Palestine, related to an Italian manuscript of ca. 1300, this example of English origin, second half of the fourteenth century. [Bodleian Library, MS. Douce 389]

Three contrasting maps are associated with his pilgrimage. Two made their debuts in the first quarter of the fourteenth century, geographically unrelated but both incorporating nomenclature from Buchard's account while it was still hot off the copyist's desk.[10] The third, the least sophisticated, came a century and a half later, the first printed map of Palestine (fig. 41), in a book that included an account of his sojourn.

The large, elongated "Buchard" map above (fig. 37) will not help get you to Palestine, but it will be an inspiring guide once you get there. The map was born of newly-proficient knowledge of the Palestinian interior, combined with the desire to attract Christian visitors. It presents the land as a virtual Christian playground, a series of interconnected welcoming cities and towns marked with their religious-historical significance and iconography, geographic accuracy honored but secondary to the pleasing use of the map's real estate. This can be seen as the beginning of what we would now call Holy Land travel or tourist maps. In later centuries, printed maps that took a remarkably similar approach were answering the same call. Compare this map, for example, to the nineteenth-century map on pages 160-161 below.

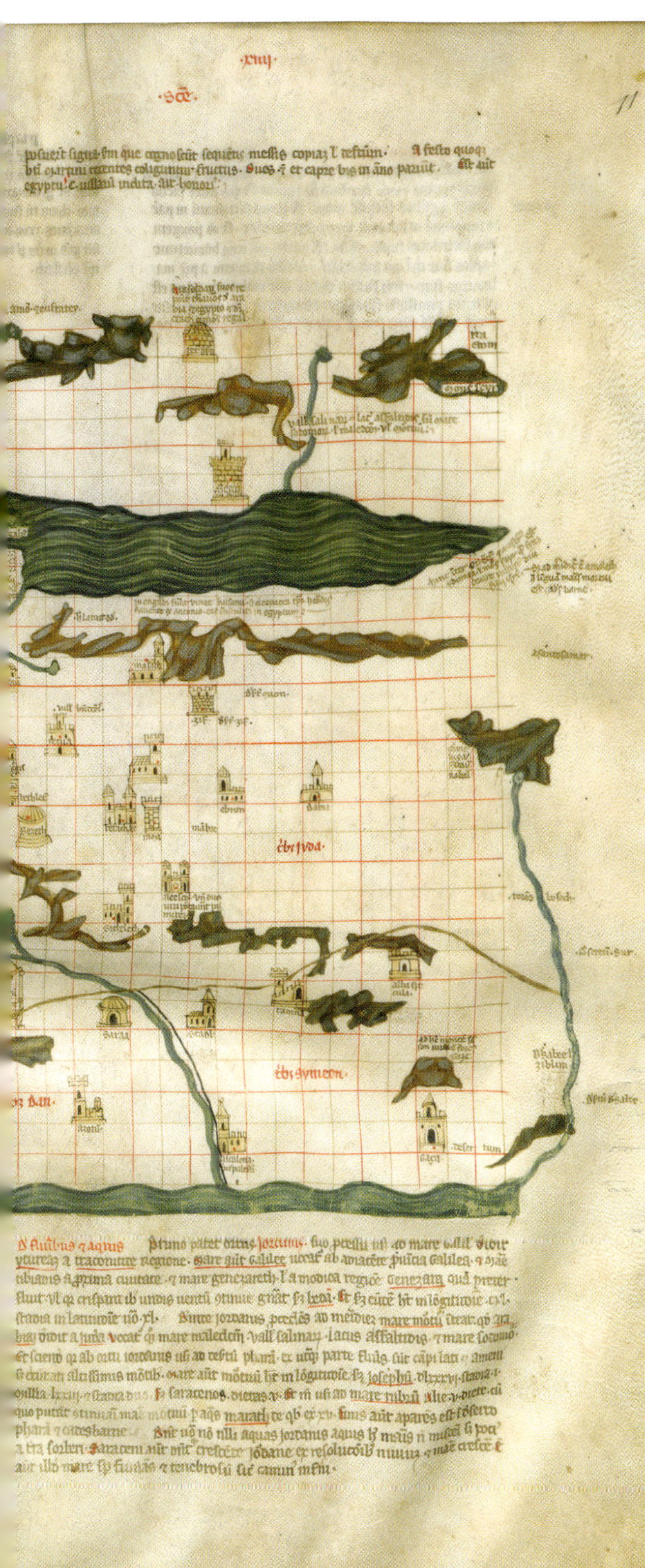

The other Buchard-based map of the period (fig. 38) served a very different but complementary purpose. It maps all of Palestine and its coasts, focusing on the correct placement of major locales, and it would become the most influential prototype—model for other mapmakers—of the late medieval period. It is attributed to the excellent Italian chart maker Pietro Vesconte and is found in various copies of Marino Sanudo's *Liber secretorum fidelium crucis*, a work that argued for renewed Crusades and laid out a methodical strategy for their success, one that coordinated military action with economic blockade. Sanudo was more than theologically or emotionally invested in the issue: he was born to an influential trading family that was active in the eastern Mediterranean, and indeed he had spent time in Acre as a teenager. Latin maps of Palestine were now integral to military plans for the European recapture of Palestine.

With the Vesconte-Sanudo map, a remarkable feature appears, entirely new to most who saw it: a grid. In his text, Sanudo provides a list of places and their positions, and explains that by dividing Palestine into squares of one league, each feature could be correctly placed. The lines are not coordinates; they are not to locate points on the earth, but simply to draw the map to scale. The Vesconte-Sanudo grid is nonetheless an important step in Latin cartography, and the question as to how the idea arose has a conjectural answer: Arabic maps, especially given that the map is the result of newly heightened intercourse with the Levant.

FIG. 38: Palestine, Pietro Vesconte. In Paulinus Venetus, *Chronologia magna*, 1328-1343. [Bibliothèque Nationale, Latin 4939]

FIG. 39: Pietro Vesconte, the Levant. In Paulinus Venetus, *Chronologia magna*, 1328–1343. [Bibliothèque Nationale, Latin 4939]

The wider region is covered by another map of Vesconte found in some copies of Sanudo's work (fig. 39, above). Its peculiarly straight, angular Palestinian and Egyptian coasts leave uncluttered space for the map's main focus, points east under Islamic rule. Its pronounced Red Sea and Persian Gulf create an Arabia one evolutionary step beyond that of the "Jerome" map, now with Mecca marked. The coverage extends to Mesopotamia, Persia, and the Tigris and Euphrates Rivers on the east, and the Egyptian coast on the southwest.

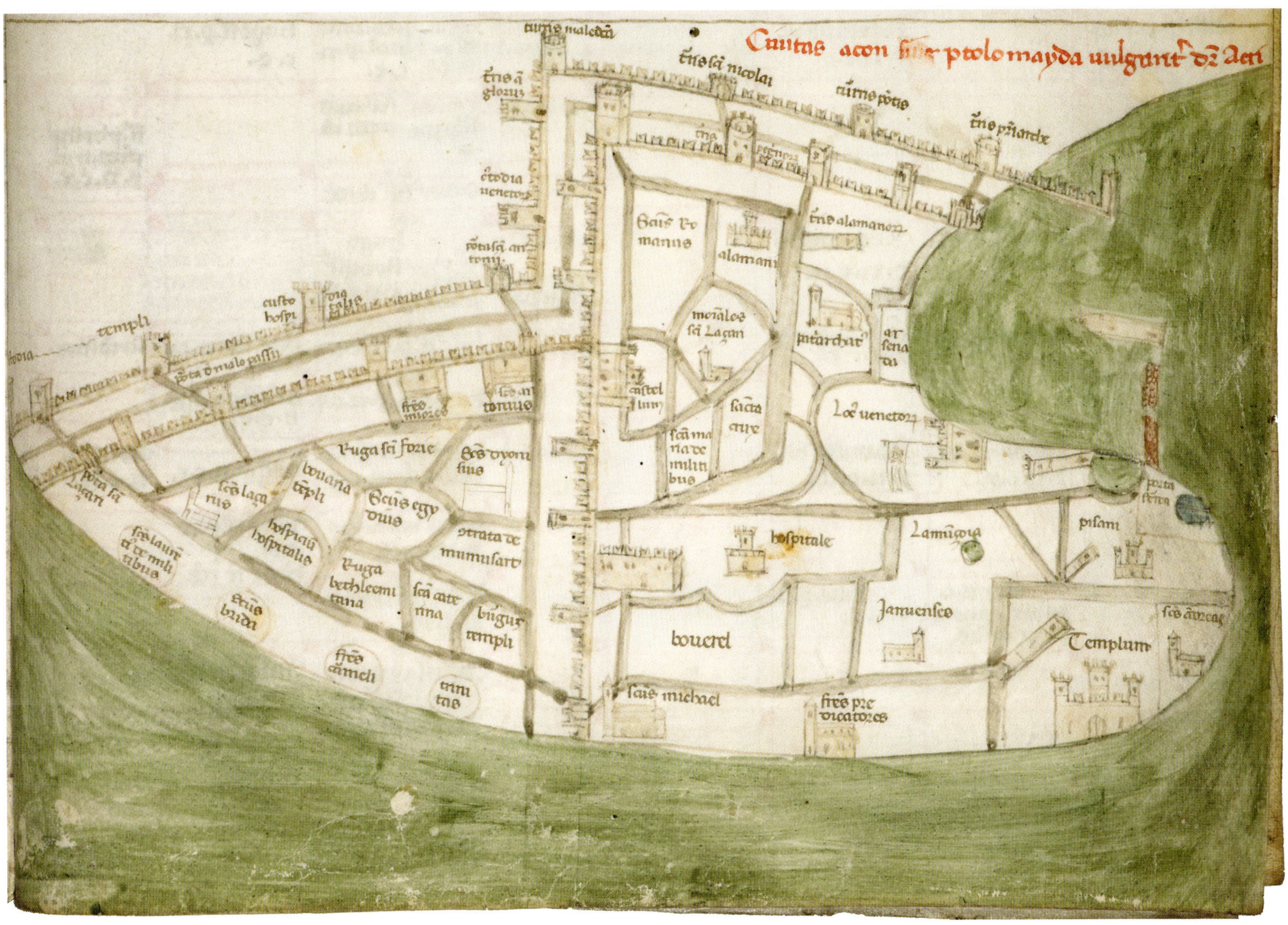

FIG. 40: Acre, Pietro Vesconte, Venice, c1321–1324. from Marino Sanudo's *Liber secretorum fidelium crucis*. [Bodleian Library MS. Tanner 190]

As for Burchard, inquisitiveness coexisted with fancy. He imagined himself to be in the land of the Bible—literally. By way of illustration, he "worked hard" to see the pillar of salt that was all that remained of Lot's wife after she disobeyed angels' commands not to look back as the wicked city of Sodom was destroyed. Burchard believed that the *actual pillar of salt* was there to be seen, not simply the site where tradition places the myth. The reason he never got to see the salt monolith from Genesis was not that the pillar wasn't there after these millennia, but that "Saracens" had warned him that wild animals, snakes, and unfriendly Bedouin ("particularly strong and very wicked men") made the area too dangerous to visit. He regretted having listened to the warnings, because he "found later [that the dangers] was not the real situation."

Cedar et tabernacula eius
heremo
Mos tabor
libanus
Fons ortoru
Nazareth
Abelina
Naym
Leopardoru
Caparnaum
decapolis
Melchisedech
Damasci
Tripolis
Cana
betulia
Anthiochi
cesaria philipi
Senerech
Dothaim
Mare galilee
Aradiu
Dor et Dan
Bethsan
Affechsuria
Hay
Galgala
Biblius
Magedon
bethel
beriebus
Couallis illustris
Emo
Anathoth
Sydon
Thorone
Symin
Bethania
sarepta
Ieshahel
Accon
Mons fortis
Laech
Garizim
caiphas
Casale lapte
Gabaa
Caphue
Dan mos
Samaria
Sichem
io iiii
Bethel
Mons sylo altissimus
Gabaa iosue
Lepua
rama
Cesaria palestini
Actuum xxi act x
Assot
sarona
Catho
Ramathaim
armatia i re i
Joppe
Japha

Amonite
Mons seyr gñ. xiiii. et deu. iii.
area polis
Cades bar ne nu. xiii.
Terra moab
Petra deserti
Mare mortuu
Desertu phares
Mons syna
Jericho ier. vi
Betagla
Statua salis mulier loth gñ. xix
Terra amalech i r xv
Vallis bñdcois
Herodiu
collis achile
Engadi. i. re xxiii.
Carmelus. i. re. xxv.
Tecua civitas. ii. re. xiiii.
Natatoria syloe io. ix
acheldemach
Batachar et Ramavilla
Betleem
Turris gregis
Ebron noua
Ebron vetus
Betsech
Mambre gñ xviii
Bethsura
Calvaria
agerdamascenus
Neelescol nu. xiii.
Sochot. i. re. xvii. io. xxi.
dos zacharie
vallis lacrimarum
Mare rubru
Cariathiarim archa. xx. ãnis
Raphaim
Bersabee
Egiptus
azotus
ascolona
accaron
Jamnia
Gaza

(Previous Page) FIG. 41: Palestine, in the *Rudimentum novitiorum*, Lucas Brandis (printer), Lübeck, 1475; Woodblock, with inserted moveable type. [Library of Congress, Incun. 1475 .R8]

FIG. 42: View of Palestine on a text leaf, Joel ben Simeon, 1478, in the so-called Washington Haggadah. (Library of Congress, LC Hebr. Ms 181]

Burchard's account, and a map of Palestine based on it, entered the age of printing with the formidable *Rudimentum Novitiorum* of 1475 (fig. 41), whose mappamundi we saw earlier (fig. 26). The woodcut map's importance is however beyond Palestine: it is the earliest printed map of certain date of anywhere, based on actual observation (which the work's mappamundi was not). That the first empirically based printed map was of Palestine is indicative of the land's importance in the European mindset.

Distinct from the earlier Buchard-based maps, the author of the *Rudimentum* (probably the printer, Lucas Brandis de Schass) drew his map in medieval style, with the

FIG. 43: Leaf from *Secreta fidelium Crucis*, Marino Sanudo, with historiated borders depicting pilgrims and Crusaders arriving in Palestine. Venice, ca. 1321-1324 [Bodleian Library MS. Tanner 190]

various realms and towns drawn as hill motifs, save for Jerusalem, depicted as the familiar circular walled city. People disembark their craft at Jaffa, and at Acre bay, the well-defined inlet on the left with the castle. Since Acre was "home" for most European pilgrims, numerals accompany several of the map's place-names to indicate their distance from the port city. Whereas the coastal areas brought greater realism, inland allowed tradition: Moses comes down from Mount Sinai with the tablets, Christ is baptized in the Jordan, and is crucified at Calvary.

Although the *Rudimentum* itself was never reprinted, both its maps were recut twice, in 1488 and 1491, for the work *Mer des Hystoires*, in which form the maps were reprinted as late as 1555, bringing its medieval image of Palestine and its Jerusalem-centered world map well into the age of global exploration.

FIG. 44: Palestine, "modern" (not Ptolemaic), from Francesco Berlinghieri, *Geografia,* Florence, 1482 [Library of Congress, G1005 1482]

The general Sanudo-Vesconte model entered the realm of the printed map seven years later, in 1482—twice, both as "modern" additions to Ptolemaic atlases. They flaunt wildly different coastlines, but share one conspicuous departure from the earlier manuscript maps: a heightened focus on the Tribes of Israel.

In Florence, the atlas was copper-engraved, the text a resetting of Ptolemy's *Geography* as dialogue composed in the *terza rima* used by Dante (fig. 44). At the same time, on the other side of the Alps, a formal edition of the *Geographia* with the full text in Latin hit the market in Ulm with the maps in woodcut (fig. 45). That the woodcuts lacked the fineness and subtlety of the copper engraving was not all bad: the bolder

FIG. 45: Palestine, “modern” (not Ptolemaic), from Ptolemy’s *Geografia, Ulm*, 1482 [Library of Congress, 48042060]

woodcut was seen by its publisher as an invitation for color. And so it is with that atlas that we first see in-house map color, the atlas offered for sale uncolored or, for a higher price, with color applied by the publisher’s colorists before the sheets were bound. While no two examples are, or indeed could be, identical, there was a consistency of style to the coloring, and a separate consistency to a second printing four years later.

Copperplates of this early period typically left behind a patina that was a pronounced—arguably positive—aesthetic artifact. Barring a buyer’s individual initiative, copperplate maps were not normally colored until the marketing considerations of Dutch and Belgian atlas publishers almost a century later.

The final influential European pilgrimage to Palestine before the clock struck 1500 was also the first of any expedition anywhere whose account and map went directly into the new medium of printing, with its immediate, wide dissemination and replication of a single image altered only by new editions, not by copyists' errors and indulgences. With the book's woodcut view-maps, Palestine also became the subject of the first printed book with fold-out illustrations, and the first with woodcuts to employ the device of hatching to simulate shading.

Breydenbach, a Dean in the Electorate of Mainz, set off for Palestine with two colleagues in April 1483. Fifteen days later they reached Venice, and found themselves among other pilgrims in the city for the same voyage. He remarked that it required much astuteness to bargain with the master of the vessel, who in his case was Augustino Contarini, whom another pilgrim, Pietro Casola, described as a "magnificent miser ... a Venetian patrician, and a very upright man of good fame." Like so many pilgrims all the way back to Arculf, Breydenbach saw his

FIG. 46: Woodblock view-map of Palestine, by Erhard Reuwich, who accompanied Breydenbach to Palestine. From Breydenbach's *Peregrinatio in terram sanctam*, Mainz, 1486. [This example Bodleian Library Arch. B ca. 25]

pilgrimage as redemption for the indulgences of his youth. The Dutch artist and printer Erhard Reuwich was one of Breydenbach's friends on the pilgrimage, and it is to Reuwich that we owe the volume's wide fold-out woodcut view-map of Palestine in fig. 46.

The map extends from Damascus and Tripoli on the north to Alexandria and the Red Sea on the south, and shows Contarini's vessel docked at Jaffa. It disregards both scale and consistent spatial plane—Jerusalem, which occupies nearly half the map and reverts to an idealized circular model, is tilted upward toward us. A fresh and imaginative use of the printed medium, the map can be seen as a self-advertisement to win the respect, the mystique, the esteem, of having traveled to the Holy Land.

FIG. 47: Imaginary view of Palestine, from a French translation by Jean Miélot of Burchard's *Descriptio Terrae sanctae of Mont-Sion.* [*Bibliothèque Nationale*, ark:/12148/btv1b100215049]

FIG. 48: Illuminated manuscript depicting a fanciful Jerusalem, the opening pages of a travel guide for a pilgrimage to Palestine. In English and Latin, it is an early such work to be in the vernacular. England, c1500. [The Queen's College, University of Oxford, MS 357]

The terms of Breydenbach's passage testify to Palestinian pilgrimage as a going business. The galley was to arrive at Jaffa within a day of a rival vessel, or else there was a penalty of 1000 florins. Eighty men would be provided for defense. En route, the vessel would stay at each port for a maximum of three days, unless the weather forced a later departure. Two meals a day would be provided, consisting of good bread, good wine, fresh meat, eggs, and other victuals. Should a pilgrim die before reaching Palestine, half the deceased's payment for passage would be returned to that person's executors; and should a pilgrim reach Palestine but die en route back to Venice, their goods would be returned. Ten ducats would be returned should any pilgrim decide to leave the group to go to the Shrine of St. Katherine, providing timely notice being given so as not to keep the galley waiting at Jaffa. Should an interpreter be required, the expense would be covered by the master as far as Jaffa and back, but not for the pilgrims' travels within Palestine. The fare was forty-two ducats, to be paid in the newly coined *tzecka*, half up front, half in Jaffa.

The most eventful printed book to include images of Palestine in the remaining years of the fifteenth century was the monumental *Nuremberg Chronicle* of 1493, a massive history of the world with woodcut views of major cities. Of Jerusalem, however, it contained only imaginary Biblical images: a circular walled city dominated by Solomon's Temple, and a view of the Roman sacking of the city.

FIG. 49: Tyre (bottom) and Jaffa (top), from a picture book of Mandeville's Travels, ca. 1410. [British Library, Add MS 24189]

PALESTINE IN LATE MEDIEVAL LITERATURE

At the end of the fourteenth century, two starkly contrasting works featuring Palestine appeared in close succession: the *Travels of Sir John Mandeville*, and Chaucer's *Canterbury Tales*.

Palestine figures prominently in Mandeville's immensely popular travel account, penned in the third quarter of the fourteenth century. Although both the "travels" and the author are almost surely fictional, its descriptions of the Levant are important simply because they were believed. Illustrated manuscripts spread imagery even more viscerally fabulous than the text, such as that in fig. 49, a glorified view of Jaffa and Tyre in a manuscript dating from ca. 1410. In the lower image, Mandeville pays duties at Tyre to enter Palestine.

Regarding Tyre, Mandeville writes:

> From Cyprus, men go to the land of Jerusalem by the sea: and in a day and in a night, he that hath good wind may come to the haven of Tyre, that is now clept Surrye. There was some-time a great city and a good of Christian men, but Saracens have destroyed it a great part; and they keep that haven right well, for dread of Christian men.

And of Jaffa,

> And whoso will go long time on the sea, and come nearer to Jerusalem, he shall go from Cyprus by sea to Port Jaffa. For that is the next haven to Jerusalem; for from that haven is not but one day journey and a half to Jerusalem. And the town is called Jaffa; for one of the sons of Noah that hight Japhet founded it, and now it is clept Joppa. And ye shall understand, that it is one of the oldest towns of the world, for it was founded before Noah's flood.

Hanging on the Jaffa city walls in fig. 49 is a giant animal bone. Repeating and embellishing existing lore, Mandeville states that

> And yet there sheweth in the rock, there as the iron chains were fastened, that Andromeda, a great giant, was bounden with, and put in prison before Noah's flood, of the which giant, is a rib of his side that is forty foot long.

As Herman Melville reminds us in *Moby-Dick*, "What seems most singular and suggestively important in this story, is this: it was from Joppa that Jonah set sail."

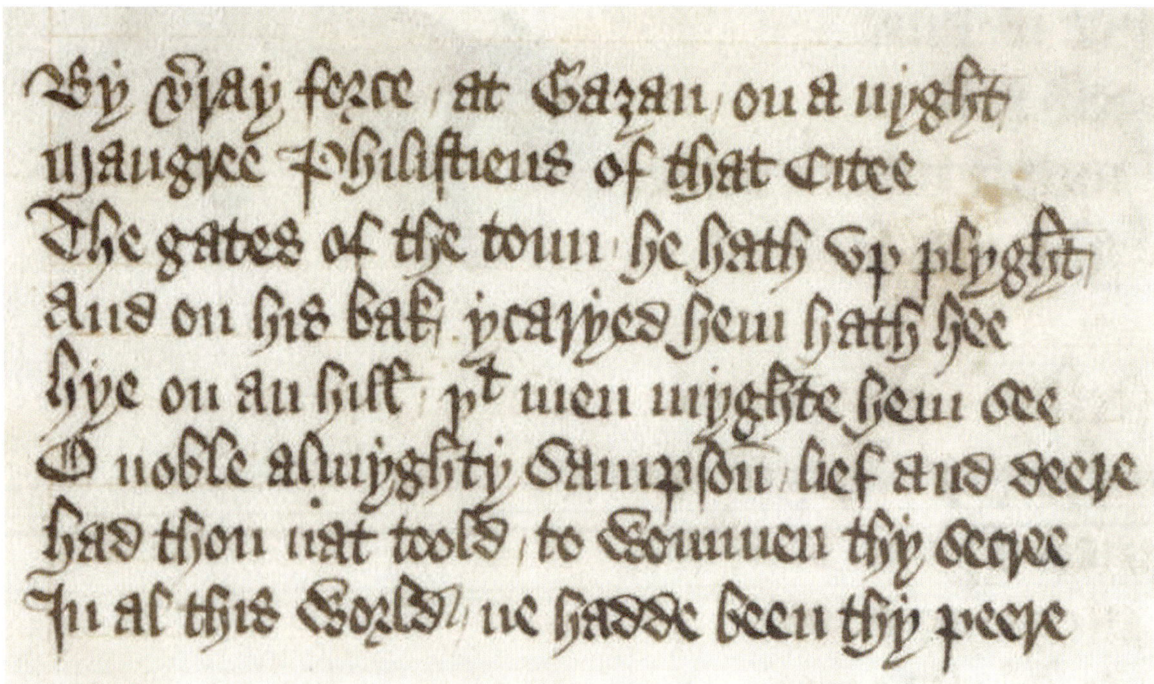

By verray force at Gazan on a nyght
Maugree Philistiens of that Citee
The gates of the toun he hath up plyght
And on his bak ycaryed hem hath hee
Hye on an hill þt men myghte hem see
O noble almyghty Sampson leef and deere
Had thou nat toold to wommen thy secree
In al this world ne hadde been thy peere

FIG. 50. From The Monk's Tale, *The Canterbury Tales*, Geoffrey Chaucer. This manuscript ca. 1400-1410 [Huntington Digital Library, mssEL 26 C 9 (The Ellesmere Chaucer)]

Palestine was not the destination of Geoffrey Chaucer's pilgrims in *The Canterbury Tales* (1387–1400), but it was indeed the destination of their storytelling en route from London to Canterbury. In the illustrated verse, Samson, in Gaza, is betrayed by his lover Delilah.

> By very force, at Gaza, on a night,
> Maugre the Philistines of that city,
> The gates of the town he hath up plight, plucked, wrenched
> And on his back y-carried them hath he
> High on an hill, where as men might them see.
> O noble mighty Sampson, lefe and dear, loved
> Hadst thou not told to women thy secre,
> In all this world there had not been thy peer.

Mixed in with the era's fanciful imagery of Palestine, literary and visual, is a woodblock allegorical map in the figure of a lion, oriented with Jerusalem at the top (fig. 51). The animal symbolized Mark the Evangelist in this cartographic device used for memorizing the events recorded in the Gospels. At the top, Jesus weeps over Jerusalem; Pilate's judgement of Jesus is to the left, the resurrection of Christ to the right. Below the lion's head is the parable of the vineyard workers, and moving farther down, the red-capped figure warns of a false prophet. The mnemonic map was printed in 1470 or within a few years following, just predating the "real" 1475 map of Palestine in the *Rudimentum*.

FIG. 51: A mnemonic “map” with Jerusalem on the top, the last of fifteen such illustrations in *Ars memorandi per figuras Evangelistarum*, a block book printed in Germany in the early 1470s. [Library of Congress Incun. X .A88]

FIG. 52: Planispheric Astrolabe, North Africa, 9th century AD. Brass, cast, with fretwork rete and surface engraving North Africa. 18.5 x 13.2cm [The Nasser D. Khalili Collection of Islamic Art, SCI 430]

CHAPTER 3

PALESTINE IN PARALLEL MEDIEVAL WORLDS

PART 2: PILOTS, TRAVELERS, SCHOLARS

PORTOLAN CHARTS: THE PILOT'S VIEW

By the late thirteenth century, radically accurate and detailed charts of the Mediterranean Sea began to appear bearing no relation to previous maps and leaving no forensic trail for a map sleuth to trace back their origin. Based on what survives—a highly unreliable gauge—it is as if they were simply invented, born fully formed.

These were the portolan charts, sea charts focusing on the coasts and their ports with little or no inland information. They are distinct from *portolanos*, books of sailing directions—pilot books, rutters, *peripli*. The two served complementary roles and could be used in concert. Their evolutions are undoubtedly entwined.

Books of sailing directions in various forms, recording any combination of ports, landmarks, direction, distance, speed, winds, stars, and sea currents, had long been essential tools for Greek, Arab, and Latin navigators. Such information could be more useful than seeing an analog of a sea coast—a map—at least until maps were sufficiently accurate as to be an aid rather than a hindrance.

Early portolan charts mapped the Mediterranean and Black Seas, in full or part, with unprecedented accuracy and detail. They were drawn to scale, with scale indicated, a rare virtue on topographical maps until the sixteenth century. Consistent with their use as onboard navigational tools, portolan charts typically lacked set orientation—the pilot would turn the chart freely according to need. A further distinguishing feature was that any embellishment was distinct from the map proper; in charts actually used at sea, typically there was none.

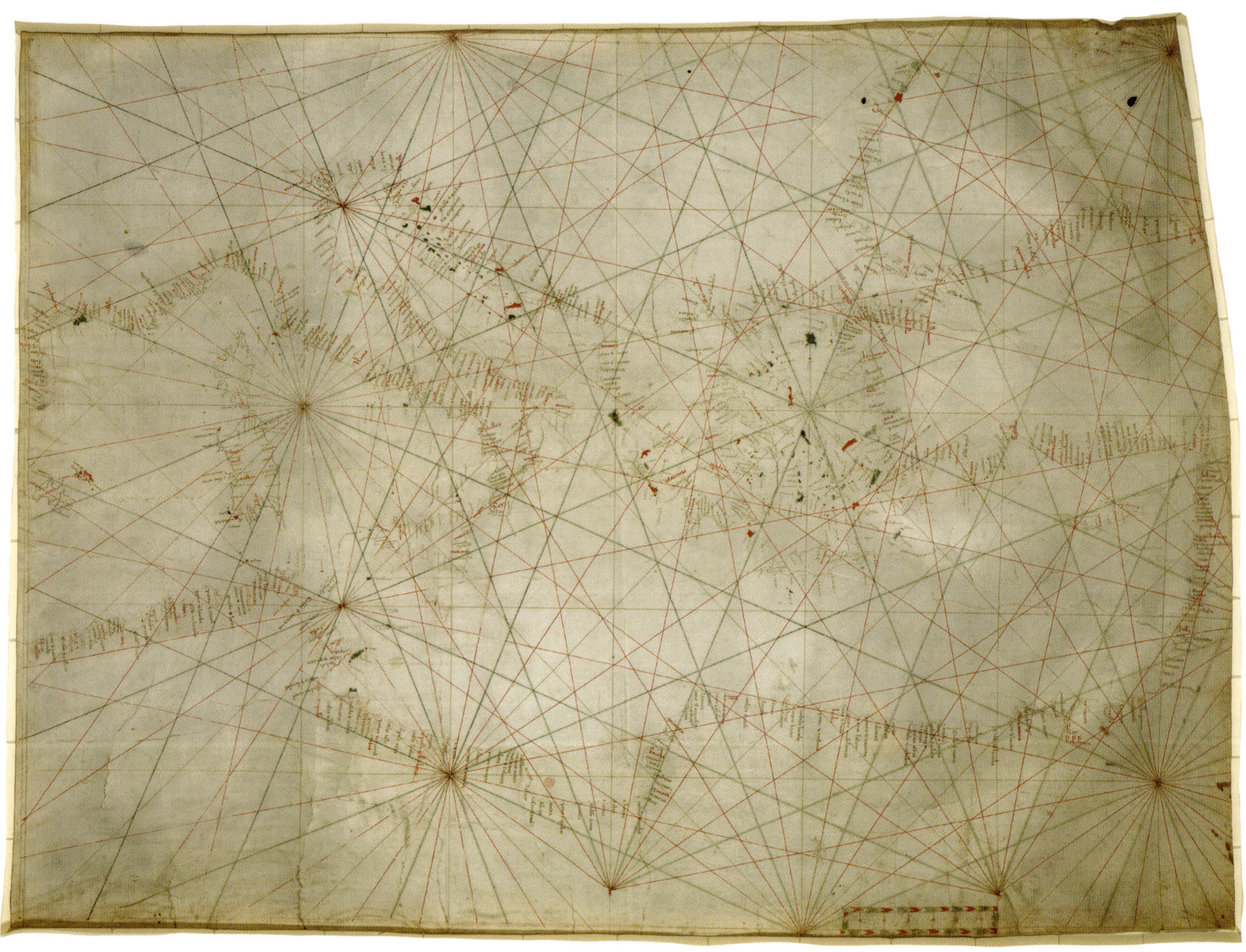

FIG. 53, 54: Portolan chart of the eastern Mediterranean and Black Sea, Italian (Genoa?), between 1320 and 1350 [Library of Congress, G5672.M4P5 13-- .P6]

FIG. 54: Palestine, detail of fig. 53.

The chart in fig. 53 & 54 is among the early survivors, here illustrated with north at the top. Note the Italian peninsula on the left, Turkey on the right, and part of the Black Sea above it. Most ports are marked in brown ink, while the more important ones are prominent in red. On the Palestinian coast, it is Jaffa that takes that honor. Sixteen crisscrossing lines—rhumb lines—pivot from central axes, the number on some charts doubled to thirty-two. Color-coding made the paths easier to select and follow. Typically, as here, eight principal directions or winds were drawn in black or (if through fading) brown ink, the eight between them in green, and if a thirty-two-line compass, the remaining sixteen in red.

FIG 55, 56:

Top: The so-called Carta Pisana, c1270 (as dated by the Bibliothèque Nationale), oriented to the south.

Bottom: The upper-left of the chart, Palestine, here turned 180° for clarity. All rhumb lines lead to Acre. Of unknown authorship, the chart is named simply for its discovery in Pisa. It is likely of Genoese origin, and is generally considered to be the oldest surviving portolan chart. Radiocarbon and other exotic dating techniques support, but cannot prove, the 1270 date, while attempts to assign a later date based on its comparison with other charts are limited by the premise that the evolution of such charts was an even process. [Bibliothèque Nationale, ark:/12148/btv1b52503226n]

FIG. 57: Detail from a portolan chart of the Mediterranean region and Europe, made in Goa by Fernando Vaz Dourado, c1580. [Bavarian State Library; image Library of Congress 2021668459]

Portolan charts can be divided into four general categories. Chronological in order of their appearance, they are:

- Those actually created for onboard use as hands-on navigational tools, such as those in figs. 53 through 56. These were typically plain, free of superfluous markings, and of manageable size. They charted only what was known. What was not known was left blank or, if suspected, marked with a dotted line. Their depiction of Palestine was entirely secular. Likely the most numerous in their day, they were the most perishable, and early examples are the rarest of survivors.
- Those designed for academics, intellectuals, and the upper-class as items of prestige and erudition. These typically covered a larger area, and by the early fifteenth century some included Atlantic islands.[11] They usually boasted embellishment, typically of anthropological or religious nature, the imagery implying orientation. An example is the 1559 chart by the Majorican mapmaker Mateus Prunes (fig. 59), oriented west, the full chart extending well beyond the Mediterranean. Palestine is easy to locate: it is directly above the word *ASIA* at the bottom.
- Those born with the advent of major European oceanic voyages, sophisticated sea charts that kept rulers abreast of their fleets' latest discoveries and imperial claims. The quest for accuracy and detail was tempered only in the service of political flattery, manipulation, and even deliberate deceit, most famously through the pushing and shoving of elusive longitude after the 1494 papal Treaty of Tordesillas divided Spain's and Portugal's "discoveries" in the Americas, Pacific, and Far East between them.
- The final offshoot of the portolan chart, which blossomed in the mid-sixteenth century, was the antithesis of its origins and purpose. Here, the sea chart became merely the canvas for precisely that which the genre had smartly excluded: gratuitous embellishment, indeed embellishment often irrelevant to the map. Not only had the empty inland spaces provided too much of a temptation, but unknown shores, especially in the southwest Pacific, were filled in by imagination, an abuse the Mediterranean was spared. We will see these in their heyday, the sixteenth century.

FIG. 58: The Eastern Mediterranean and Black Sea, portolan chart by Joan Martines, Messina (Sicily), c1580. [The Huntington Library, mss HM 33 (which dates it "between 1575 and 1599")]

That the first type became a must-have tool of Mediterranean pilots is reflected in a series of late-fourteenth-century documents relating to a consignment operation of a Barcelona merchant. Batches of four *cartes de navegar*, presumably drawn by local chart makers, were consigned to one or two mariners to sell on to pilots in the course of their travels. Portolan charts had become one of the essential tools upon which Mediterranean pilots relied for efficiency of business, and possibly their lives.[12]

FIG. 59: Portolan chart of the Mediterranean by Mateus Prunes, Majorica, 1559. Note the Red Sea and Mount Sinai on the south (left). [Library of Congress, G5672.M4P5 1559 .P7]

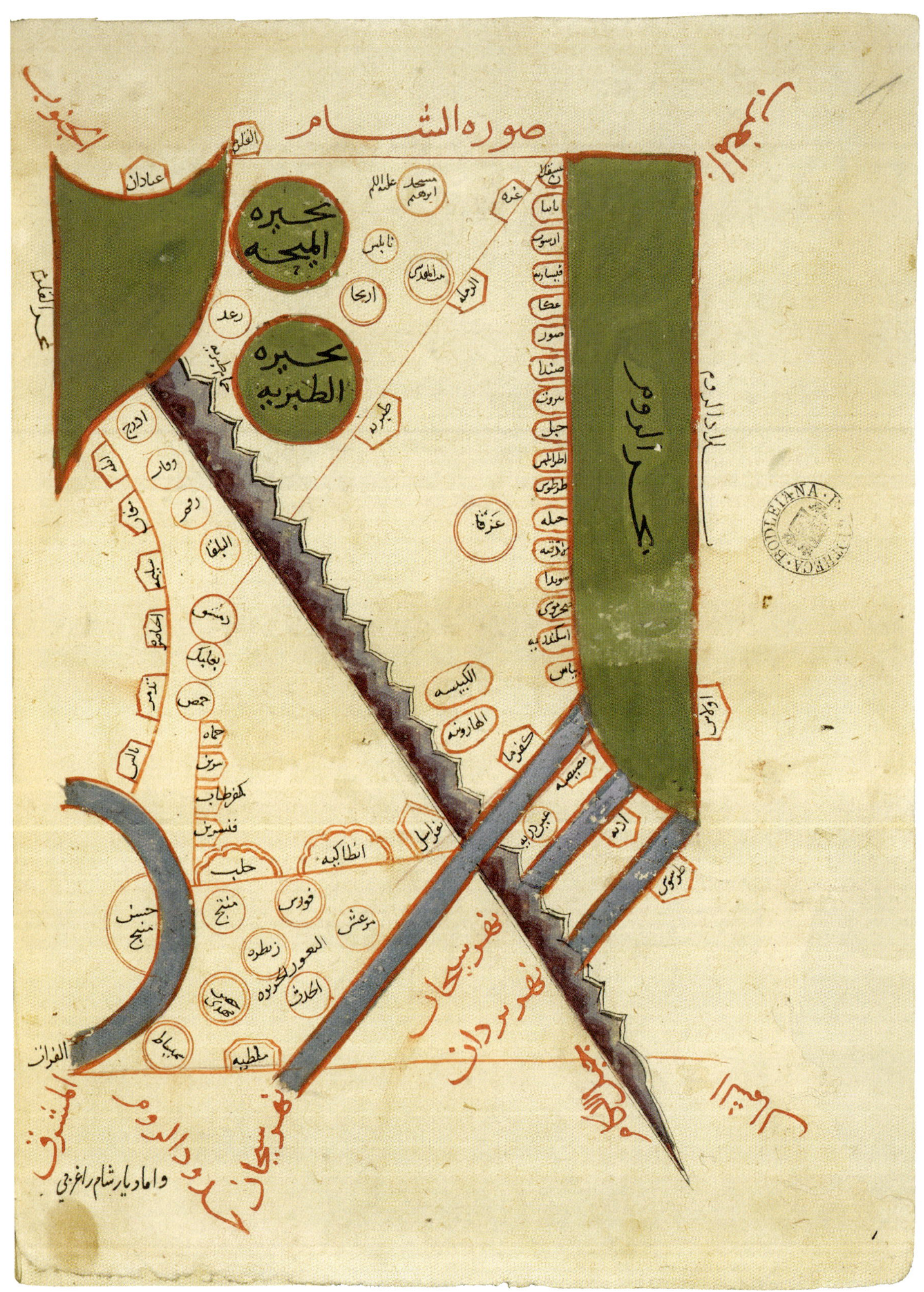

FIG. 60: Map of the Levant, Iṣṭakhrī, mid-tenth century (but 1272). [Bodleian Library, MS. Ouseley 373]

ARABIC MAPPING

Portolan charts were such useful tools that some Arabic ("Islamic") mariners copied them wholesale, making no change except to translate the place-names. There was no reason to reinvent them, and their secular nature was familiar—Arabic cartography was in general not theologically premised, even when by Muslims mapping cities key to Islam.

Until the cross-civilization melting of cartographic traditions of the late Middle Ages, Arabic and Latin cartographic traditions evolved largely to their own philosophies. Unlike their Latin counterparts, Arabic geographers early on sought to use formal methodology, and by the ninth century were compiling tables of places and coordinates, largely inspired by the Alexandrian geographer Claudius Ptolemy (ca. 100–170 CE).

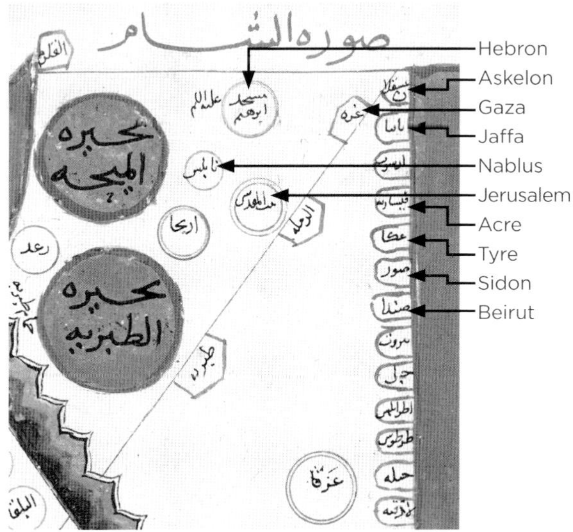

Key for fig. 60

The oldest known surviving maps by Arabic geographers are four dating from ca. 1037, in a copy of the *Book of the Description of the Earth* by al-Khwārazmī, a writer of diverse interests who was active in the first half of the ninth century. He was influenced by Ptolemy but compiled his own tables of the land and stars, and proposed a shorter, more accurate longitudinal breadth of the Mediterranean than Ptolemy's. His extant maps are of the "Island of the Jewel" (unidentified or semi-mythical island in the extreme east), the world (Indian?) ocean, Sea of Azov (northern Black Sea), and the only one that touches on the periphery of our subject, the Nile and its delta.

Al-Khwārazmī systemized the use of color on maps, and we can speculate that he was a likely source of the use of color coding by Latin portolan chart makers. We know that during the twelfth century, a period during which portolan charts were evolving, some of his writings were translated and became known to Latin scholars, such as his highly influential book on algebra—indeed the very word is a transliteration of the title of that book, *Al-Jabr*.

Map survival was kinder to al-Iṣṭakhrī, the tenth-century geographer and traveler whose *Book of Routes and Kingdoms* includes the map of the Levant in fig. 60. As is typical of Arabic maps, al-Iṣṭakhrī's were highly stylized, shapes and geometric patterns taking the place of literal geographic contours, with calligraphy often taking a prominent role.

In contrast to al-Khwārazmī, al-Iṣṭakhrī was far less concerned about theory as he was in depicting regions familiar to Arabic audiences in a format that was simplified, easy to memorize, and easy to duplicate. With these goals, his maps' extreme stylization was not merely aesthetic, but functional.

His map of the Levant is illustrative: it is "wrong" as a geographic analog, but conceptually clear in the way that a modern transit route map is wrong in order to be clear. Although there was no parallel in Latin chart-making as a genre, the technique was used when beneficial, such as in the sea chart of trading ports in fig. 78.

Al-Iṣṭakhrī's vertical sea on the right is the Mediterranean, with the eastern Mediterranean ports marked. The two round seas are the Dead (upper) and Galilee, with the Persian Gulf to their left.

FIG. 61: "The Golden Dome [Dome of the Rock] in Jerusalem," Aǧayib al-Maḫlūqāt wa ǧarayib al-Mawǧūdāt, 1388 [Bibliothèque Nationale, Persian Supplement 332, F. 140v.]

In contrast to the well-established Arabic mapmaking traditions known to us today, an elaborate, Egyptian (Fatimid) cosmographic manuscript survives that testifies to a wide diversity of medieval Arabic cosmographic thought: the *Kit b Ghar 'ib al-fun n wa-mulaḥ al-'uy n*, roughly translating as the *Book of Curiosities of the Sciences and Marvels for the Eye*, a copy of ca. 1200 of a work completed ca. 1020–1050. Its unknown author exudes a great individual curiosity about the cosmos, ordering creation from the heavens and working down to the earth, a sophisticated ordering of the universe and the interchange of celestial events with the terrestrial. Among the work's highly individual maps is one of the Mediterranean (fig. 62).

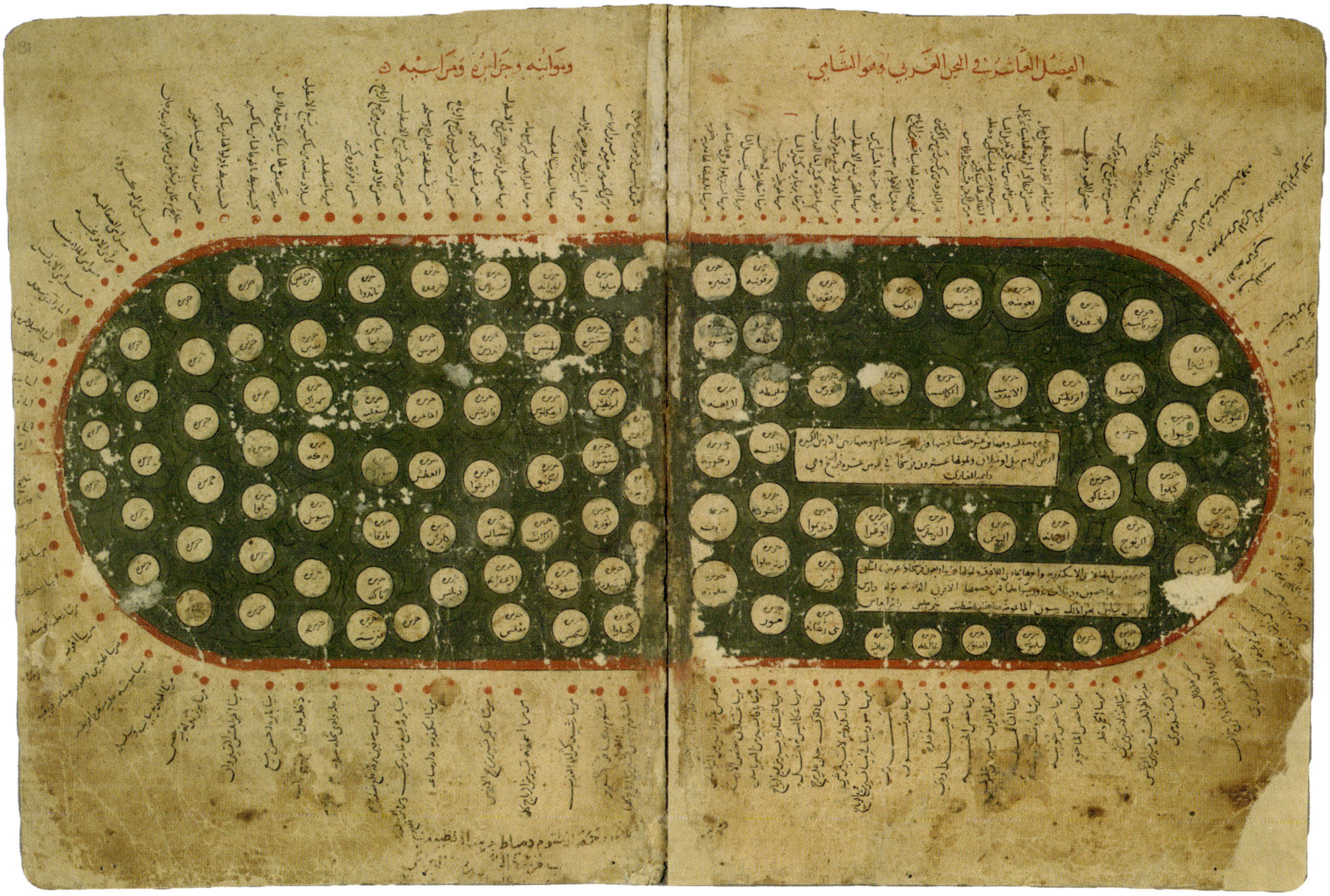

FIG. 62 (& keymap): Map of the Mediterranean Sea, *The Book of Curiosities*, Egypt, 1020-1050 (copy of c1200). [Bodleian Library, MS. Arab. c. 90]

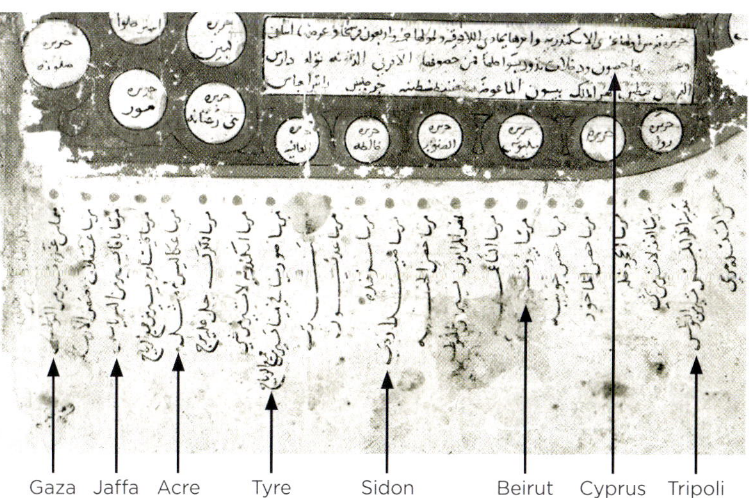

The visually closed Mediterranean includes Byzantine as well as Arabic ports of call, with the Levant lying below Cyprus, the lower of the two rectangular islands (the upper is Sicily). Gaza, Jaffa, and Acre are among the red place-marks along the bottom, immediately to the right of the centerfold. Along the upper left bend are the Lombards, the Slavs, the Franks, the Galicians, and al-Andalus. Constantinople is among those below the left red heading.

FIG. 63 (below), 64 (detail on right): World map from *The Book of Curiosities*. South is at the top. The map is extraordinary for the fine red lines running along the top from western Africa on the right, through the source of the Nile in the top center, and ending at the Indian Ocean (detail, fig. 64, above). This is a remarkably early use of a longitudinal grid, a graticule, in its theory more sophisticated than the grid we saw on the later map of Vesconte (page 60-61).

Europe is in the lower right, with Constantinople at its leftmost point, behind the reddish-black vertical, slightly curved wall. From there, moving across the sea diagonally to the left, the general area of Palestine has ten cities indicated but not labelled, except for the Negev, which is marked "Wandering" (the vertical word by the red mountain). The vertical red-bordered land in the upper left is the enigmatic "Island of the Jewel" mapped by al-Khwārazmī (p87). In the extreme lower left lies the gate built by Alexander to keep away the apocalyptic monsters Gog and Magog.

Egypt, 1020-1050 (copy of c1200). [Bodleian Library, MS. Arab. c. 90]

Two factors distinguish the popular influence of maps such as these, and their related ideas of the structure of the cosmos, from the popular influence of maps in Latin Europe: the much higher rate of literacy among the Egyptian public, and the use of paper rather than expensive vellum, helping to democratize knowledge by making multiple copies more economically practical.

Roughly one century and half a sea separate our unknown Egyptian cosmographer from the most celebrated of Arabic geographers, al-Sharīf al-Idrīsī, the grandson of the last ruler of a dynasty that governed Málaga until 1058. Evidence points to al-Idrīsī's father having moved from there to Sicily, being welcomed by Roger I, and his son growing up in the circle of the future king Roger II.[13] Sicily was already a multifaith, multilingual center of learning, and it was there that Latin civilization got its first insight into Ptolemy—not the *Geography*, but the *Almagest*, a mathematical and astronomical treatise. The young al-Idrīsī was apparently valued by Roger II when he assumed power, as he ultimately charged al-Idrīsī with the mapping project that would become both their legacies.

According to al-Idrīsī, Roger II's initial interest in surveying was for the enlargement of empire. His was modest as empires go: some conquest in North Africa and Calabria. When these were no longer sufficiently gratifying, he set his eyes on the entire world—the mapping of it. To that end, scholars were called to his

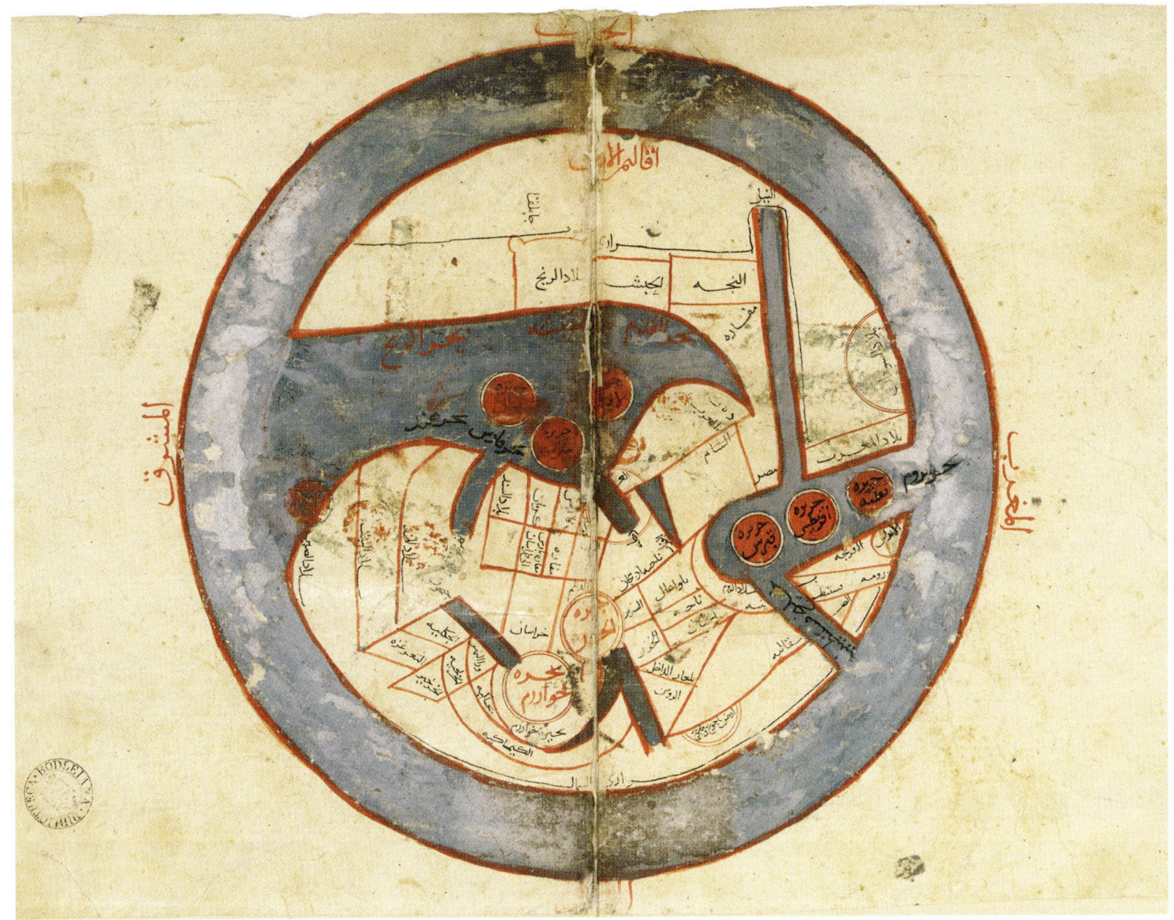

FIG. 65: World map from the *Ṣuwar al-buldān* by Ibrāhīm ibn Muḥammad Iṣṭakhrī. Europe is the diminutive triangle in the lower right, with the islands of (right-to-left) Sicily, Crete, and Cyprus above it. Above Crete is the conspicuously stylized Nile, and Palestine is the parallelogram above Cyprus, marked "Levant". Mid-tenth century (but 1272). [Bodleian Library, MS. Ouseley 373]

service and voluminous texts were scoured. These proved inadequate for the ambitious project, and so he then sent scouts to survey the world, whatever they could reach of it in their assigned directions. As the travelers returned, their data was compiled, collated, compared, and pieced together into a coherent whole. Iron drafting tools were used to create the resulting map, from which the image was recreated on a disc of silver of about thirty-three pounds.

> [It had] the seven climes, their land and regions, shorelines and hinterlands, gulfs and seas, watercourses and rivers, inhabited and uninhabited parts, frequented routes, distances, lengths of journeys, harbors between one locality and the other …[14]

No such map survives, however, despite the durable medium that could easily have withstood the millennium. The likelihood is that the silver itself was its downfall, a temptation to subsequent marauders to melt and reuse. But however glorious the silver disc must have been, what *has* survived is more important: copies of al-Idrīsī's *Kit b nuzhat al-musht q*, an atlas roughly translated as "excursion of the one who yearns to penetrate the horizons," also known as the *Tabula Rogeriana* after its sponsor.

FIGS. 66, 67, 68: Three copies of al-Idrīsī's twelfth-century map of the Levant, demonstrating the differences through copyists of what in theory was the same map.

Above (FIG. 66) is the earliest, ca. 1250. [National Library of France; image Library of Congress]

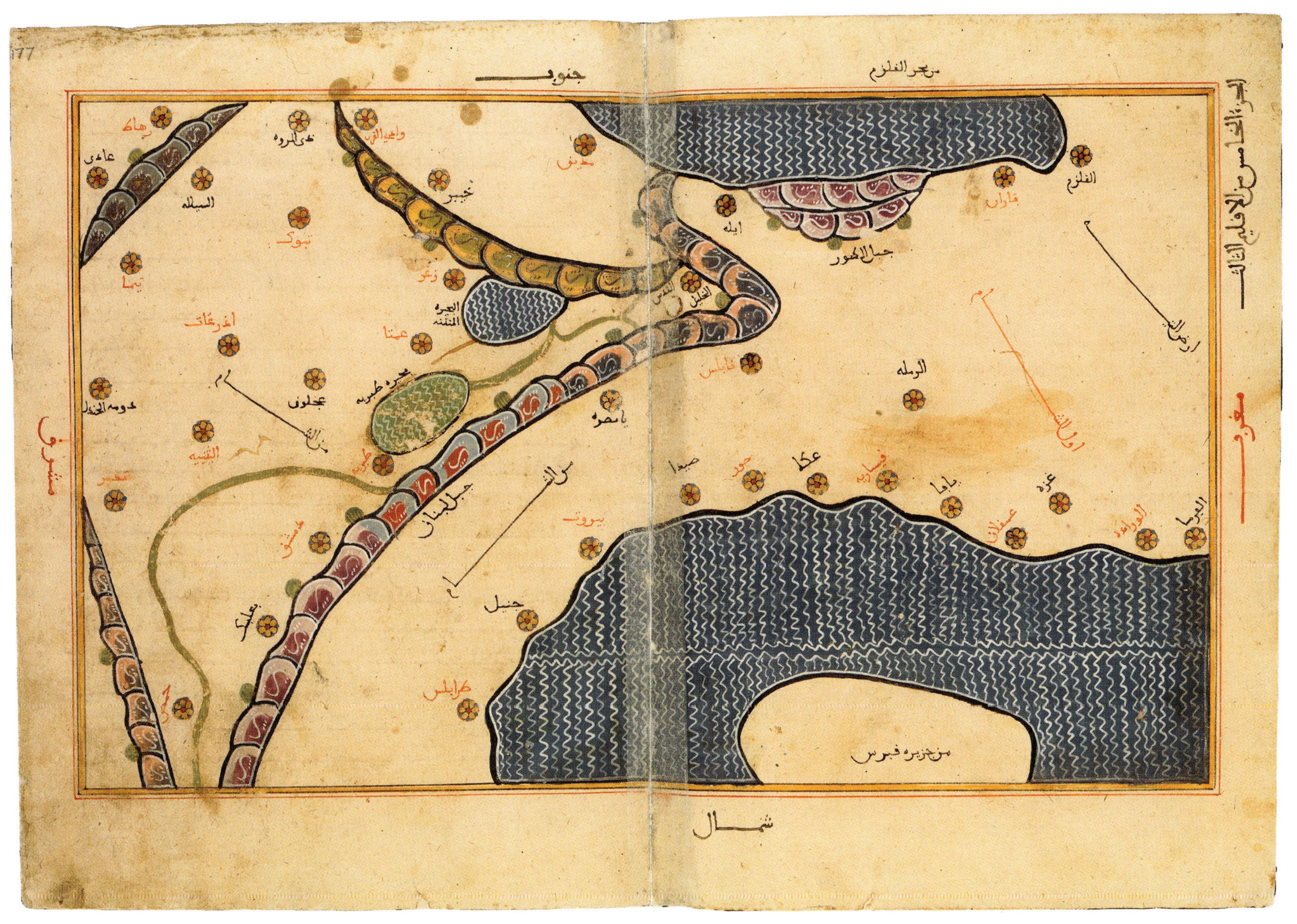

FIG. 67: 14th–15th century. [Bodleian Library, MS. Greaves 42]

جنوب
من خليج القلزم بحر فارس
مشرق
شمال
الحورا
صحرا تبوك
جبل الشراه
قبر ابرهيم
ايله
الطور
خيبر
تيما
الحجر
زغر
البحيرة الميتة
اريحا
القدس
الرملة
عمان
اذرعات
الاردن
بلاد الغور من الشام
بحيرة طبرية
طبرية
قيسارية
يافا
عكا
صور
صيدا
بيروت
اطرابلس
عرقة
حمص
تدمر
بعلبك
دمشق
الجولان
جبل اللكام
الروم
جزيرة قبرس
طرف البادية

FIG. 68: Dated 1553. [Bodleian Library, MS. Pococke 375]

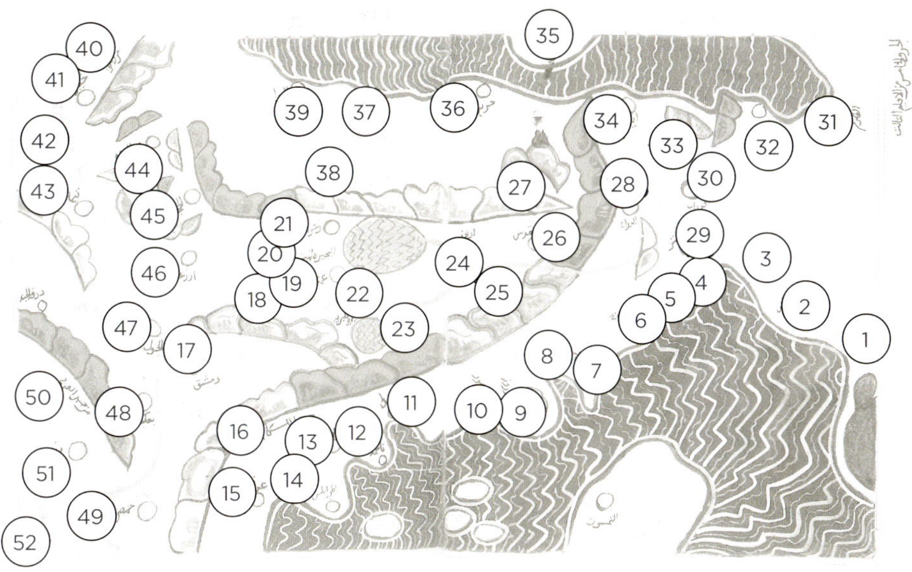

Key map for fig. 68: Though the furthest chronologically from the original, it is closer to the earliest (now largely illegible) copy than the middle example.

1. al-Farma
2. al-Arish
3. Rafah
4. Ashkelon
5. Jaffa
6. Qisarya (Haifa)
7. Janfawiyya
8. Acre
9. Iskandaron (Alexandroschoene)
10. Tyre
11. Sidon
12. Na'ma
13. Beirut
14. Tripoli
15. Araka
16. Allukam Mountain
17. Damascus
18. Land of the rift valley from the Levant
19. A'mna
20. The dead lake
21. Za'ra
22. Lake Tiberias
23. Tiberias
24. Jericho
25. Jordan
26. Jerusalem
27. Ibrahim's grave (Hebron)
28. Aldawam
29. A'naz
30. Imdrab
31. Al Qalzam
32. Faran /Qaran
33. al-Tur
34. Aylah
35. al-Nu'man (island)
36. Harin
37. Tabuk desert
38. Mt Sharah
39. al-Hora
40. Mazardu [?]
41. Khaibar
42. Land of Tamud from al-Hijaz
43. Tayma
44. Dur al-Marwa
45. al-Hajar
46. Adza'at
47. al-Jul
48. Baalbek (Lebanon)
49. Homs (Syria)
50. From Alaarj Mt (min Jabal ala'arj)
51. Tarmus
52. The edge of the [Badiya?]

FIG. 69, 70: The world map of al-Idrīsī, 1154 (this copy 1553), and the world map of Vesconte, ca. 1320, both rotated so that north is at the top for easy comparison. The al-Idrīsī is probably very similar to the lost map made on a silver disc. The Veconte's original orientation is east, of al-Idrīsī, south. [left, Bodleian Library, MS. Pococke 375; right, Bibliothèque Nationale, ark:/12148/btv1b55002483j]

Unprecedented in its scope, this was a methodical, comprehensive, uniform assemblage of geographic and demographic analysis of as much of the world as could be gleaned by tapping all available sources: explorers, scouts, and merchants, plus testimony, rumors, and existing maps and texts. It divided the earth into seven climate zones latitudinally, as per Ptolemy, and each *clime* into ten sections longitudinally. Each of the resulting 70 maps was supplemented by text recording the socioeconomic, physical, cultural, and political situation of the region. Whatever its limitations, it is difficult to identify a mapping project equally ambitious in its scope until another Italian atlas in a much different world, the 1646 *Arcano del Mare* of Robert Dudley.

Al-Idrīsī's map of Palestine, the fifth map in the third climate zone, betrays no sense of the political irony of a Muslim mapmaker employed in a Christian court on an island at which Latin soldiers refreshed en route to Palestine. Three copies of the map are known extant (images 66, 67, 68), spanning three centuries from ca. 1250 to 1553. No two are alike, illustrative of the pitfalls of manuscript copying and/or disparate originals, and they are not in sequence of consecutive copies: the first and third are related, while the middle one is distinct.

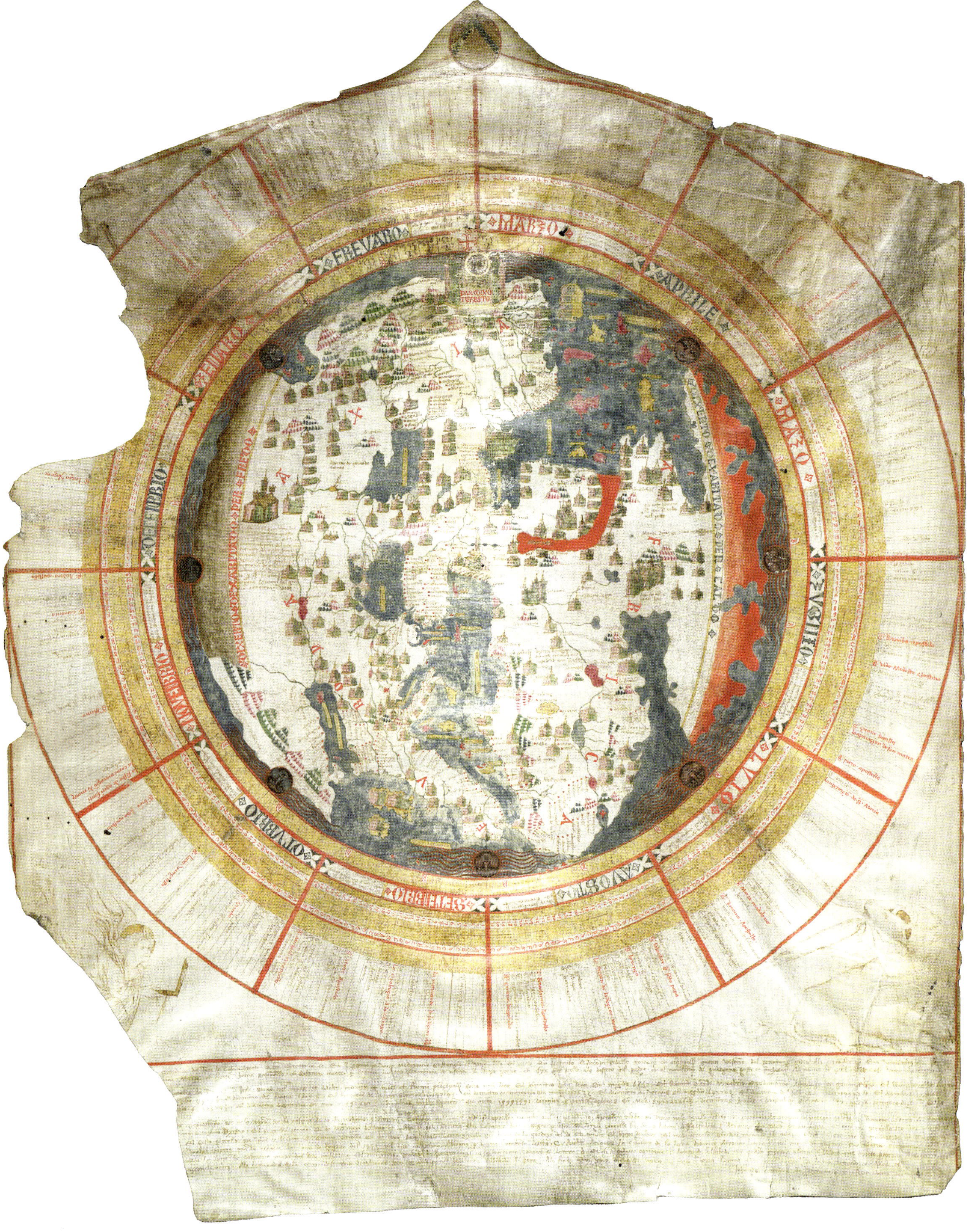
FREVARO
MARZO
APRILE
PARADIXO TERESTO

FIG. 71: Mappamundi, Giovanni Leardo, 1452-53. This map forms a continuation of the progression illustrated on the previous two pages, here shown oriented to the east as intended. Paradise sits at the top, and Palestine occupies the center.

The concentric circles surrounding the earth are calendars. The innermost circle indicates the dates of Easter for 95 years, until April 10, 1547. The second circle shows months, beginning with March (the first month of the year in the Republic of Venice), as well as the day, hour, and minute the sun enters the signs of the zodiac. Circles three through six are to calculate the phases of the moon. The seventh indicates dominical ("Sunday") letters in order to determine the day of the week for particular dates, and the eighth and ninth give the lengths of the days through the year. [University of Wisconsin-Milwaukee; photo, Library of Congress]

GEOGRAPHERS PIECE IT ALL TOGETHER

Al-Idrīsī's ghost was in Venice in the early fourteenth century when a new, radical species of world map began appearing that melded various influences of the larger Mediterranean world into a coherent whole, and in which Palestine, arguably to its benefit, boasted no special mystique. The Latin geographers who composed them drew heavily from their Arabic colleagues, from Mediterranean pilots, and travelers of all varieties—and what better place to do so than Venice, a window to the Mediterranean world and within easy reach of Sicily, where al-Idrīsī' had worked.

The two world maps illustrated in figs. 69 & 70, that of al-Idrīsī working in Sicily in the mid-twelfth century, and Vesconte, working in Venice in the early fourteenth, demonstrate this clearly. Vesconte borrowed from his colleagues to the south for the essential concept, with its open Indian Ocean, well-defined Arabian Peninsula, and complete Africa, and benefitted from the intervening years with emerging hints of the rounding of West Africa. He drew on portolan charts for his superior rendering of Mediterranean and Black Sea coasts, and other Latin sources for the rest of Europe. Palestine is roughly at the center, but not for theological reasons—indeed in this example, Palestine is not even marked.[15]

Other Latin maps followed in the same pattern. As late as the mid-fifteenth century, world maps such as those by Giovanni Leardo (e.g., fig. 71) retained the same core Arabic DNA while continuing to evolve.

PALESTINE AS A STOP-OVER

In the previous chapter, we looked at medieval travelers who set out with Palestine as their destination. During the same period, others passed through Palestine as a point of great interest, but not their actual destination. Prominent among them was Benjamin of Tudela, who left his native Spain about 1165 and wrote of his travels and the Jewish communities he passed. He described Jerusalem as

> a small city, fortified by three walls. It is full of people whom the Mohammedans call Jacobites, Syrians, Greeks, Georgians, and Franks, and of people of all tongues: It contains a dyeing-house, for which the Jews pay a small rent annually to the king, on condition that besides the Jews no other dyers be allowed in Jerusalem. There are about 200 Jews who dwell under the Tower of David in one corner of the city. The lower portion of the wall of the Tower of David, to the extent of about ten cubits, is part of the ancient foundation set up by our ancestors, the remaining portion having been built by the Mohammedans ... In Jerusalem is the great church called the Sepulchre, and here is the burial-place of Jesus, unto which the Christians make pilgrimages. Jerusalem has four gates: the gate of Abraham, the gate of David, the gate of Zion, and the gate of Gushpat, which is the gate of Jehoshaphat, facing our ancient Temple, now called Templum Domini.

> From Jerusalem, it is a trip of two parasangs [6–7 miles] to Bethlehem, which is called by the Christians Beth-Leon, and close thereto, at a distance of about half a mile, at the parting of the way, is the pillar of Rachel's grave, which is made up of eleven stones, corresponding with the number of the sons of Jacob. Upon it is a cupola resting on four columns, and all the Jews that pass by carve their names upon the stones of the pillar. At Bethlehem there are two Jewish dyers. It is a land of brooks of water, and contains wells and fountains.

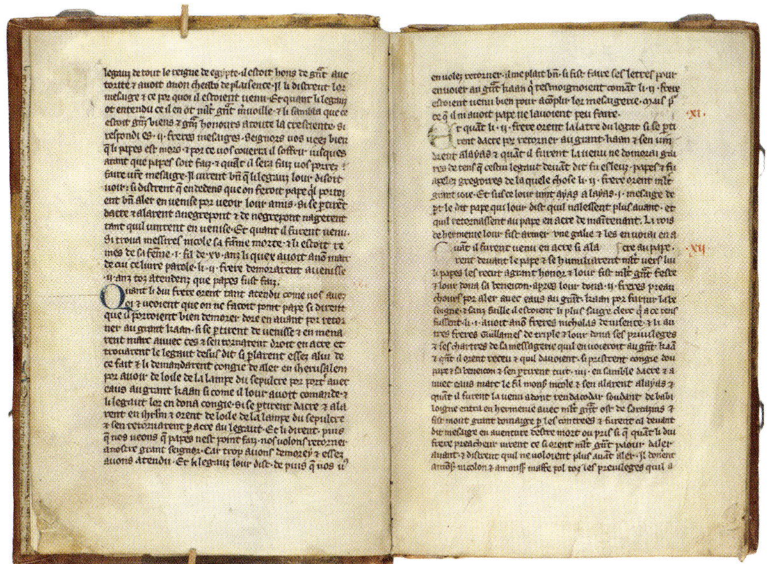

FIG. 72: An early manuscript of Marco Polo's travels, opened to pages recording his time in Palestine. After being captured by the Genoese during a naval battle between Venice and Genoa in 1298, he befriended a fellow prisoner, Rustichello da Pisa, a romance writer, to whom he dictated his account and observations. [National Library of Sweden, Shelfmark: M 304; Image Library of Congress]

Ibn Jubayr passed through Palestine in 1183, as did the better-known Ibn Battuta in 1325. The most influential was Marco Polo, whose odyssey widened the Mediterranean view of the world and broadened the Latin perspective of Palestine's place as a crossroad.

In 1271, Marco, his father, and uncle made Palestine their first major stop en route to points east, allegedly to get oil from the lamp at Christ's sepulchre in Jerusalem to bring to Kublai Khan. A letter from the pope to the khan would have been protocol, but there was no pope—political infighting among cardinals had thrown the Catholic Church into the longest papal election in its history, 1268–1271. The stalemate was not resolved until the cardinals were locked in their Viterbo palazzo, their rations of bread and water reduced, and (lest that be insufficient) the building's roof removed. The Polo trio had already abandoned hope and set off when Gregory X was named the new pope—who, ironically, was in Acre, from which they had just left. Word reached them, they returned to Palestine, secured the new pope's letter to the "Great Khan," and set off overland for China.[16]

When more than two decades later, Marco was allowed by the khan to return to Europe, it was to accompany the Mongol princess Kököchin to Persia by sea from China. Prevailing Latin belief would have deemed that impossible, because the Indian Ocean was believed to be a closed sea (as can be seen, for example, in fig. 79). His account of his odyssey proved otherwise, vindicating Arabic maps. Since Polo had already reached Persia, he continued overland, but his sea route from China demonstrated that one could travel by sea from the east coast of Asia to, for example, Aqaba.

Manuscripts of the reports of Odoric, ibn Battuta, and Polo were clearly available in 1375 in the Jewish quarter of Palma on the island of Majorca, where a monumental, encyclopedic world map now known as the "Catalan Atlas" was being created and which incorporates reports from these travelers (figs. 73 & 74). Attributed to Abraham Cresques on a commission from Prince John of Aragón, the full work consisted of six vellum leaves, originally mounted on wood. The map is a combination portolan chart and mappamundi. Jerusalem is marked with a church, Damascus with a crescent flag. Two rivers join from the north to feed Lake Hula, from which the Jordan continues to the Sea of Galilee and Dead Sea.

FIG. 73: One section of the world map known as the "Catalan Atlas," attributed to Abraham Cresques, Majorca, 1370–1380. Oriented here with south at the top, as implied by the map's principal text, though when laid flat as intended, orientation is irrelevant. Palestine is easy to locate by starting from the conspicuous Red Sea in the upper left. [Bibliothèque Nationale, ark:/12148/btv1b52509636n]

FIG. 74: Palestine from the Catalan Atlas, turned 180° for easier viewing.

FIG. 75: Palestine, the lower half of a leaf from Gregoria Dati, *La Sfera*, ca. 1480 [National Library of Finland, Mscr. 1]

After the Florentine merchant Gregorio Dati (1362–1435) made his fortune in the silk trade, he served as consul of the Silk Merchants' Guild, as overseer of the charitable hospital *Ospedale degli Innocenti*, and became head of the town council or *Signoria*. He also was a writer, most famously of *La sfera* ("The Sphere"), a cosmographic-geographic textbook in *ottava rima*, eight-line rhyming stanzas intended to educate young Florentine merchants on natural phenomena, navigation, and the topography of the Mediterranean.

While the work allowed for wide artistic variation, the example in fig. 75 is representative of most: the geography is seen from above, contrasted by vignettes seen three-dimensionally at an angle. Note the possible Arabic influence in the map's stylized promontories and bays, a single pattern repeated for each, with shading that imparts three-dimensionality of the coast. We will see a similar technique in maps by Piri Reis (p134).

FIG. 76: Palestine, leaf from *La Sfera,* Gregorio Dati, Florence, ca. 1440. [New York Public Library, Spencer Coll. MS. 198]

FIG. 77. Woodcut view of Mount Sinai, illustrating the exaggerated dimensions and Biblical narrative also seen in the Dati map in fig. 76. Thunder, lightning, jets of flame, and trumpets announce God's descent to Mount Sinai. Moses appears twice: at the bottom, placing barriers so that others do not ascend the mountain, and on the mountainside, looking upward. From *Libro delli comandamenti di Dio del Testamento Vecchio et Nvovo et sacri canoni*. Florence, Antonio di Bartolommeo Miscomini, 1494. [Library of Congress, 48032652]

A different copyist drew the far more dramatic rendering of Dati's imagery in fig. 76, in which the entire map is three-dimensional. St. Catherine's church sits atop a towering Mount Sinai, and Sodom is in flames at the mountain's base. The adjoining text reads:

> Larissa [al-Arish] is surrounded by marshes and swamps, among lands that are deserted until you reach the ill-fated and justly rebuked valley, the place that was punished by God with fire [Sodom]. Here there is a high mountain, and then a little further north are the flanks of Mount Sinai, on top of which the Divine Law was issued by God to Moses. and Saint Catherine [of Alexandria] is buried.
>
> Halfway between Larissa and Beirut is the port of the Holy Land [Jaffa]. This should be the property of the one who claims to be the leader of the Christians [probably criticism of contemporary popes' failure to call a new Crusade]. This is where the High King [David] held his throne, who made the work that is sung every day. [It was believed that King David was the author of the Psalms that were sung daily.] This is also where the Holy Sepulcher of Jesus is and where he was crucified for us.
>
> This is Zion [Jerusalem], the capital of Judea, toward the East and a little to the right. To the left of that is Galilee and to the east of that is the Jordan River. Along the coast lies Caesarea as well as Acre, Tyre, Sidon, and Mount Lebanon, where the [Jordan] river issues from two sources. Here are Mount Carmel and other holy mountains.[17]

FIG. 78: Arnald Domenech, Piero Roselli, 1484, sea chart recording the weights and measures in use at 27 Mediterranean ports, including the Palestinian port of Acre (second from the left, bottom row). The absence of coastlines and consistent orientation allows for greater clarity in charting established trade routes, for which geographic accuracy is secondary.

Rhodes is the elaborately-connected port in the lower center. The island was at the time both a major commercial hub and the base of the Knights Hospitaller, a Christian military order founded in the crusader Kingdom of Jerusalem in the 12th century.

Orientation is nominally west, as was typical for such charts, yet fluid. The Levantine coast (bottom row), left-to-right, is Alexandria, Acre, Domas (Sidon?), Beirut, and Cyrus. Going up the right vertical row from Cyprus, the nominal orientation still holds: Crete, Constantinople, Venice, Naples, PIsa, and Genoa. But successive ports then continue counter-clockwise: France and Spanish ports dominate the top and left row.

To the extent that the chart's visual image is of a "closed" Mediterranean with fluid orientation, it can be compared with the Arabic map in fig. 62.

While the city vignettes were drawn with some regard to the actual place, the only realistic city view is that of Siena, at the top.

*Asiento present hordenat a payon les responsions dels pezos e mezures: delahun boch al altre de tots los presents bochs nnomenats los quals son cap e regiment de la mercadoria hordenat. [*Library of Congress G5672. M4P5 1484 .D6]

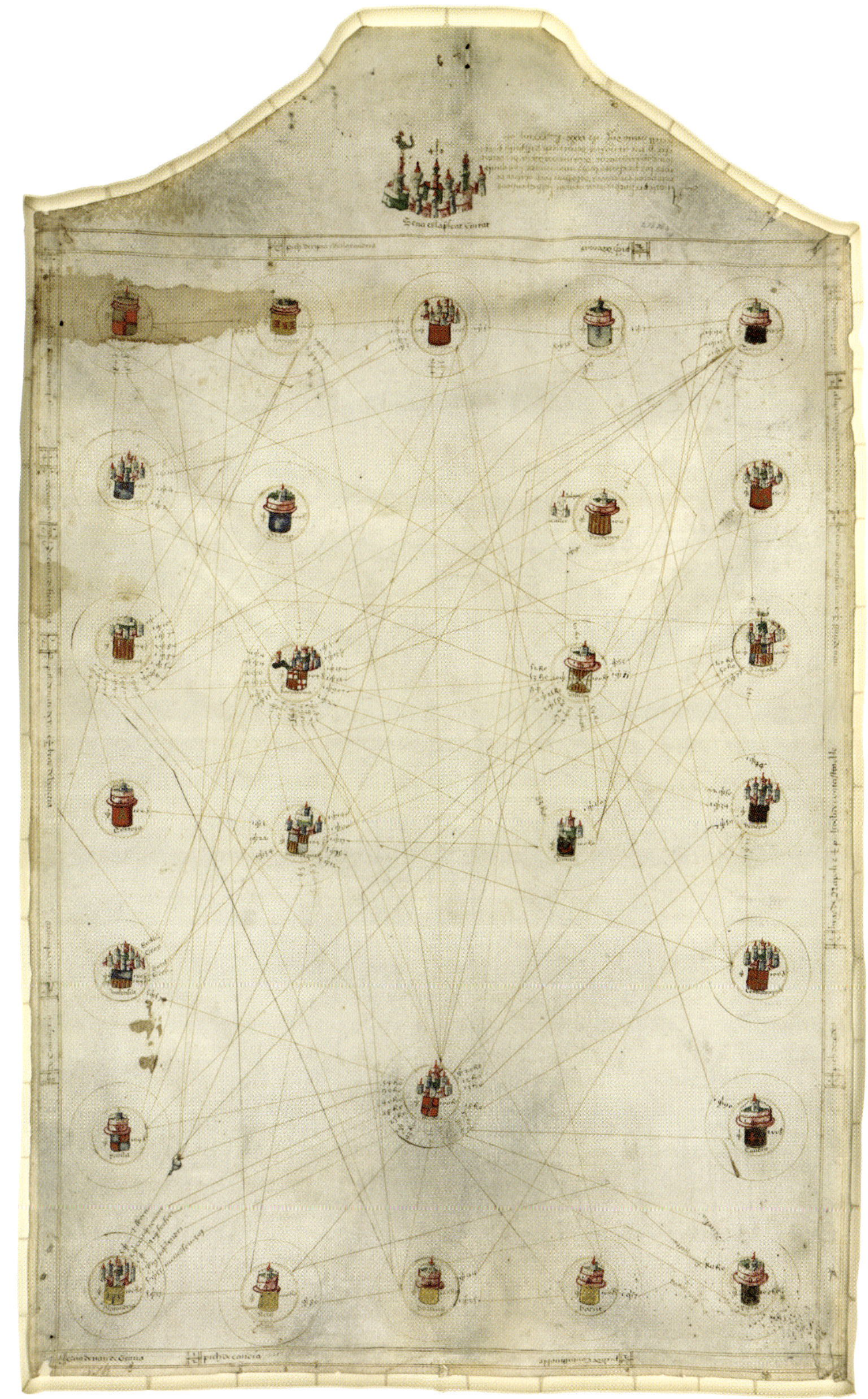

FIG. 79: The world according to Ptolemy, an Italian manuscript of ca. 1460. Note the land stretching from Africa in the lower center to Southeast Asia in the extreme right, rendering the Indian Ocean the closed sea referred to on page 101. In the map's mindset, Marco Polo sailed through that land at about where the right-most wind cherub is drawn. [National Library of Naples, image Library of Congress, 2021668203]

PTOLEMY: AN OLD FLAME, REKINDLED

European cartography's final push to the Renaissance came from a then-thirteen-hundred-year-old text originating in the Lebanese port of Tyre, now a peninsula, but two millennia ago an island blessed with two bustling ports. Its cosmopolitan environment influenced the Greek-speaking Roman geographer, Marinus of Tyre, who was an early proponent of mathematical geography. His work, now lost, provided the basis for the most influential of Greco-Roman geographers, Claudius Ptolemy, who headed the library of Alexandria between about 127–150 CE.

When Ptolemy's *Geography* was translated into Latin in the early fifteenth century, it galloped into European consciousness as fresh and revolutionary. The book provided a vast inventory of places and their coordinates, so that a map could be "digitally" constructed from the text, and described methods for plotting these points on a flat surface—that is, it codified the very idea of maps as mathematical projects. It is also with Ptolemy that, for better or worse, north became the default orientation.

FIG. 80: Ptolemy's fourth map of Asia, showing Palestine (left) and the land east as far as the Persian Gulf (lower right). An Italian manuscript of ca. 1460. [National Library of Naples, image Library of Congress, 2021668203]

The principles laid out in the *Geography* were more important than the accuracy of his figures. Ptolemy's were skewed by his underestimation of the size of the sphere, as well as by guesswork extrapolation in measuring longitude in the furthest reaches of his known world—the bane of all geographers until the advent of the chronometer in the late eighteenth century. He used the Canary Islands as the prime, a logical and nonpartisan choice because they were simply the most westerly point known. But it would have been impractical to measure longitude from the Canaries; Instead, his point of reference was a "stone tower" said to be the midpoint of the old Silk Road, whose location remains uncertain.

Vellum manuscripts of the *Geography* with its twenty-seven maps—the world, ten of Europe, four of Africa, twelve of Asia—circulated among European intelligentsia during the fifteenth century. Its influence expanded dramatically once the book was available in printed form on paper: first in Bologna (1477, fig. 81), and then Rome (1478, fig. 82), both using copperplate reproduction for the maps. The 1477 engraving gives the appearance of a work done in haste, as if to beat their competitors in Rome to the market.

FIG. 81: Bologna, 1477 [National Library of Finland]

Figs. 81, 82. Palestine, detail of Ptolemy's fourth map of Asia from the two earliest printed editions of his *Geographia*.

Fig. 81, previous page: Bologna, 1477

Fig. 82, left: Rome, 1478

(Next page) Fig. 83: Chart of the Mediterranean from the so-called "Miller Atlas," produced for King Manuel I of Portugal in 1519 by cartographers Pedro Reinel, his son Jorge Reinel, Lopo Homem, and miniaturist António de Holanda. A towering Christian cross sits atop a mountain neighboring a grand Jerusalem, and on Mount Sinai are the two stone (here gold) tablets inscribed with the Ten Commandments given to Moses, as related in the Book of Exodus. The Palestinian coast combines some arbitrary undulation to define the various ports, and some realism, in particular at Haifa and Acre. [National Library of France; image the Library of Congress, Control Number 2021668723]

Of the twenty-six regional maps, the Asia *Tabula IV* covers the eastern Mediterranean and Middle East. As is easily seen in the 1477 and 1478 copperplates (figs. 81 & 82), there is wide variation among the various renderings of the map, a result of the limited coordinates from which the analog must be reconstituted—imagine drawing a continuous abstract image that must pass through widely spaced pixels. Place-names were engraved with stylus on the 1477 map, as would remain the norm, but through mirror-image letter stamp on the 1478, so there is a neat "printed look" consistency to its lettering.

The close of the fifteenth century presaged a frenetic revolution in Europe's knowledge and mapping of the earth. The blossoming of printing technologies brought advancements in geographic knowledge to a wider public, whose world view would be unrecognizable to their grandparents. Although this evolution of geographic knowledge was not always forward—some blunders were the result of informed, intelligent deduction—the prevailing mindset was of discovery and accuracy, an obsession with "filling in the map" as correctly as possible. The sixteenth century would determine whether that applied to Palestine.

19 PARALELVS HABENS MAXIMVM DIEM HORARV
OCCENVS GRMANICVS
IBRNIA ISVLA
ALBION INSVLA
OCCEANVS BRITANICVS
GALLIA BELGICA
TRILEVCI CATIRIDES
MARE IBERICVM
MARE LVSITANIV
MARE AFRICA
HERCVLEVM
MARE LEGVSTICVM
SARDOVM
PANONIA
SIRTIS MAGNA
3 SEPTIMVS PARALELVS HABENS MAXIMVM

ETENTRIONALIS PARS ORIENTALIS
ASI
ATICA
PALVDES MEOTIDES
SINVS CARCINITVS
MAR EPONTI CVM
SCYTHIA INTRA
IMAVM MONTEM
HYRCANIVS MARE
M
ARMEN IA
MAIOR
E IRCANIA
DIA
ASIA PROPRIE
CAPADOCIA
PHINICIA
CILICIA
LICIA
ME SO PO TANIA
SVRIA
SIRIA CVM
EVPHATES
BABLONIA
PER SIDIS
TIGRIS
N IVM
AEGYPTIACVM
IVDEA
ARABIA DE SERTA
NILVS
LIBECI MONTE
PETREA
ARABIA
MARE PSICV
FELIX MARI
THI MONTES
MEREDIONALIS PARS ORIENS

FIG. 84: Title from the engraved frontispiece to Thomas Fuller's *Pisgah-sight of Palestine*, 1650. The title is a play on the story of Moses being shown the Promised Land from atop Pisgah, the peak of the Jordanian Mount Nebo.

CHAPTER 4

PULLED IN ALL DIRECTIONS, 1500-1800

Seemingly independent forces at play in the sixteenth century tugged at Palestine's future: the normalization of Western imperialism, the long, if bumpy, trend toward a more secular, scientific mindset, combined with the power of printed maps by virtue of their mass dissemination, and one particular movement that harnessed that power: the Reformation, in which a major schism in the Christian church broadly divided the faith between Catholicism and the new offshoot, Protestantism. Messianic evangelism pulled the mapping of Palestine one way, the quest for empiricism the other.

Like language, mapping reflects its creators' wishes and subconscious cultural assumptions. Like language, what a map "says" on the surface may not be its primary message—its subliminal "unspoken" mission may be more powerful than that which it shows the eyes. Both language and maps do role-reversals: We create them, and then allow them to become our masters, telling us what to think.

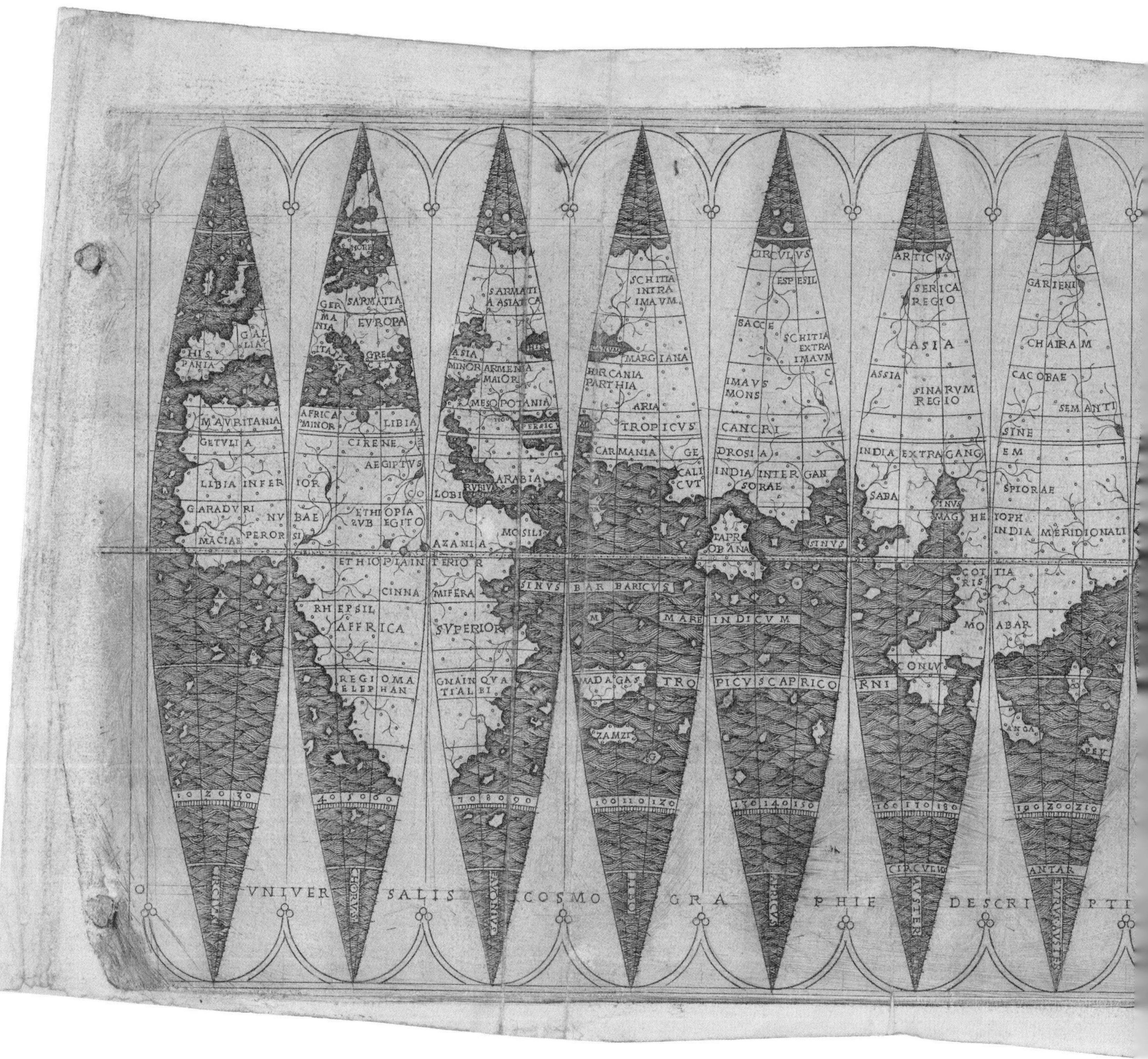

FIG. 85: Globe gores, *Universalis cosmographie descriptio tam in solido quem plano,* 1517(?), after Martin Waldseemüller, 1507. The use of gores served two purposes: they could be cut from the sheet and pasted on a sphere sized for the purpose, making a globe; or, viewed as is, the disjointed format effectively eliminated the distortion of a continuous projection. [New York Public Library catalog ID (B-number): b14353394]

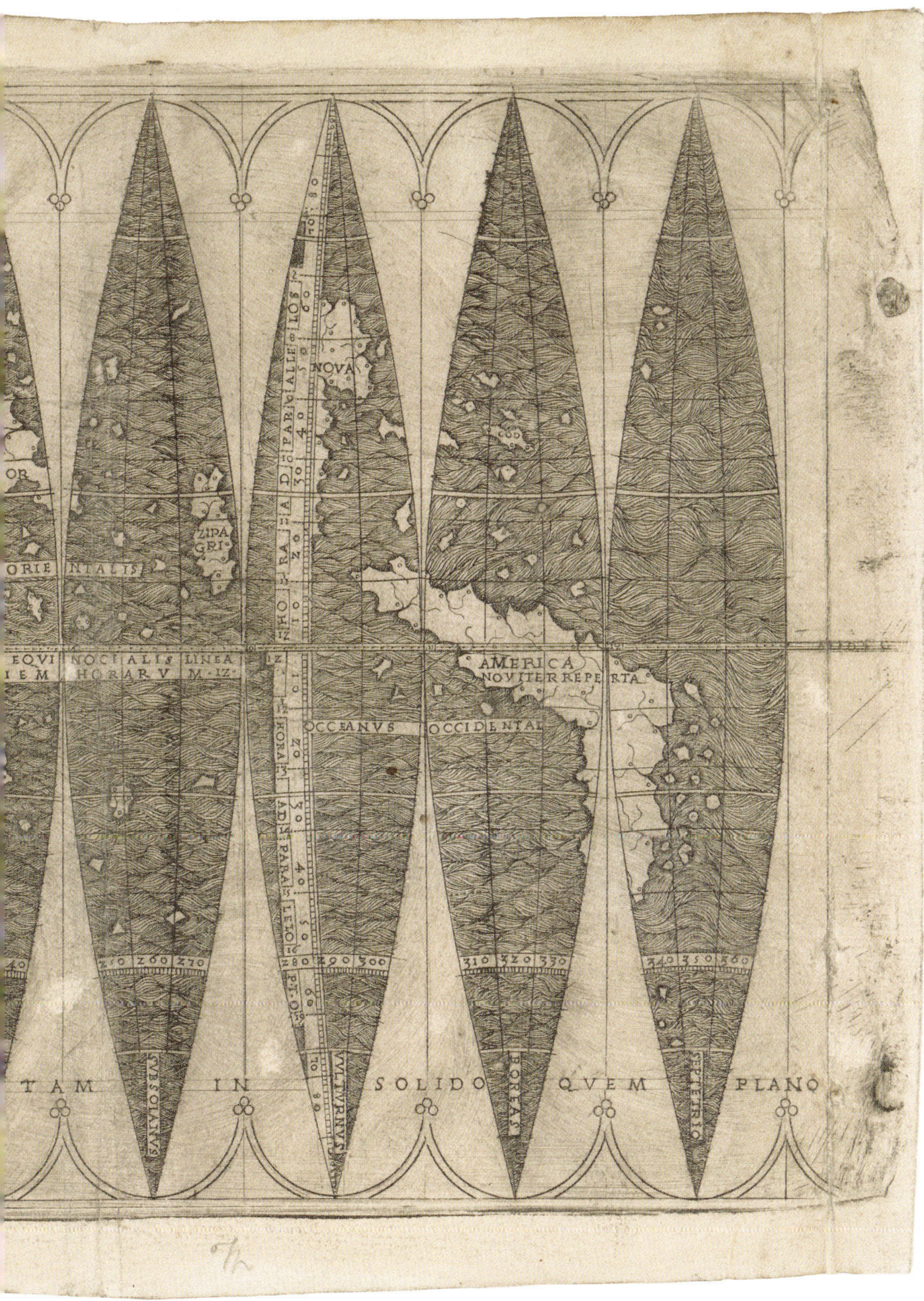

As if the turn of the century had some transformative effect, printed maps took a leap in adventurousness and size shortly after the clock ticked "1500." In 1507, the humanist Martin Waldseemüller pushed the limits of the woodblock medium to create a sophisticated, twelve-sheet woodcut map of the world, the most influential world image among the several circulating during the cartographically tumultuous period spanning the first three decades of the century. It incorporated into existing manuscript models the latest Spanish reports from the Americas and Portuguese exploration around Africa, and treated Palestine as any other place on the earth.

Fig. 85 is a much-reduced copperplate adaptation of it in globe gores, which is better adapted for our purposes. It illustrates the shocking triviality in which Palestine suddenly found itself in the world image in a matter of just a few decades. The region of Palestine is marked with the single word *Mesopotamia*, a tiny speck in an abruptly widened world.

The new ability to print large maps using multiple blocks or plates quickly inspired a series of such maps of Palestine. Six blocks were used for a north-oriented map by an unknown cartographer, the woodblocks attributed to Lucas Cranach the Elder, ca. 1515 (following page).

SEPTENTRIO MITTNACHT
DAS GROS MEER
ABENT OCCIDES
HEMATH
ROT MEER
MERIDIES · MITTAG
DIS GEBIRGE · ARABIE
SAMARIA
JERUSALEM
HEBRON
IOPPE
SICHEM
JERICHO
BETHLEHEM
GENESARA
64
65
66
67
68
69
70

(Previous Page) FIG. 86: Map of Palestine of unknown authorship, the woodblock attributed to Lucas Cranach the Elder, ca. 1515. A single example of the map survives, of which the lower third is in Amsterdam, the upper two-thirds in Jerusalem. The present image is the author's hybrid of a high-resolution image of the lower third, and a line reproduction of the whole map, both supplied by, and with the kind permission of, the University Library Vrije Universiteit Amsterdam (which holds the lower third). [LL.05413gk]

FIGS. 87, 88, 89: The sixteenth century's dramatically-expanded world brought the need for better tools to understand the earth and make astronomical calculations. One method was volvelles (fig. 87), primitive analogue computers in which "tools" of paper, printed and cut to shape, pivot around a string knotted through the centerpoint. In this volvelle from the *Cosmographicus Liber* of Peter Apianus, 1524, the innermost moving part is a world map, seen by itself (from a separate example) in fig. 88. Palestine is three concentric circles (latitudes) above the center.

The volvelle's uppermost moving part—a long, narrow piece that measures latitude—has a hexagram on the round hub through which the string is sewn (fig. 89). This is the mystical Seal of Solomon, drawn to simulate three-dimensionality, the opposing triangles interlaced. While the mythology of the Seal dates back to antiquity, the consensus today is that its image as an hexagram (typically interlaced) originated with medieval Arabic tradition, from which it was adopted by Jewish Kabbalistic tradition in medieval Spain.

FIG. 88

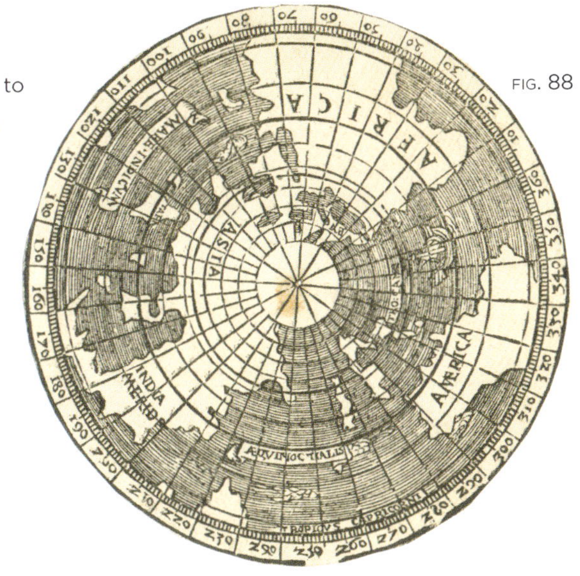

FIG. 87

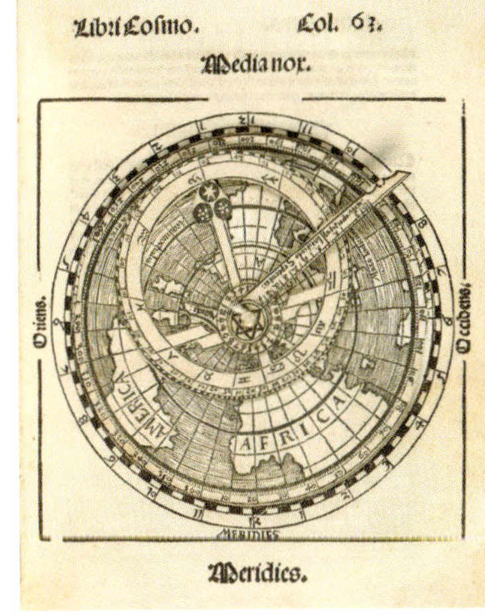

FIG. 89

At a moment when maps of Palestine were based on Burchard or Ptolemy's fourth map of Asia, the Cranach map began what would become its traditional "look": a north-oriented map of the southern Levant. It does retain influence from Ptolemy, but it is a more advanced map than its predecessors, especially as regards placement of interior towns. The Tribes are marked, while elaborate Biblical imagery is confined to the Sinai. Jerusalem is given no favors, drawn to about the size of coastal Apollonia (Arsuf, Arsur). A European galley docks at Jaffa.

Whatever the map's geographic improvements, the association with Cranach would make it the first Reformation map of Palestine. Not only was Cranach a staunch supporter of Martin Luther, but one of his patrons, Prince-elector of Saxony Friedrich III, was as well, and indeed aspects of the map's improvements likely originate in Friedrich III's 1493 pilgrimage to Palestine.

At about the time of this map—1516—the Ottoman occupation of Palestine began.

During the next couple of decades, the excellent geographers Orontius Finaeus and Peter Apianus both made maps of Palestine, almost surely woodcuts. No copies are known extant, but they are cited later in the century by the geographer Abraham Ortelius.

FIG. 90: *Quarta Asiae tabula*, Bernard Sylvanus (Ptolemy), Venice, 1511. First map of the region printed in color. [Norman B. Leventhal Map & Education Center]

Experimentation in printing processes now led to the first attempt to print maps in color, a 1511 Venetian edition of Ptolemy's *Geography* by Bernard Sylvanus. Two strikes were used to print each map: first a woodblock of the geography and most place-names using black ink, and then a second strike with only the typeset of the more important place-names, printed with red ink. The visual effect was to imitate rubrication, red ink manuscript embellishments of letters (see, e.g., fig. 41). Aligning the two strikes was an imprecise ritual, and so the placement of the red place-names varied. The atlas's Ptolemaic *Quarta Asiae Tabula* was the first map of Palestine printed in color (fig. 90), with *Palestina*, *Judea*, *Samaria*, and *Galilee* winning the honor of red ink.[18]

Of the seven woodcut editions of Ptolemy's *Geography* printed between the Sylvanus and 1541, two, 1535 and 1541, were published by Miguel Servet (Servetus).[19] Their publication did not bode well for the respected Spanish scholar. On October 27 of 1553, he was burnt alive at the Plateau of Champel at the edge of Geneva (atop a pyre of his own books, according to tradition). His crimes were three-fold: denying the Trinity, opposing infant baptism, *and* because the verso text of the atlas's *Tabula Terre Sanctae* challenged the fertility of Palestine.

Excepting two *isolarios* (books of islands), between 1477 and 1532, the only printed atlases were Ptolemaic, with the "modern" rendering of Palestine added to editions first published in 1482, 1513, and 1522.

The year 1532 broke that doldrum with Jacob Ziegler's atlas, *Quae intus continentur Syria, Palestina, Arabia, Aegyptus, Schondia, Holmiae...*, containing eight woodcut maps, seven of which were devoted to Palestine and the Sinai region. Ziegler did not seek to escape Ptolemy, but rather to correct it, to juggle Ptolemaic data with other sources to compile a "new Ptolemy," a project never finished.

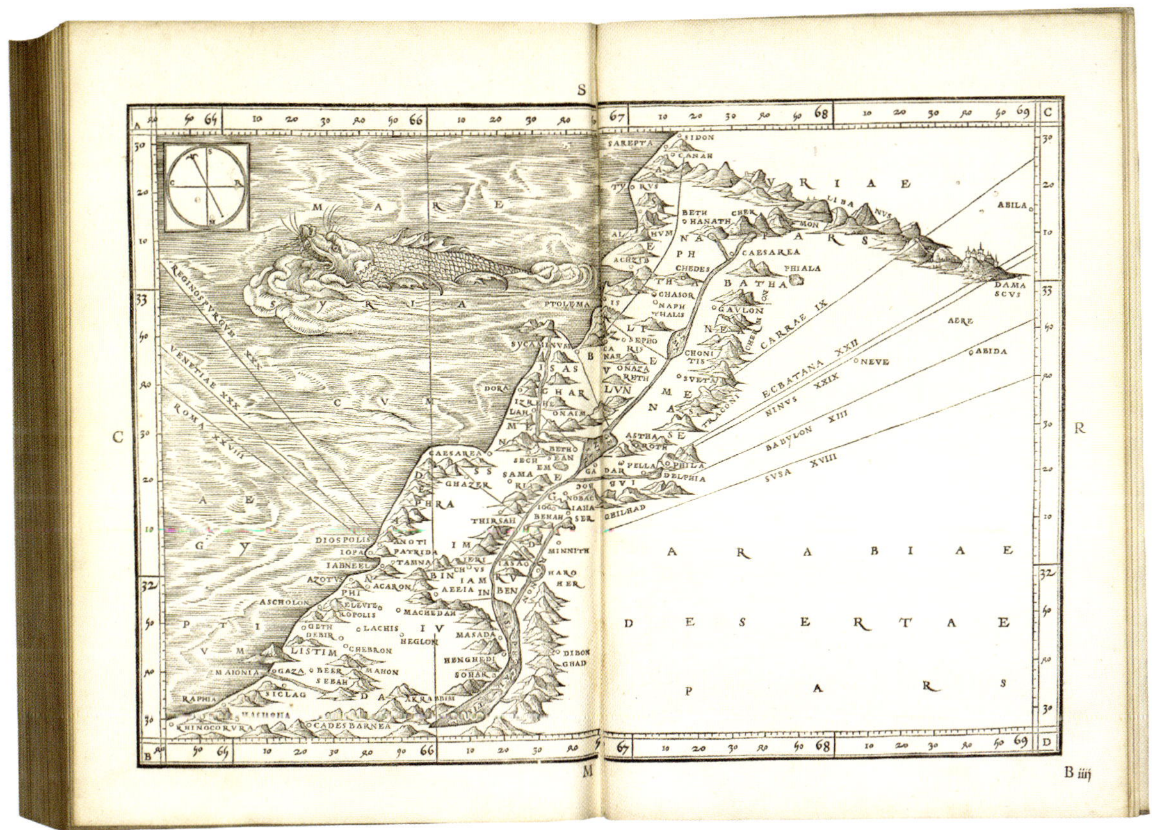

FIG. 91: Jacob Ziegler, Palestine, the fifth map from his *Quae intus continentur. Syrie, ad Ptolemaici operis rationem*, 1532

The atlas's fifth map introduced magnetic declination to printed maps (upper left of fig. 91), and his seventh map furthered the welcome trend, seen in the lower part of the Cranach map, to separate the Gulfs of Aqaba and Suez. Ziegler's geography was however a few steps forward, a couple backwards—all geographers' fate when faced with conflicting data. He introduces angular undulations to the Mediterranean coast, exaggerates the promontory that is Haifa (for him, the Roman *Sicaminum*), and creates an erroneous bend to the Dead Sea that would be copied by other geographers. A convert to Protestantism, his geographical works were placed on the Catholic Church's *Index Librorum Prohibitorum*, the list of prohibited books.

ISRAELITIS CVM SAMARIA EX OBSERVATIONE I. ZIEGLERI.

FIG. 92: manuscript map, one of several maps attributed to Jacob Ziegler, here shown with the title from its verso, *Israelitis cum Samaria ex observatione I. Ziegleri*. No date, but relevant to 1532. [Bibliothèque Nationale, CPL GE DD-2987 (10418 B)]

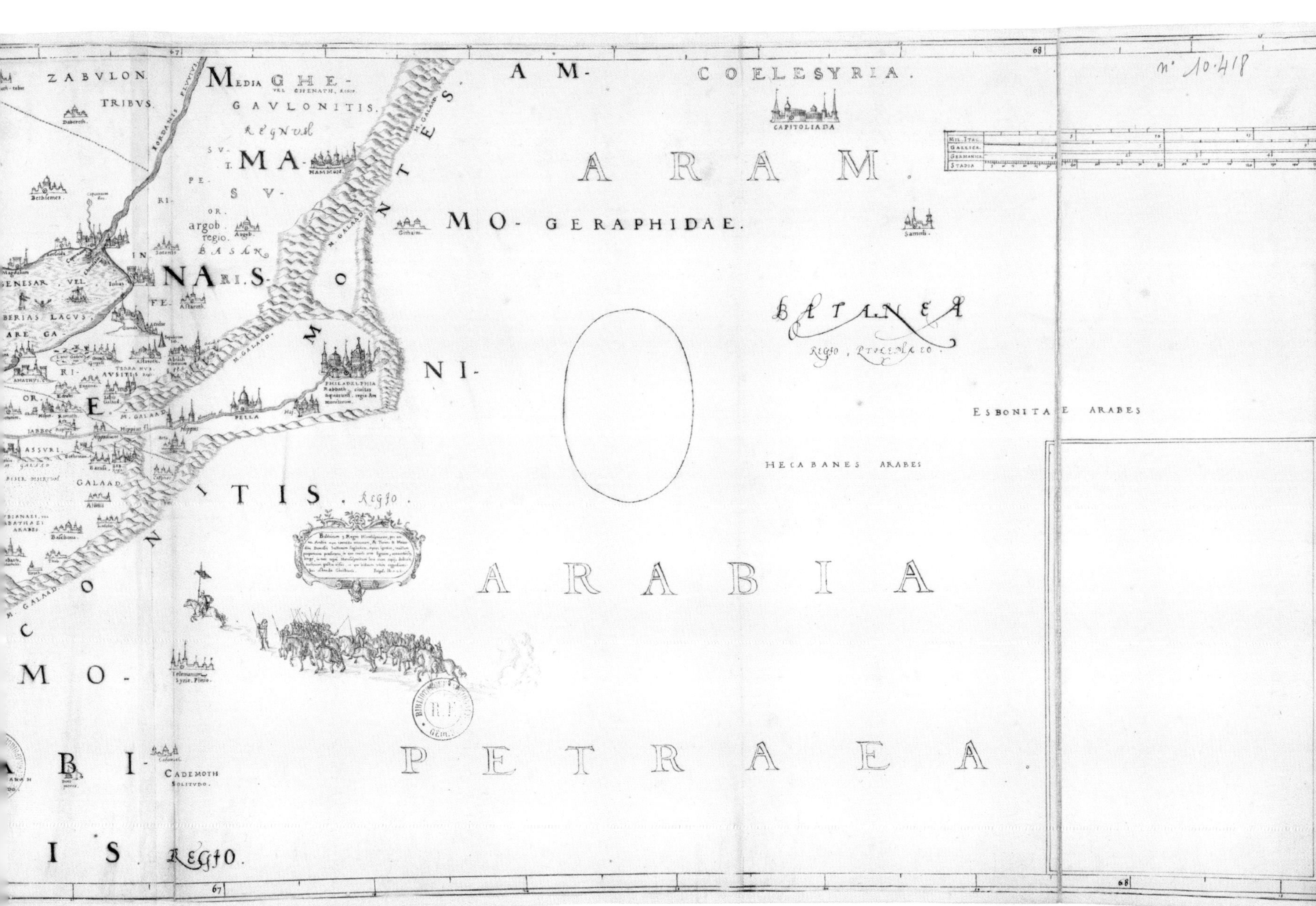

Among several manuscript maps of Palestine associated with Ziegler is that in fig. 92 (previous page). It is genetically linked to the *Tercia tabula continet samaria* of the printed atlas, not just geographically, but in its title's use of the Biblical *Samaria* to define the land, a name that would be invested with political weight in the twentieth century. On the right of the manuscript, the desert army is that of Baldwin IV, known as the Leper King, king of Jerusalem in the late twelfth century. At Jaffa, Andromeda is chained to a rock as a sacrifice to Cete to appease Poseidon, who was furious at boasts by Andromeda's mother that her daughter was more beautiful than the Nereids. The huge frenzied sea monster is nearly at the prize, but viewers of the map were reassured by the image of Perseus on a flying horse above the monster, racing to Andromeda's rescue. Above, Jonah is about to be swallowed by the whale, and at the top, we see the whale again, now with the symbolism stated: just as Jonah was three days and three nights in the fish's belly, so will Jesus be three days and three nights in the heart of the earth. The empty rectangles on the upper left and lower right were likely intended for a title, dedication, and/or explanative legends in a printed rendering.

Ziegler's maps provided the basis for a few major works that followed in close succession, beginning with Gerard Mercator in 1537—the important geographer's first published map (fig. 94.). Mercator assembled Ziegler's seven woodcuts into a single map, incorporated his own modifications, oriented it to the northwest to make better use of the rectangular space, and had it engraved on copper.

(Previous page) FIG. 93: Chart of the Mediterranean, Italy, 1505 (author unknown). Three cities in the Levant merited vignettes: top-to-bottom, Aleppo, Damascus, and Jerusalem. The distinctive shape of such charts is simply that of the sheep skin from which it was made, the neck used for the geographically sparser end, or for inscriptions. [Bavarian State Library; image the Library of Congress, Control Number 2021668460]

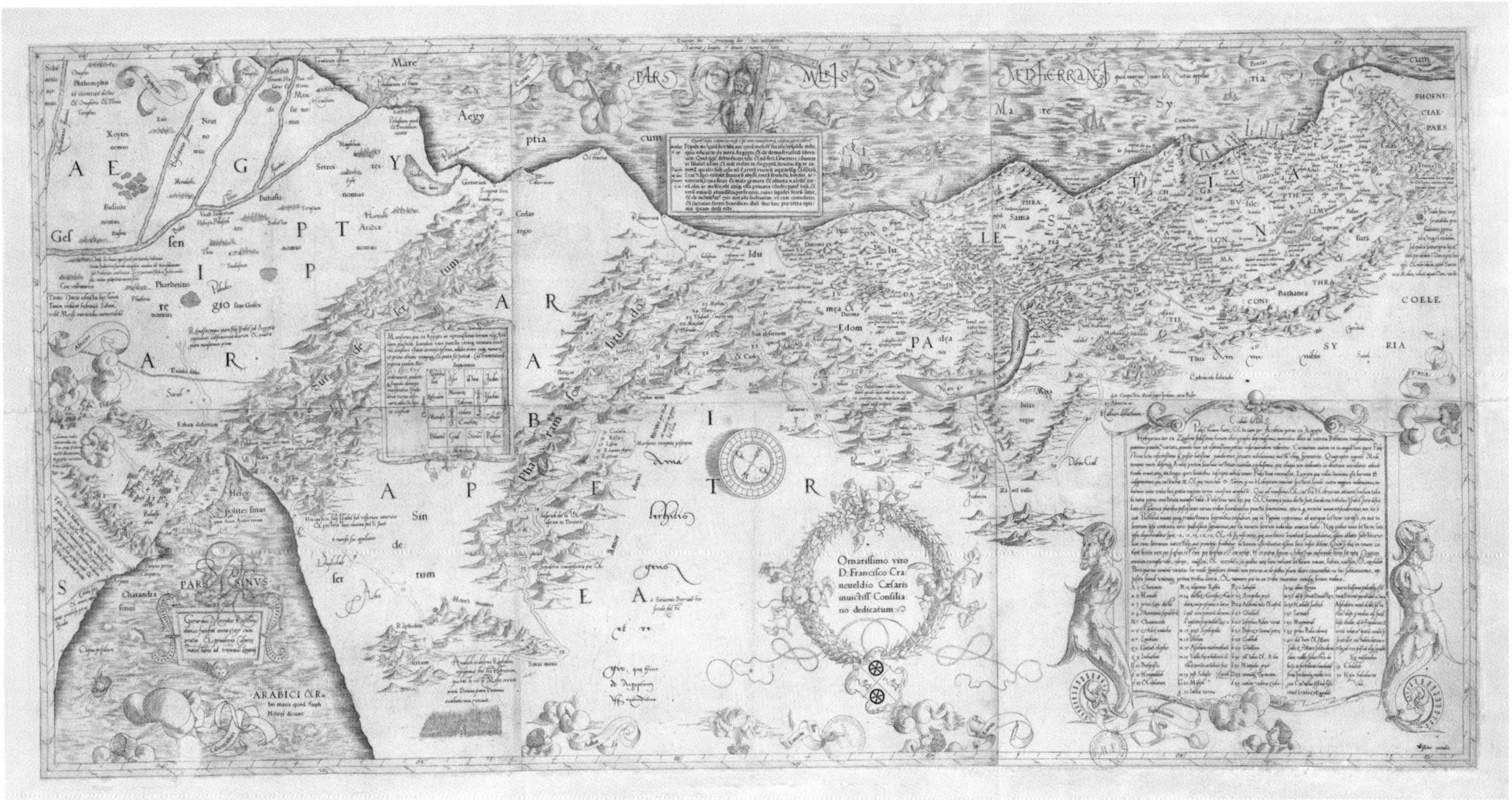

FIG. 94: Gerard Mercator, Candido lectori S. Palestinam hanc, et in eam per Arabicas petras ex Aegypto Hebreorum iter ex Zieglero fidissimo horum chorographo deprompsimus... 1537. Six years later (1543), Mercator's association with Lutherans earned him a spot on the Inquisition's list of heretics, and imprisonment. In the detail above, New Testament iconography first takes a dominant role on a printed map: Christ overlooks the land from the top center. [Bibliothèque Nationale, CPL GE DD-2987 (10405-10406 B)]

FIG. 95: Wolfgang Wissenburg, *Descriptio Palestinae nova / per Wolfg[ang] Wissenburg Basiliens*... 1538. [Bibliothèque Nationale, CPL GE DD-2987 (10402 B RES)]

The following year (1538), the Reformed preacher and theology professor Wolfgang Wissenburg published a wall map based on Ziegler's (fig. 95). He dedicated it to Thomas Cranmer, a leader of the English Reformation and once Archbishop of Canterbury, who would be burned at the stake in Oxford in 1556. Wissenburg improves on Mercator by including Ziegler's distinction between the Gulfs of Aqaba and Suez while correctly resisting his odd Dead Sea. The Biblical Exodus, which would become a fixture on European maps of Palestine, is illustrated as a series of camps, but most of the map's otherwise empty space is filled with arbitrary motifs of trees, vegetation, hills, and waves. (His mountains, real or not, were not motifs.)

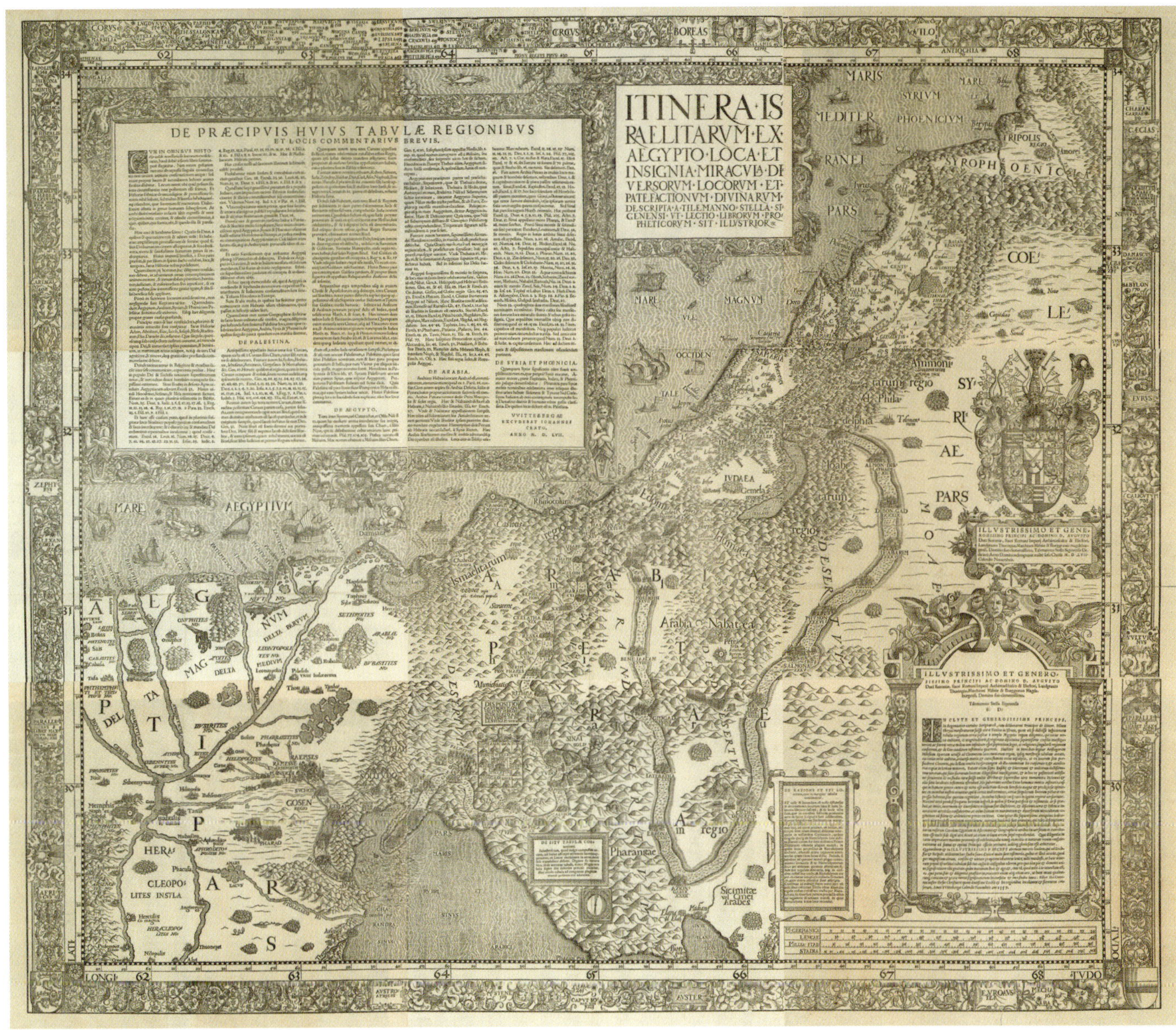

FIG. 96: Tilemann Stella, 1557, *Itinera Israelitarum ex Aegypto loca et insigna miracula diversorum locorum et patefactionum divinarum descripta a Tilemanno Stella / excudebat Iohannes Crato.* [Universitätsbibliothek Basel, UBH Kartenslg AA 104]

In composing his influential 1559 wall map of Palestine (fig. 96), the German mathematician Tilemann Stella embraced Wissenburg's elaboration upon the Biblical Exodus, while trusting Ziegler regarding the Dead Sea. Given that the map was his crowning contribution to a project of furthering Biblical studies, its title is revealing: whereas Wissenburg presented his *pièce de résistance* as a map of Palestine upon which he features the Exodus, Stella now reframes it. His is titled as a map of the Israelites' journey out of Egypt, with the associated miracles and divine revelations. Rather than Biblical stories taking place in Palestine, Palestine is defined by them.

FIG. 97: Palestine, after Lucas Cranach; from Christoph Froschauer, *Das Alt Testament dütsch, der vrsprünglichen Ebreischen waarheyt nach vff das aller trüwlichest verdütschet,* Zürich, 1525 [Trinity College, Cambridge, A.10.18]

No surviving printed Bible included a map of Palestine (or anyplace else) until 1525, and when it did, it was a fiasco (fig. 97). The choice of prototype was fine—the Cranach map of a decade earlier—but it appears that the craftsman employed to cut the woodblock had previously only cut illustrations, never a map, because he took the shortcut of cutting the block directly from an image of the original, without reversing it. Most nongeographic images pass commercial scrutiny in mirror-image, if to the consternation of the artist; but the result here was a mirror-image map. This was not the first time: Venetian woodcutters had already done this to the Macrobius world map in 1489 and 1500.

FIG. 98: Palestine, Sebastian Münster, 1540

The blunder may have inspired Sebastian Münster, a geographer and professor of Hebrew, when he composed his new map of Palestine for his 1540 edition of Ptolemy's *Geography* (fig. 98.). Münster took the same "look" but made it work by changing the orientation—not reversing east and west as would be expected, but changing north to west, the result "correct" but overstating the Levantine coast's slight NE-SW bend by about forty-five degrees.

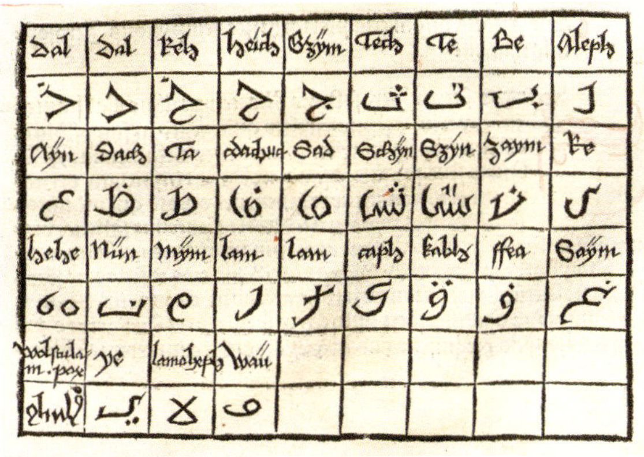

FIG. 99: A first step toward printed travel guides that incorporate dictionaries in the language of the place to be visited, Breydenbach's *Peregrinatio in terram sanctam* included this transliteration of Arabic sounds. [Mainz, 1486].

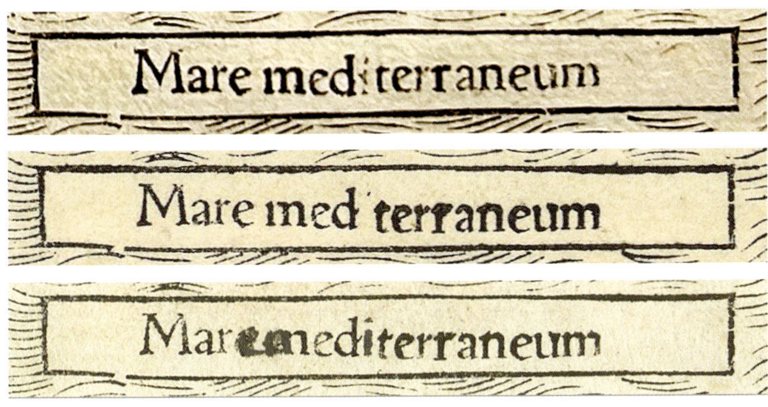

FIG. 100: The Mediterranean Sea label from three examples of the map of Palestine from the first edition of Münster's Ge*ography* (1540), illustrating the challenges of inserted type.

- **top:** All's fine, except the type "i" is sunk slightly too far into the woodblock, causing a faint print.
- **middle:** The type has slipped further in. There is no "i", and *terraneum h*as sunk down, as the type is no longer held tight.
- **bottom:** The missing "i" is replaced in manuscript, and the same hand has also reinforced the now-ailing type of the fourth and fifth letters. [Library of Congress / Bibliothèque Nationale / LOC]

The esteemed Franciscan-turned-Lutheran had his own printing challenges. He opted to make place-names by inserting metal type in the woodblock, rather than being cut as part of the block. This had huge advantages: it was clearer, allowed for extended text to be changed according to the language of the edition, and saved the most laborious part of the block-making. But the inserted type had to be exactly level with the raised image of the block. It was often not secure, and might fall out during printing or get pushed further into the block and lose contact, both when inked and when struck, pitfalls illustrated in fig. 100.

There would be two more renderings of Ptolemy's *Geography* doubling as a vehicle for new, non-Ptolemaic maps: that of Giacomo Gastaldi in 1548, and its spinoff by Giacomo Ruscelli in 1561 and subsequent, both in copperplate. But the genre had run its course. Seeing the need and the market for a major cosmographic atlas that broke free of classical constraints altogether, Münster created his immensely popular, non-Ptolemaic *Cosmography* of 1544. Republished and enlarged through 1578, it did much to democratize geographic knowledge—and error—with editions in the vernacular: German (1544+), French (1552+), and Italian (1558+).[20]

Christian suppport for the Zionist "return" of the Jews would have a dual motivation: the obvious theological, but also anti-Jewish bigotry. As Münster prepared the *Cosmography*, the first had already been voiced by the German theologian Martin Cellarius in the 1520s. But in 1543, Martin Luther himself made the explicit call for Jews to go to Palestine prompted by bigotry:

> The country and the roads are open for them to proceed to their land whenever they wish. If they did so, we would be glad to present gifts to them on the occasion; it would be good riddance. For they are a heavy burden, a plague, a pestilence, a sheer misfortune for our country.[21]

FIG. 101: Antonio Lafreri, *Disegno de l'Isola di Cypro con li confini della Caramania, Soria, Giudea et Egitto nel quale si vede ancho l'ordine che ha tenuto alcuna volta l'armata delli Clarmi. Sri. Venetiani nel marciare...* Rome, 1570 [Bibliothèque Nationale, ark:/12148/btv1b55000181t]

FIG 102: *Vile do Gaza chef du royaome*. Manuscript sketch of Gaza from a personal account of travels, *Les voyages e peregrinassions de Vincens Blac.* Seventeenth century. [Bibliothèque Nationale, ark:/12148/btv1b10463836m]

As Münster's *Cosmography*, with its woodcut maps and views, all created for the book and thus uniform in format, was enjoying great success, ad hoc non-Ptolemaic atlases of copper-plate maps were being put together on demand in Italy, where loose-sheets formed the major part of the map market. Through the 1550s to the 1570s, sellers offered an array of maps of the world and its parts by various Italian geographers, many published by Antonio Lafreri. Map customers, rather than simply leaving the shop with their selection of loose-sheets, might opt to have them bound, producing what is now referred to as "Lafreri atlases." The maps were superior in content and production, but as atlases they were simply albums of unrelated maps. Since the maps were conceived as individual loose-sheets, they were neither uniform in size nor format, and so extra margin was added to smaller maps, while larger maps might be folded to facilitate binding.

As the Lafreri map of the eastern Mediterranean in fig. 101 was being engraved on copper in *portlano* style, Pope Pius V was organizing a coalition of Catholic states to challenge the Ottoman Empire, in what the following year would be the Battle of Lepanto. The map depicts this in anticipation, as if a good luck charm to ensure a Latin victory. At first the map's magic seemed to work, but it didn't last.

Manuscript portolan charts continued to be produced by European, Ottoman, and North African geographers. Of the Ottomans, none of the era surpass those of corsair and navigator Piri Reis (Muhiddin Piri). Only a fragment of the famous 1513 world chart attributed to this Gallipoli native survives, the Levant among the lost bulk of the map. But copies of his combination navigational book and portolan atlas, *Kitab-i bahriye* (Book of the Sea), more relevant to our topic, are intact.

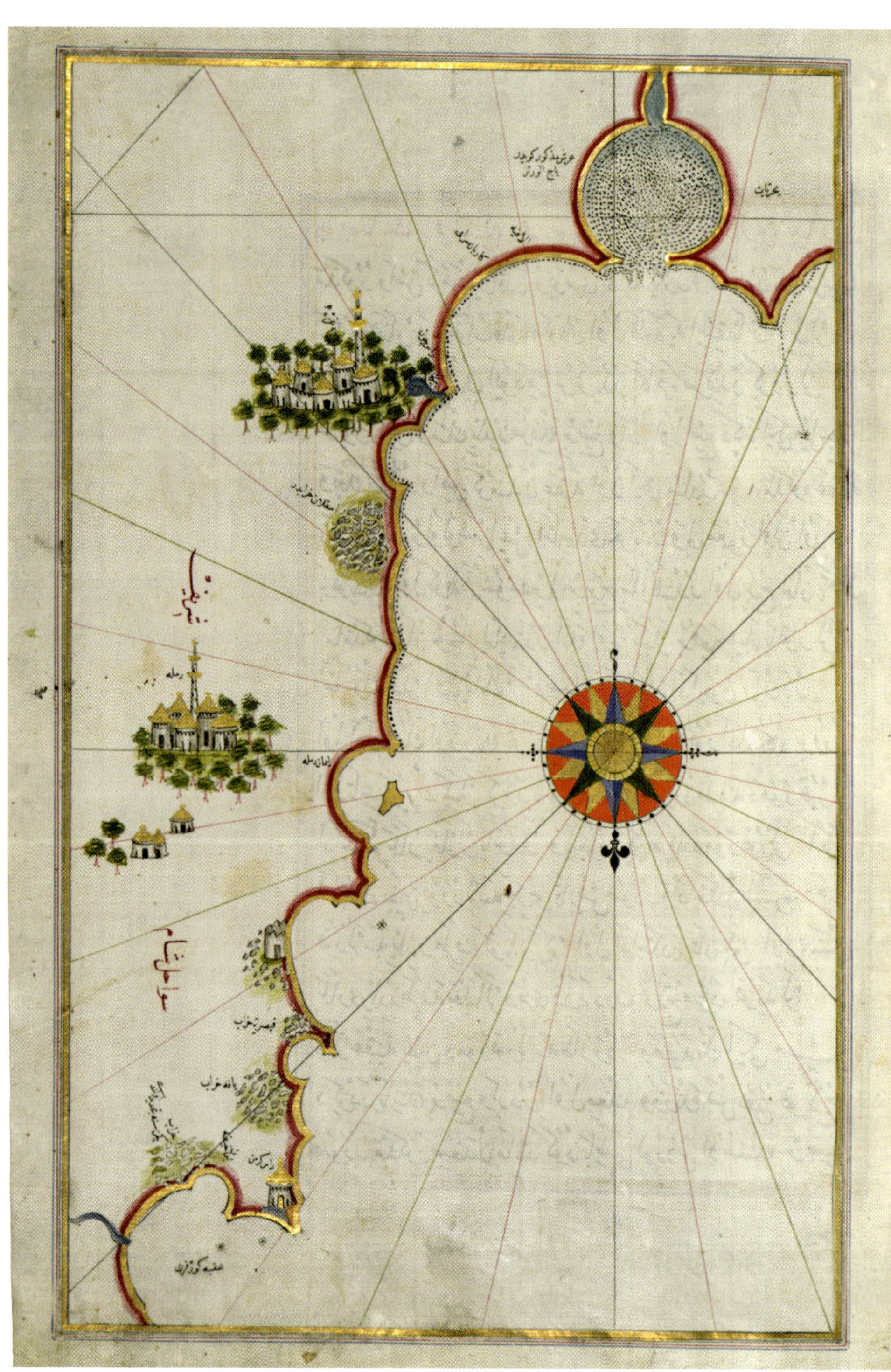

Oriented with south at the top, two of his maps cover Palestine: figs. 103 (southern) and 104 (northern). The large inlet at the top is the Nile Delta, and moving north (down), the large city vignette is Gaza, the rocks below it Ashkelon. Ramla is the lower vignette, followed by a small cape marking Caesaria, and then Jaffa. The down-facing cape and bay at the bottom is Acre. Overlapping to the northern sheet (104), Acre is repeated at the top, then extends north to Tyre, the large three-pronged promontory at the bottom.

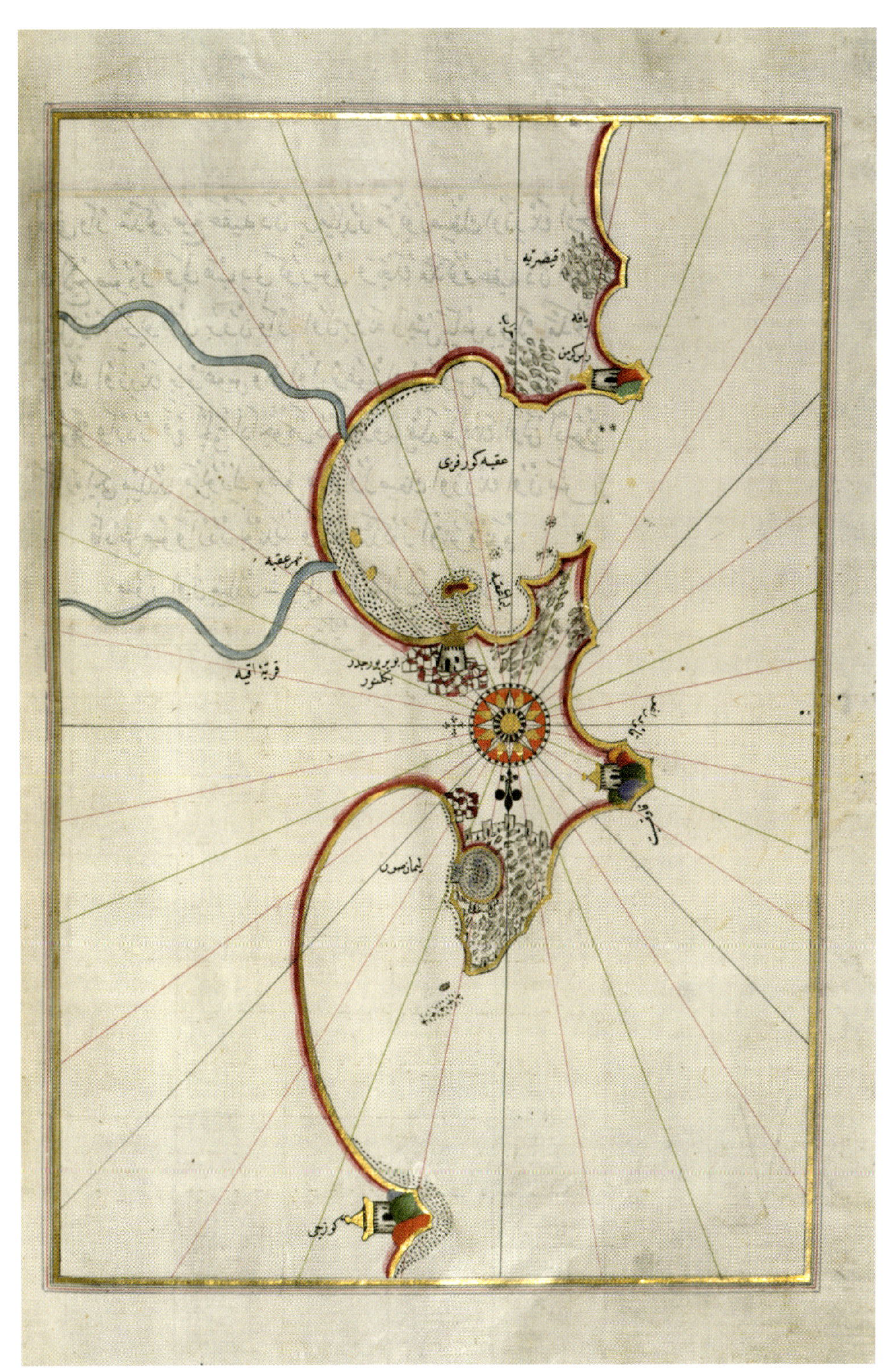

FIG. 103, 104: Sea charts of the Palestinian coast from Piri Ries's *Book of the Sea (Kitab-i bahriye)*, a seventeenth-century copy of a ca.1526 original. [Walters Art Museum, W.658.312A, W.658.313B

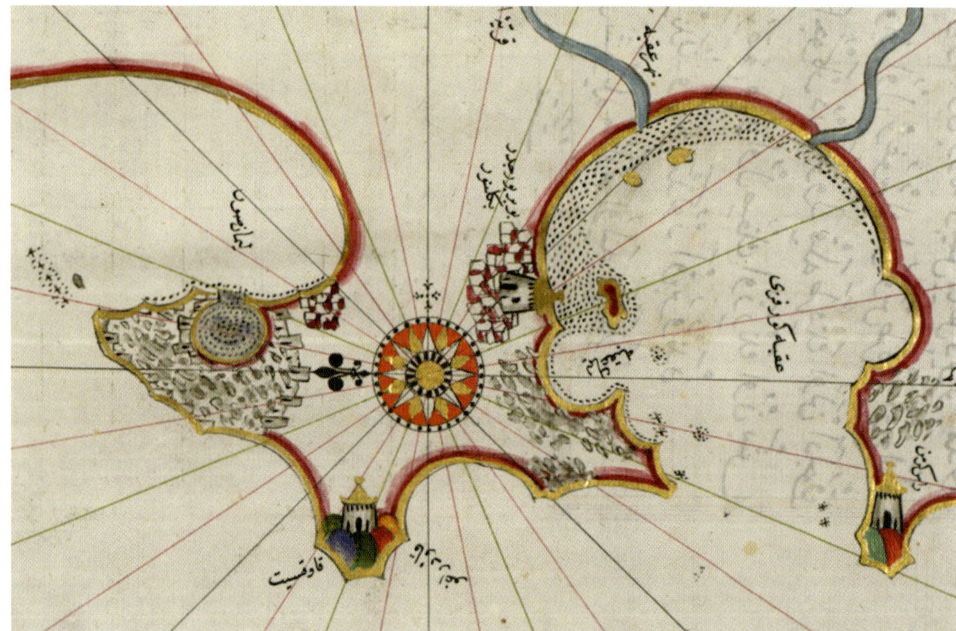

FIG. 105: Stylized Palestinian capes from the fifteenth-century Venetian, Gregorio Dati (top, a detail of fig. 75 on page 104), and the sixteenth-century Ottoman, Piri Reis (bottom, a detail of fig. 104, page 133, turned 90°)

It is interesting to compare the stylized capes in the *Book of the Sea* of Arabic lineage to those of the fifteenth century Venetian Gregorio Dati we saw in the previous chapter (p104, above). Dati's were unusual for a Latin mapmaker, whereas for Reis, the stylization was part of a long inheritance of Arabic mapping, examples of which Dati or the copyist likely saw—and liked. As for Piri Reis, this most famous of Ottoman mapmakers came to an inglorious end. Following a perceived military failure at Hormuz, he was beheaded in Cairo in 1553.

FIG. 106: The Eastern Mediterranean, from an atlas of sea charts, ʿAlī ibn Aḥmad al-Sharqī al-Safāqisī, 1571–72. South is at the top. [Bodleian Library, MS. Marsh 294; A similar atlas is held by the Bibliothèque Nationale, Arabe 2278]

The port city of Sfax, south of Tunis on the winding Tunisian coast and nominally within the Ottoman sphere, was home to the al-Sharqī al-Ṣifāqsī family of chart makers. The al-Ṣifāqsī chart of the eastern Mediterranean in fig. 106 preserves a clue suggesting that such charts were passed around transculturally: an early European hand has translated a few of the Levantine ports to Latin characters, most visibly *Ascalon*. The chart is wholly modern and designed for its utilitarian purpose, yet the little sea atlas from which it comes also contains a rough world map harking back four centuries to al-Idrīsī, a map of no value at sea or land but preserving what had come before.

In the same spirit, Ptolemy remained spiritually relevant to many Latin mapmakers as Europe "discovered" and idealized Classical Greek and Roman civilization. For no practical end, Gerard Mercator produced a labor-intensive, copperplate edition of Ptolemy's *Geography* at the stunningly late date of 1578, even after having gotten himself tied in cartographic tangles on parts of his famous 1569 world map (that first codified the projection named for him) through his unwillingness to let go of the ancient Alexandrian geographer.

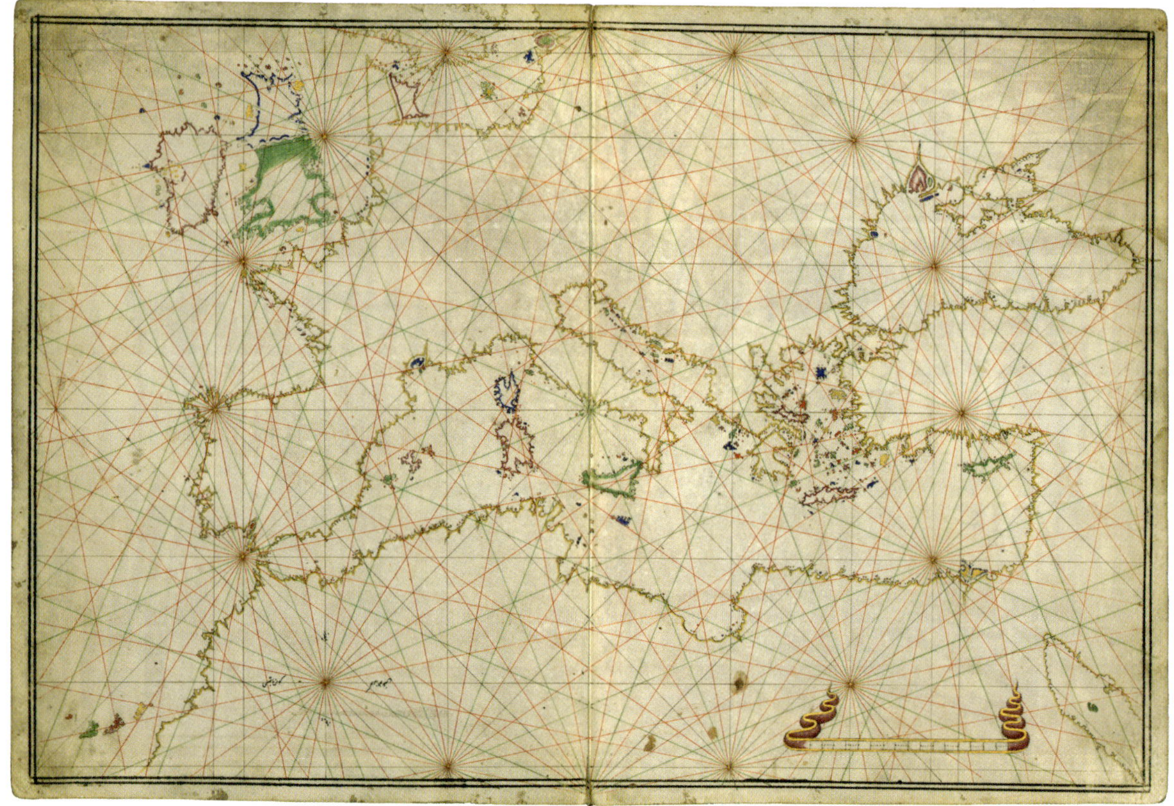

FIG 107 (left), 108 (right): Two charts from an Ottoman sea atlas, 1550–1600. [Walters Art Museum, Ms. W.660; photo Library of Congress, 2021668462; Break in the center joined in the images]

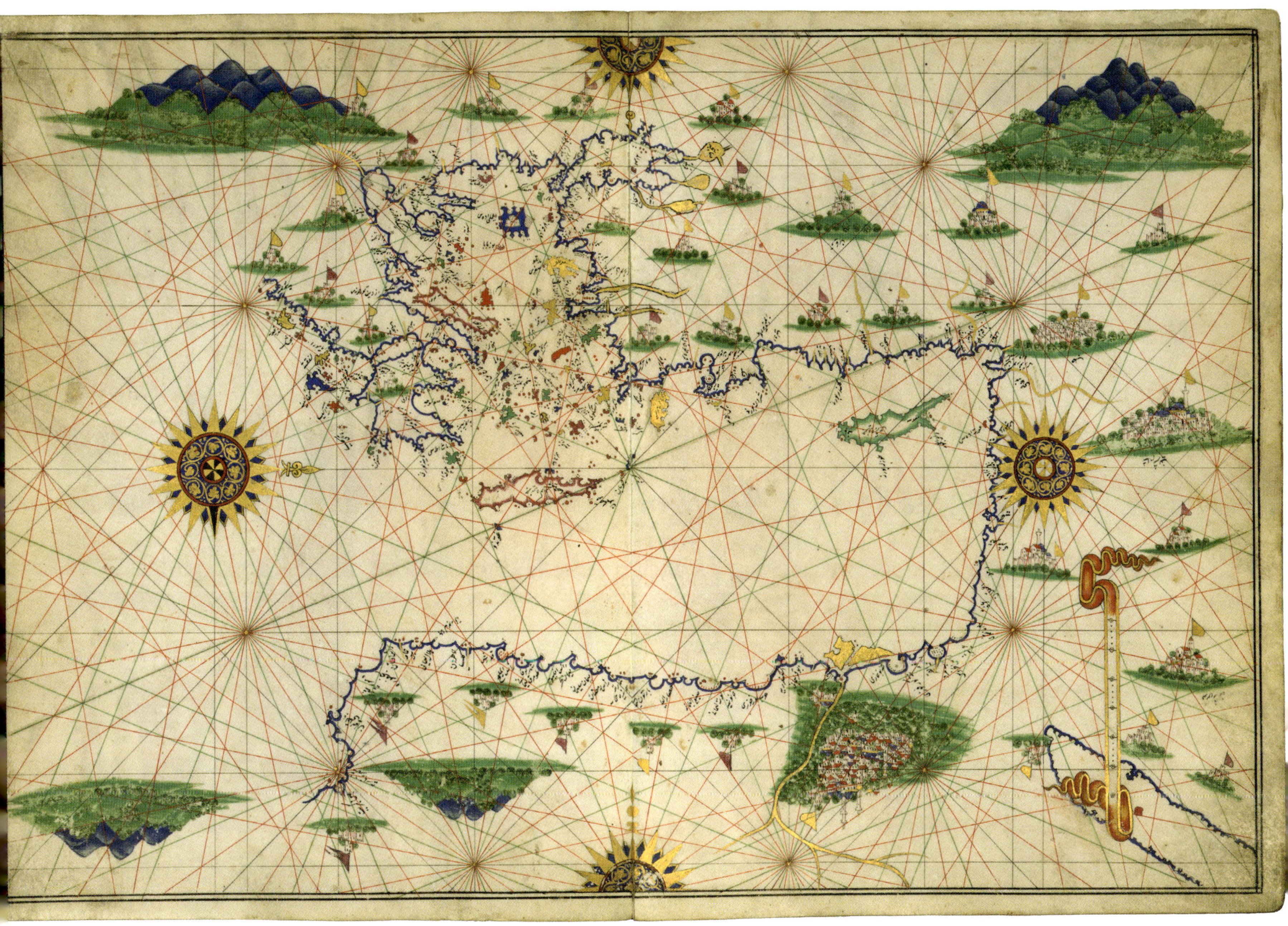

This was an era in which sea charts were increasingly used as objects of art. An Italian-influenced Ottoman atlas of the second half of the sixteenth century contains a chart of Europe in draft form (fig. 107), the skeletal coasts and rhumb lines drawn, but nothing more. From there, the eastern Mediterranean was extracted for the completed chart in fig. 108, coastal names inserted in nasta'līq script, and vignettes of numerous cities drawn in remarkably fine detail.[22]

SEPTENTRIO
mare galileo
mare tiberiadis
TRIBVS NEPT ALIN
NAZARETH
ASER
TRIBVS ISAC
TRIBVS GAD

FIG. 109 (left): Palestine, uncertain authorship, in a portolan atlas by Battista Agnese, ca. 1550. [The Huntington Library, HM 10]

FIG. 110 (below): The Palestinian coast from Acre and south, detail from a chart of the eastern Mediterranean by Battista Agnese, ca. 1544 [Library of Congress, G1001 .A4 1544]

FIG. 111: Chart of Europe and northern Africa from a Portolan atlas inscribed "Nicolas Vallard de Dieppe, 1547," likey referring to its first owner, not its (possibly Portuguese?) maker. Palestine is in the upper left. [The Huntington Library, mssHM 29]

Battista Agnese, of Genoese origin working in Venice, was a prolific maker of small portolan atlases destined for wealthy families' studies. The intricately drawn map of Palestine in fig. 109 (previous page) was bound in an Agnese atlas of ca. 1550 and appears to have been created for it, though its authorship is uncertain. Compare it to fig. 110, the Palestinian coast from a typical chart of the eastern Mediterranean by Agnese of ca. 1544.

chart from a no-frills navigational tool to the opposite—wildly embellished maps of nil value to a pilot but nonetheless strewn with rhumb lines for effect—reaches its apogee in the northern French port of Dieppe, associated with names like Nicolas Vallard (fig. 111) and the explorer, navigator, and privateer Guillaume Le Testu. Le Testu's map of the eastern Mediterranean (fig. 112) squeezes in the expected Levantine coastal names but devotes itself to Biblical iconography. The Red Sea is mis-figured and mis-oriented even for the day, but serves to illustrate the crossing of the sea by the Israelites and drowning of the Egyptians. The Persian Gulf fares more badly still: it is nowhere to be found.

The printed medium would not begin to embrace sea charts until the end of the century, and when it did, Palestine was not a focus. The period's major event in the commercial map market was the publication in Belgium in 1570 of a new work that established the essential concept of an atlas as it would be understood until the advent of digital maps: the Antwerp geographer Abraham Ortelius's *Theatrum Orbis Terrarum*. Its maps covered the entire world, were uniformly conceived and formatted, methodically arranged, with sources cited and with explanatory text. They were engraved on copper, richly embellished, and designed to be saleable with or without in-house color, to be purchased either way, according to preference and budget.

FIG. 112: Palestine, the Levant, Egypt, and inland, Guillaume Le Testu, 1555. The indulgent extreme of the portolan chart as an artist's *carte blanc.* From his *Cosmographie universelle, selon les navigateurs tant anciens que modernes.* [Bibliothèque Nationale, ark:/12148/btv1b8447838j]

FIG. 113: *Nova descriptio amplissima Sanctae terrae, quam Mr. Petrus Laicksteen astronomus perambulavit ac visitavit an°. 1536.* Christiaan Sgrooten, this example published in Paris by N. Berey, 1656. [Bibliothèque Nationale, GE DD-6011 (1-9 RES)]

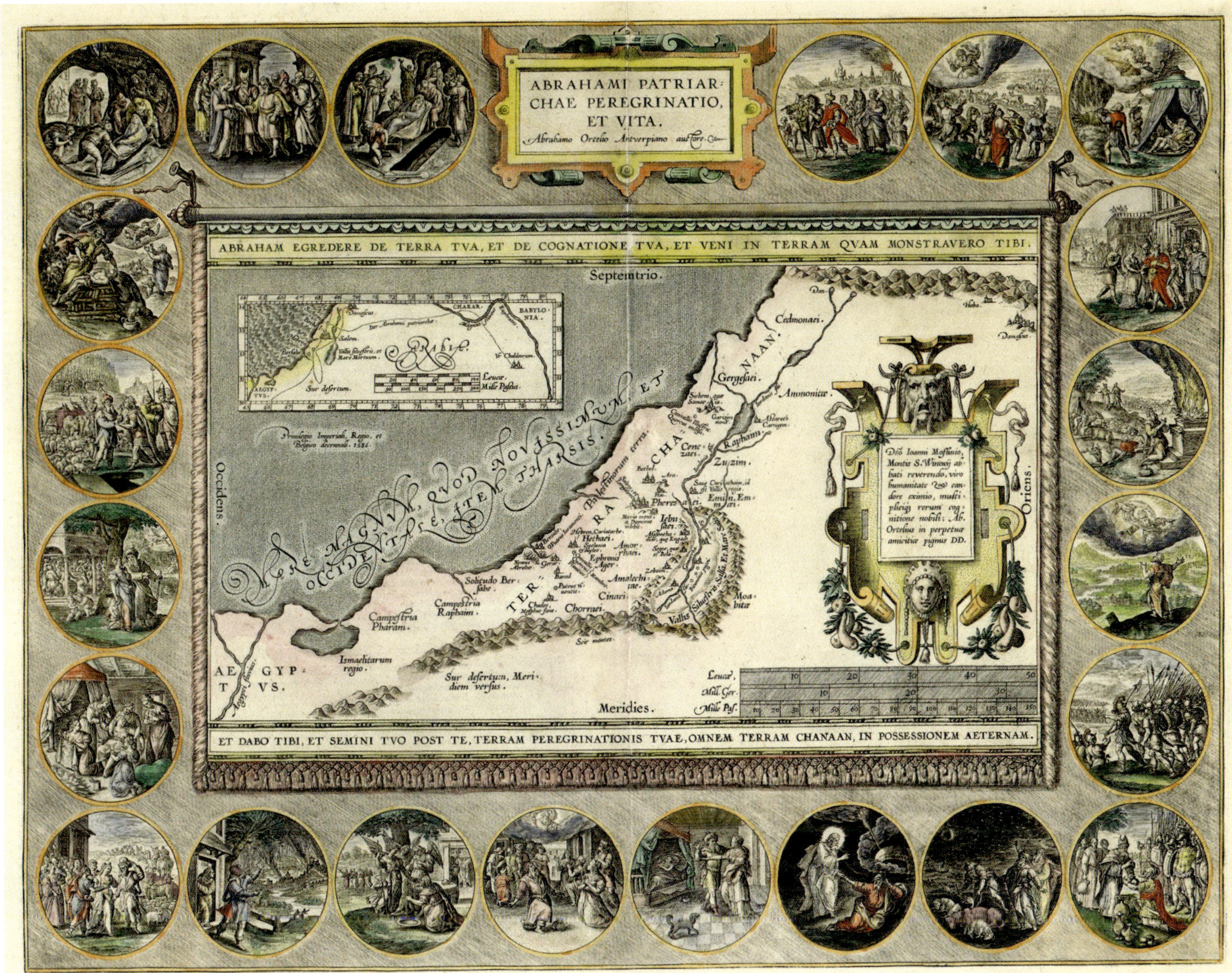

FIG. 114: Abraham Ortelius, 1590, *Abrahami Patriarchae peregrinatio et vita.* The most elaborate of the maps of Palestine in Ortelius's atlases. [Library of Congress]

The *Theatrum* was an instant success. It appealed to both the intellect, real or feigned, and was a feast for the eyes. A must-have object of art and symbol of erudition for those of means, it set the course for the slew of like-minded atlases that followed in its wake, spawning a half century of unrivalled supremacy for the Low Countries in the commercial atlas market.

The *Theatrum* was expanded and updated throughout its forty-two year run, during which Ortelius added an atlas of the ancient world, the *Parergon*, as well as a fat pocket atlas, the *Epitome*. He was the first to produce an atlas in English—the *Epitome* in 1601 and the by-then massive *Theatrum* in 1606. All contained maps of Palestine, bringing reductions of the work of Tilleman Stella (1570+) and, beginning in 1584, that of Christiaan Sgrooten (fig. 113), who served as court geographer of the (Catholic) Spanish King Philip II in the Netherlands. Sgrooten's *Nova descriptio amplissimae Terrae Sanctae* was the century's final large, separate prototype of Palestine in the Cranach-Wissenburg-Stella tradition, and the only one said to incorporate new, empirical reports, namely those of the astronomer Peter Laicksteen during travels in 1556. Frustratingly, little more is known of him, and Ortelius's text adds nothing beyond acknowledging him on the map. Ortelius's accompanying text to all his maps of Palestine is couched in Biblical reference.

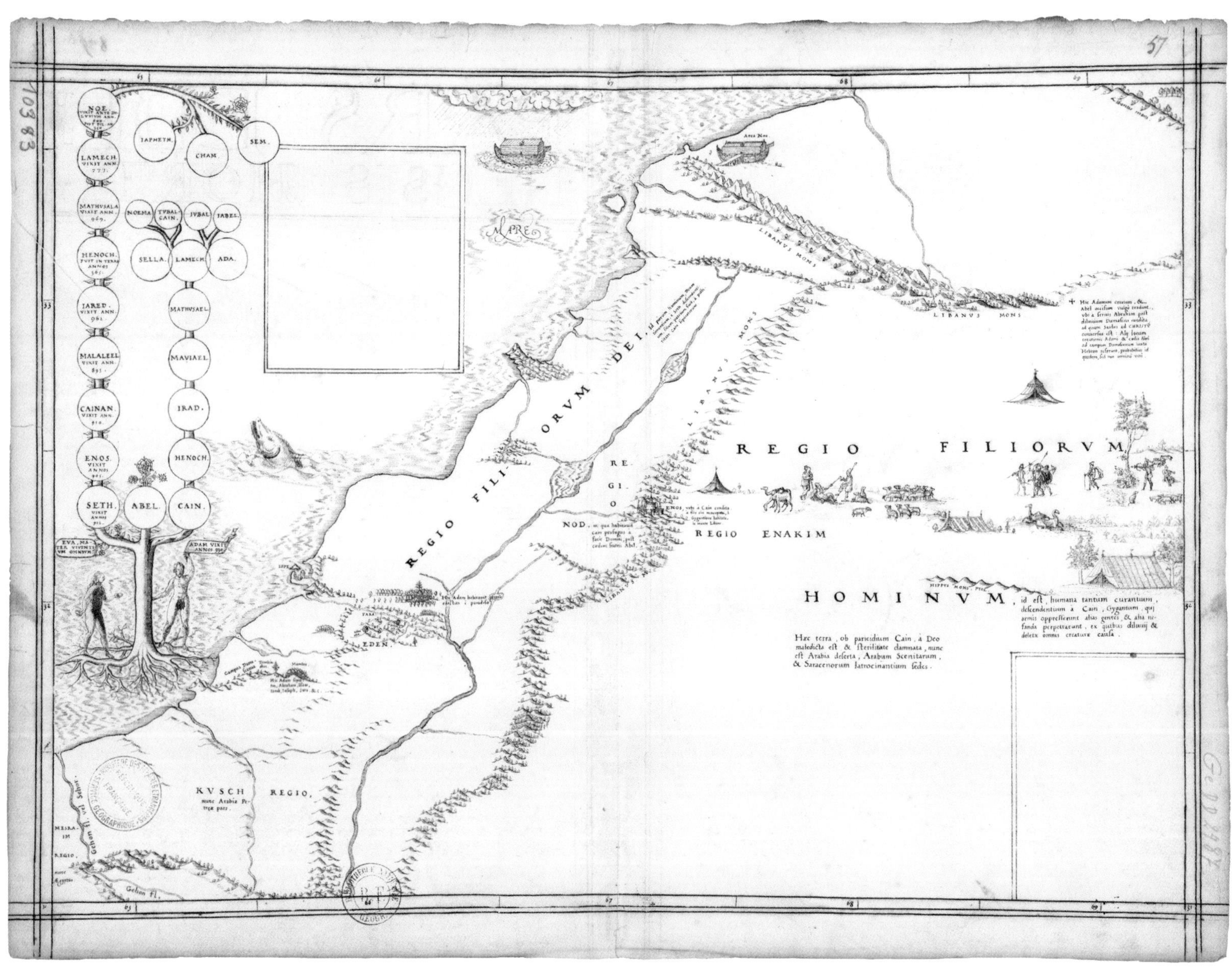

FIG. 115: Pars Edenensis horti, c1600(?). Manuscript map of Palestine concerned with the location of Paradise. As its author's inscriptions explain, many believe that the place where Adam was created and Abel was killed was where Damascus was founded by Abraham's servants after the flood. More likely, the mapmaker says, it was near Hebron, and so the Garden is shown just inland from Jaffa. Adam and Eve stand by the Tree of Knowledge, from which sprouts a family tree. In the north, Noah's Ark appears twice, at sea during the Deluge, and beached afterwards. Attributed to, or associated with, the historian André Favyn. [Bibliothèque Nationale, CPL GE DD-2987 (10383)]

FIG. 116: Adam and Eve are expelled from the Garden of Eden. From *De Bibel int corte ghetranslateert. Wten laine ende walsche metten figueren. Antwerpen, Gheprent bi Claes de Graue,* 1516. [Library of Congress, BS1092 .G5]

BEYOND PALESTINE

Renaissance and Enlightenment thought might have led to a less theologically constrained mapping of Palestine. Instead, it broadened the inquiry into Biblical issues. Reconstructions of an imagined Biblical Jerusalem, or of Solomon's mythical temple, remained popular, and theories of the whereabouts of the Bible's Eden flourished—or had the Deluge, as some claimed, so altered the earth's surface that it no longer exists? Theories regarding the Biblical story of the dispersion of the Tribes of Israel widened dramatically with Europe's expanding knowledge of the earth. In 1571, the Spanish orientalist and polymath Arias Montanus composed a world map for the purpose of tracing the locations of the Tribes and other Palestine-relevant sites throughout the world.

The whereabouts of Paradise was another question that invariably involved Palestine. The holy book placed the Garden of Eden in the east, and early on, this was often envisioned as near Palestine—after all, how far could Adam and Eve have gotten before the story continued? Many medieval mappaemundi associate the four rivers of Paradise with Palestine, as does the Jerome map (fig. 33). On quite a different level, John Milton's epic *Paradise Lost* (1667) uses the expulsion of Adam and Eve from Paradise to explore such concepts as free will, predestination, human agency, and the very nature of good and evil. When Milton invokes the sea monster Dagon, the monster is "dreaded through the Coast / Of Palestine, in Gath and Ascalon, / And Accaron and Gaza's frontier bounds."

If many Biblical questions were pursued with a view to the afterlife, the one most concerned with worldly comfort in the present was Ophir, from where Solomon's ships were said to have imported the gold and other riches to Palestine to build the apocryphal First Temple. In this theological mindset, Ophir was a place that existed in the post-Deluge world and thus one where, in theory, mortals could still approach—*and* it promised fabulous wealth. As phrased in the King James Bible:

> And the navy also of Hiram [Phoenician king of Tyre], that brought gold from Ophir, brought in from Ophir great plenty of almug trees, and precious stones ... And Huram sent him by the hands of his servants ships, and servants that had knowledge of the sea; and they went with the servants of Solomon to Ophir, and took thence four hundred and fifty talents of gold, and brought them to king Solomon.

Early writers generally believed Ophir to lie in Africa or Southeast Asia, but as the European worldview expanded, so did the theories. John Dee, for example, court astronomer to Elizabeth I who delved into alchemy and divination, was typical of many in attempting to reconstruct King Solomon's tracks to Ophir by using the Judeo-Christian Bible as a literal travelogue.

Arias Montanus marked Ophir twice on his world map: once in the coastal northwest of North America, and once on the coast of Peru. One could make an educated guess as to his reasoning: Logically, Solomon's ships would have sailed into the Indian Ocean (Ophir was clearly not in the Mediterranean), even to its eastern end. For reasons beyond the scope of this book, that eastern Indian Ocean coast "became" the west coast of Central and South America and, for Montanus, by extension the Pacific Coast of North America.

Indeed, Montanus was simply committing to the map what had already become theory among some Spanish pilots and cosmographers. In the 1520s, Rodrigo de Santa Ella, founder of the University of Seville, deduced that Ophir lay in the middle of the Pacific, and the fabled land was soon sought there by explorers such as Sebastian Cabot and Ruy López de Villalobos. But short of happening upon some unearthly glistening shores brimming with riches, they had no idea what they were looking for, other than pinning the Ophir identity onto whatever they found where they expected to find it—which is what happened.

In 1567, Álvaro de Mendaña y Neyra set off into the Pacific from Peru, confidence strengthened by Amerindian legends that allegedly spoke of a rich land to the west. His expedition "discovered" well-populated lush, mountainous islands which—though far from the image they'd conjured as the source of the fabled temple's riches—"became" the Solomon Islands at the hands of cosmographers back in Spain and were already marked as such on a 1575 chart by López de Velasco (fig. 117).

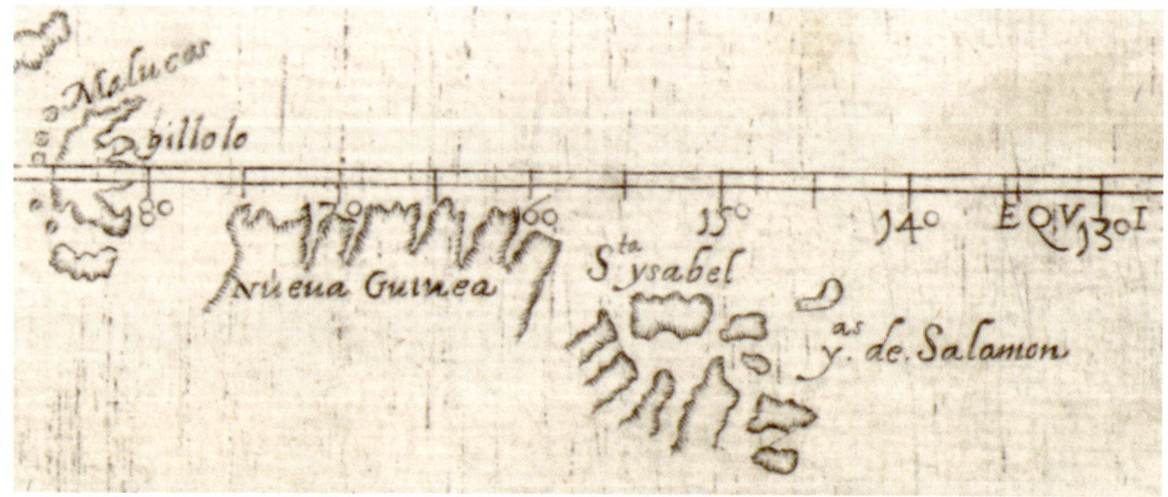

FIG. 117: A detail from a copper-engraved rendering of a 1575 chart of the Pacific by López de Velasco, showing the Solomon Islands east of New Guinea. Antonio de Herrera y Tordesillas, Madrid, 1601

To whatever extent those involved—explorer, cartographer, royal patron—actually believed that Mendaña's archipelago was the source of the fabulous riches of the imagined temple in a fabled Palestinian past, there was not to be a reckoning. As if fate were toying with them for their absurdity, they then "lost" the islands. For precisely two hundred years, neither Mendaña nor any subsequent European mariner could find them again.

FIG. 118: Petrus Plancius, *Tabula Geographica, in qua Paradisus, nec non Regiones, Urbes, Oppida, et Loca Describuntur...*, c1590.

By 1600, the Spanish had barely ventured into the realm of printed maps, despite (or because of) their then-supremacy in overseas imperialism. Excepting the anomaly of a 1498 Zaragoza printing of the 1486 Breydenbach map (a copy of fig. 46, above), none of the few printed maps produced by Spain had theological content.

In contrast, Dutch geographers such as the Reformation minister Petrus Plancius actively exploited the power of printed maps. As adept in the challenge to Spanish overseas exploits as he was in religious affairs, at the turn of the century he created a series of copper-engraved illustrated /instructive maps of Palestine to accompany a Dutch Bible (fig. 118). The maps continued to solidify Palestine as a land defined by Judeo-Christian mythology, drawing the viewer into the Palestinian earth as inseparable from the Old and New Testament.

A partcularly influential map of Palestine was the work of a Catholic priest, Christian van Adrichem, who had been director of a convent in Delft. As was the norm, Adrichem's map was new only in the sense of its reinterpretation and re-juggling of medieval and ancient writings. Harking back to older errors, the coast of Egypt continues straight from Palestine's, and what Josephus described as a peninsula at the southern end of the Dead Sea Adrichem misinterprets as a peninsular-shaped water extension. The map would be the basis for several more by Reform geographers, even into the nineteenth century. The first, however, was by a rabbi.

Jacob ben Abraham Zaddiq was a Dutch Jewish banker and merchant of Portuguese descent. He took Adrichem's map, translated it to Hebrew, replaced New Testament iconography and inscriptions with those of the Old Testament and, as he lived in Amsterdam, had the resulting map produced by one of the city's finest engravers, Abraham Goos. The resulting map (fig. 119) is a markedly superior production to the Latin-text Adrichem, and as a large loose-sheet map, copies would often have been displayed in open view. For the book shelf, a much-reduced Hebrew map of Palestine, also

FIG. 119. Palestine, Jacob ben Abraham Zaddiq, 1621. As can be seen in the lower right and in the detail on the left, off the coast of Gaza and the Sinai one galley flies a flag with a hexagonal star. This is likely a symbol of Jewish identity generally, not yet a Star of David in the modern sense, a concept that evolved during the seventeenth century. [Bibliothèque Nationale, GE BB-246 (XVII, 43-44 RES)].

Adrichem-based but with the Egyptian coast corrected, appeared in the so-called Amsterdam Haggadah of 1695.

Posterity remembers Zaddiq as less admirable than his map, having spent a year in prison for repeated violence against his wife. But his crime was not as bad as that of Othello in William Shakespeare's play of that name, written circa 1603. The gist of the play—false claims of infidelity moves the Moorish general in the Venetian army to murder his devoted wife—was adapted from an Italian novel by Giraldi, itself inspired by Scheherazade's story of "The Three Apples" in the *One Thousand and One Nights*. Given the play's Orientalist bent, it is not surprising that Shakespeare invokes Palestine, nor surprising that he does so in context of desire.

Will not go from my mind: I haue much to do,
But to go hang my head all at one ſide
And ſing it like poore *Brabarie*: prythee diſpatch.
Æmi. Shall I go fetch your Night-gowne?
Deſ. No, vn-pin me here,
This *Lodouico* is a proper man.
Æmil. A very handſome man.
Deſ. He ſpeakes well.
Æmil. I know a Lady in Venice would haue walk'd barefoot to Paleſtine for a touch of his nether lip.
Deſ. The poore Soule ſat ſinging, by a Sicamour tree.
Sing all a greene Willough:
Her hand on her boſome her head on her knees,
Sing Willough, Willough, Willough.
The freſh Streames ran by her, and murmur'd her moanes

FIG. 120: From *Othello, Mr. William Shakespeare's comedies, histories, & tragedies.: Published according to the true originall copies.* [Bodleian Library, Arch-G-c-8, 00874, fol-vv3r (1623)]

After Othello tells his wife Desdemona that she should prepare for bed, as he will return "incontinent" (quickly, or lustfully), her maidservant Emilia helps her prepare. They discuss marital fidelity, Emilia arguing that women have the same physical desires as men do. Desdemona mentions that Lodovico, her cousin whom they had just seen, "is a proper man," to which Emilia adds "a very handsome man," and Desdemona, "He speaks well." It is then that Palestine enters the play, courtesy of Emilia:

> I know a lady in Venice would have walked barefoot to Palestine for a touch of his nether lip.

Beyond expressing the difficulties the Venetian woman would have willingly endured for that "touch," the rejoinder hints at the exoticism, even eroticism, of the destination. That Venice was a standard point of embarkation for Palestine by ship makes enduring the barefoot journey all the more poignant.

As for the mythical Othello's real-life Ottoman co-religionists, their supremacy in the eastern Mediterranean continued to solidify during the last quarter of the sixteenth century after the short-lived setback of the Battle of Lepanto. In contrast, Ottoman initiative in the charting of both land and seas lost momentum. Its occupation of Palestine was entering its second century, and occupiers need to keep track of empire, but the extent to which the Ottomans relied on surveys rather than written records for cadastral purposes in Palestine is unclear.[23] Over the next two centuries, as European kingdoms sought the world as empire, the Ottomans repurposed their maps, some of which they acquired as gifts by European merchants to win favor. When in 1803-4 the Ottomans produced their first "modern" printed world atlas, the *Cedid atlas tercümesi*, it was presented as what it was: a re-engraving of British printed maps, translated into Turkish using Arabic script. The Ottomans' own mapping of lands under their control continued through to the twilight of their empire (e.g., fig. 144, p171).

FIG. 121 (above): The House of Samson in Gaza, and the Church of St. George in Lidda. Page from a *Proskynetarion*, a pilgrim's guide book to the holy places in Palestine. Greek, 1693. [Bodleian Library, MS. Canon. Gr. 127]

FIG. 122 (left): The eastern Mediterranean, from the monumental world map (*Kunyu Wanguo Quantu*) of the Italian Jesuit priest Matteo Ricci, Beijing, 1602. [Library of Congress, National Digital Library Program, 2010585650]

The mapping of Palestine reached China with the arrival of the Jesuits in the form of a twelve-foot-wide woodcut world map produced under the direction of the Italian priest Matteo Ricci, finished in Beijing in 1602 (fig. 122). Of Palestine, the map states that "God came down from heaven and was born in this country; therefore men call it the Holy Land."

PALESTINE AND THE REFORMATION

The end of the sixteenth century brought the first influential Reformation voices arguing for the "restoration" of the Jews to Palestine in context of millennial theology, notably the English clergyman Thomas Brightman. At first, such ideas were condemned and remained in manuscript form; and Brightman died in 1607, too soon to see his voluminous writings disseminated in print and his views popularized. In his book *The Revelation of Saint John...*, whose lengthy title includes "the restoring of the Jewes," he asks, and answers:

> What shall they [the Jews] return to Ierusalem againe? There is nothing more certaine, the Prophets doe every where directly confirme it, and beat upon it.[24]

Brightman then clarifies *why* they must come. They "shall not come thither to have their ceremoniall worship restored," but rather to "worship Christ purely," that is, to convert or face damnation.

The religious precedent set, the next step was to involve the state. "That your Petitioners being conversant in the City, with and amongst some of Izraell race, called Jewes...". So began a petition sent to the English government in January 1648 by Johanna and Ebenezer Cartwright, English Baptists living in Amsterdam, calling upon it and the Netherlands to take an active role in transporting Jews first to England, and then to Palestine. Their petition was published the following year, the beginnings of the idea of state sponsorship of what would become known as Zionism:

> And that this Nation of England, with the Inhabitants of the Nether-lands, shall be the first and readiest to transport Izraells Sons & Daughters in their Ships to the Land promised to the fore-Fathers...[25]

European mapping of Palestine continued to evolve in appearance while following the inertia set in the sixteenth century. The vast majority of printed maps of Palestine produced during the seventeenth and eighteenth centuries, no matter how superficially dissimilar, are of the same cast: maps of Biblical nomenclature and related elements reconfigured, redesigned, turned one way or another, newly embellished, "improved," and repackaged. Images of these "antique maps" are popular today, imbued with messianic overtones whose repercussions stretch far beyond anything imagined by their baroque makers.

FIG. 123: Thomas Fuller, *Galilaeae Descriptione ...*, 1650. Lettered diagonally across the map, the whole of southern Palestine is "Judea" and northern Palestine is "Samaria." Copperplate.

Maps of Palestine in books (or loose-sheet) tended to be more interesting, less formulatic, than those in atlases. A good example is the map in fig. 123, one of several in the 1650 *Pisgah-sight of Palestine* by the English orator, preacher, and historian Thomas Fuller (see also title, p114). The frontispiece to another of Fuller's works, *The Historie of the Holy Warre*, is an itinterary view-map showing the Crusaders marching from Europe to the Church of the Holy Sepulchre and the bloody battles among humans, angels, and skeletons that ensued.

In 1714, the Orientalist Adriaan Reland, the son of a Protestant minister, published the fruit of his many years' research into Palestine's ancient geography, linguistics, sociology, and history: the *Palaestina ex monumentis veteribus illustrata*. His meticulous reconsidering of evidence from the early Christian era, and his several maps' relative freedom of rote embellishment (e.g., fig. 124, overleaf), helped focus the ensuing Reform mapping of Palestine on a (still proto-) scientific path.

But the most revealing aspect of Reland's more "scientific" work—revealing about us, not him—is that today, his work is cited to further the ethnic cleansing of Palestine.

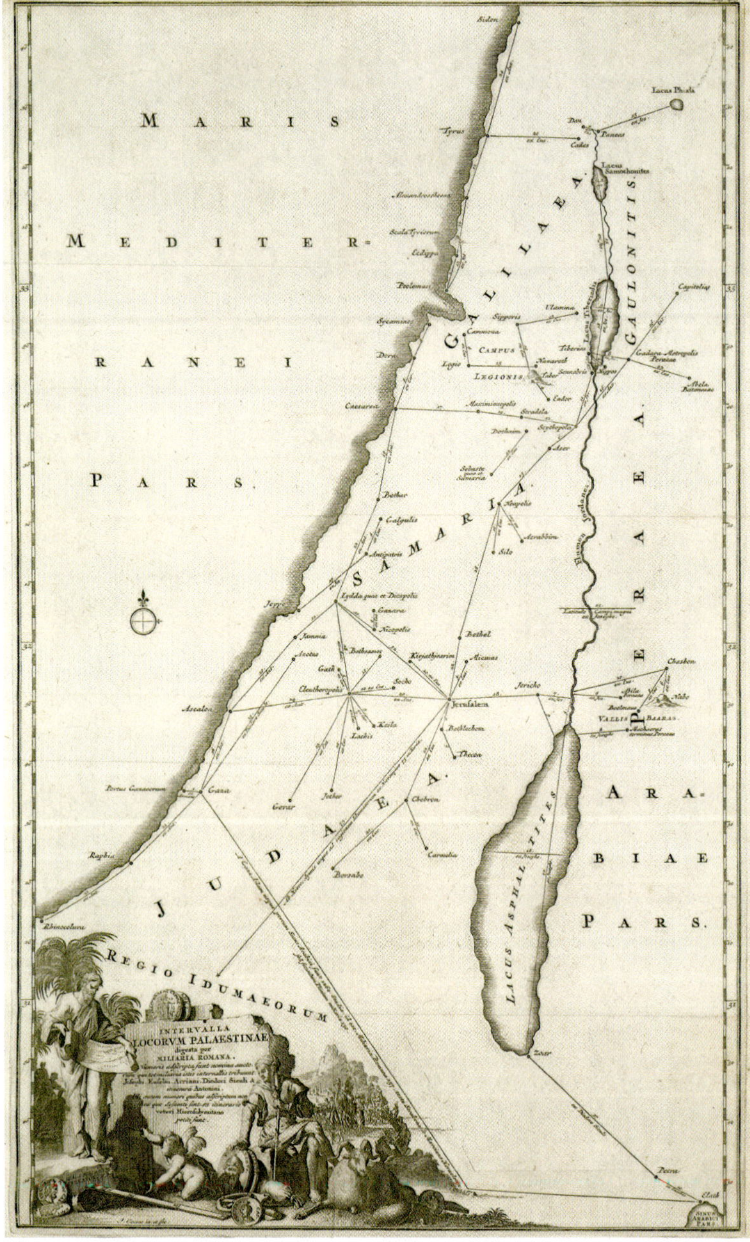

FIG. 124: *Intervalla locorvm Palaestinae digesta per miliaria romana*, map of Palestine showing distances in Roman miles and based on ancient sources. Adriaan Reland, Utrecht, 1714.

Put in crude terms for brevity, modern arguments supporting the expulsion of non-Jewish Palestinians from the land are invariably founded on the claim that "Palestinian" is a made-up identity and "Palestine" a made-up "country." The value of Reland to those making the argument is this: proof of Palestinian nonexistence is said to come from "the Arabs" themselves. For example, a 2010 article in the *Jewish Chronicle* invokes Reland as its hard proof for a piece that, right in its headline, puts "Palestinian" in quotes and dismisses the very concept of such a people as a "myth"—and, citing Reland, that this is the case "even according to the Arabs." A 2023 *Times of Israel* piece illustrates Reland's book (that, the author says, was "discovered") and states that it "debunks the occupation fallacy"—the Israeli state cannot be occupying what does not exist. Reland, the author contends, "completely refutes theories about 'Palestinian traditions' [and] 'Palestinian people' [and there is] almost no link between the land and the Arabs." Any thought to the contrary "is like inherent antisemitism built in people's minds," and if by the end of the article you are still unconvinced, "you are blind to the facts and truth."[26]

The extraordinary aspect of this argument, heard relentlessly today with or without Reland, is the geographic hard-wiring that it exposes: People's right to live on their own land is a matter of whether selected geographic terms, and selected labels for ethic identity, match. A people may have thrived on the same hillside for thousands of years, but can be thrown off the land at the invocation of ethno-geographic terminology.

So ingrained is this hard-wiring that opponents of the ethnic cleansing typically accept the racial-cartographic premise, and argue instead on "facts"— expose Reland's errors, the mis-framing and limitation of his data, and point out that he never stepped foot in Palestine. We will see more of this stealth ethno-geographic-psychological manipulation in the final chapter.

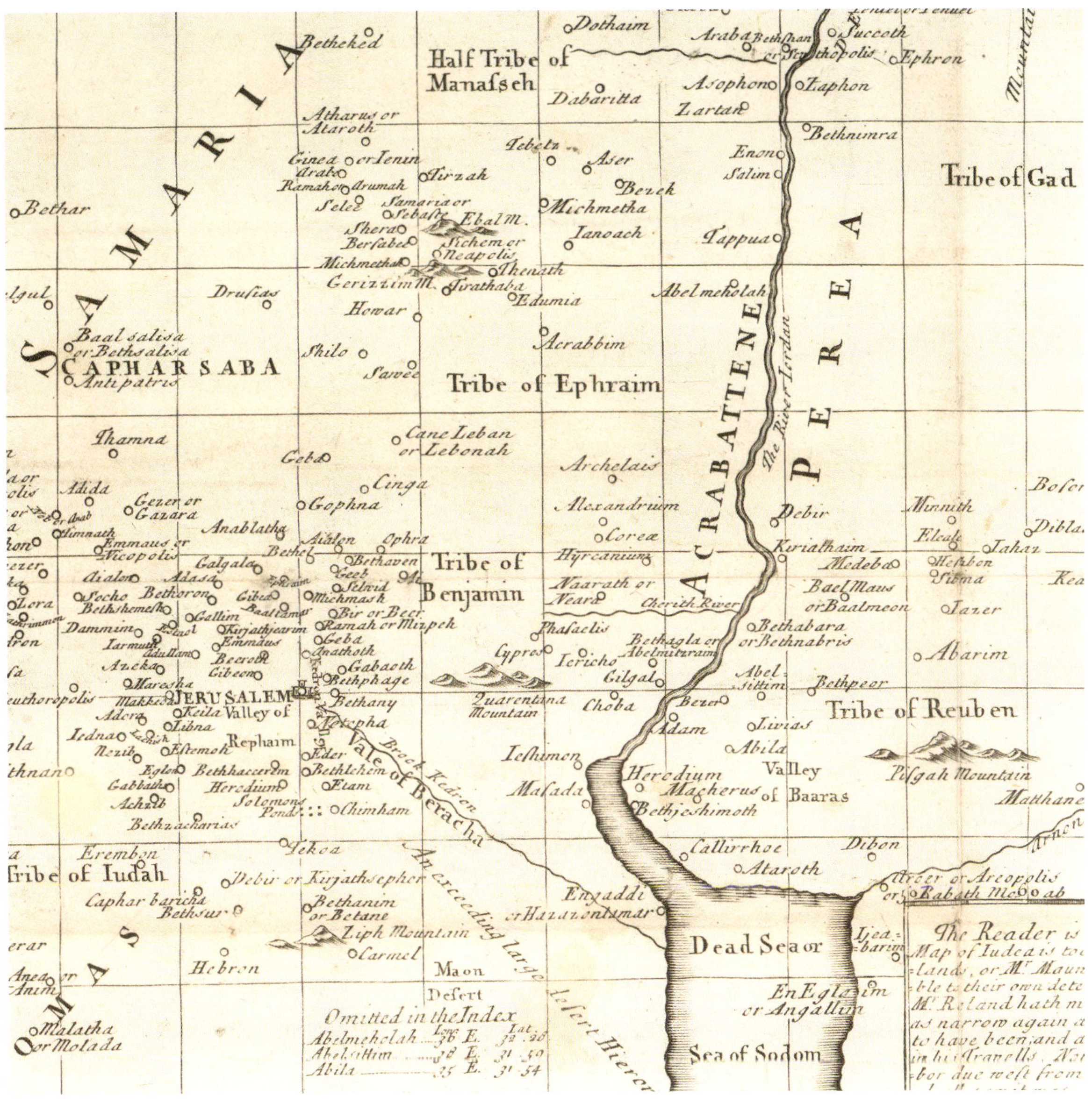

FIG. 125: Detail, William Whiston, 1737, *Cellarius's, Reland's, and Maundrell's, Maps, of Palestine Corrected and Improved by Mr. Whitston. With the Addition of an Alphabetical Index of the Several Places; with their Longitudes East or West from Jerusalem; and their Latitudes North: for the Ready finding them in the Map.*

William Whiston evaluated the works of Reland and others, parsing their parsing of ancient geography. In 1737, he combined the result into a large comprehensive map of Palestine that further expanded the new "scientific" look (detail, fig. 125). No one could accuse Whiston, a mathematician and a proponent of Isaac Newton's theories, of being glued to tradition—indeed he pursued a mad proposal to solve longitude by anchoring a network of hulks at predetermined points in the ocean, from which fireworks, developed to explode at a particular height, would be ignited. When it came to Palestine, however, his mindset shifted. He stretched any empirical notion of the land's breadth and its fertility in order to support fabled imagery of its Biblical population, and included an extensive legend in his map to explain "one reason why the Land of Palestine has been esteemed much smaller than it really was." Whiston used Jerusalem as the prime meridian—the Enlightenment version of placing Palestine at the center of the earth.

FIG. 126: *A map of Canaan: with the adjacent countrie's very usefull for the understanding of the Old Testament.* The map records forty-two sites visited by the Israelites following their exodus from Egypt. Philip Lea, London, c1692 ("Sold by P. Lea, at the Atlas and Hercules in Cheap-side; and in Westminster hall") [Norman B. Leventhal Map & Education Center]

FIG. 127: In the lower right corner of his map of Palestine, *Iudæa Seu Palæstina,* Johann Baptist Homann, a convert to Protestantism, illustrates two Biblical figures studying a map of southern Palestine showing the route of the Israelites across the Red Sea and on to Jerusalem. The map is copper-engraved, while the illustration is achieved through etching, in which that area of the plate is covered with a film of wax, a needle then used to draw the image, exposing the metal, and acid is applied. Since the resulting lines are much finer than those of the engraved geography, etched illustrations were not colored even when the map was, and wear to the plate visibly affected the etched lines before those of the main map. [Library of Congress 2011585236]

FIG. 128: Wall map of Palestine, "Ancienne" and "Moderne". Nicholas de Fer, Paris, 1701 [Bibliothèque nationale de France GE B-1114 (RES)]

The sixteenth through eighteenth centuries had been a reckoning among possible Palestinian futures. European civilization might have come to see the land as a region like any other, with its own complex history, traditions, and myths. Instead, Palestine's medieval ink dried, its "other-worlding" now serving as the backdrop to a long-cultivated messianic destiny in the collective Western subconscious.

Christian calls for the Jews to "return" to Palestine resurfaced with newfound militancy as the eighteenth century drew to a close. The French Revolution and other upheavals reinvigorated eschatological (end of time) theories and were interpreted by Protestant theologians in context of the Scriptures, such as the Revelation of St. John and the famous dream of the Babylonian king Nebuchadnezzar II as interpreted by his captive, Daniel. In 1529, Martin Luther had used the dream to explain the Ottoman siege of Vienna that year, and indeed published an allegorical "Dream of Daniel" map for the purpose. That passed—but the world was now much different. A great sense of actuality emboldened the millennial movement, as events unfolding before their eyes confirmed that the time had truly come. Palestine was again the center of the earth.

FIG. 129: Jerusalem, from the north. Photography by the American Colony, between 1898 and 1914. Negative, glass, dry plate; 5 x 7 in. [Library of Congress, LC-DIG-matpc-07474]

CHAPTER 5

MAPPING THE MEDIEVAL PRESENT

1800+

> The proximate signs of the coming of Jesus Christ being nigh at hand, marked out in the scripture prophecies … the Jews will be put in motion, and return to take possession of their ancient country.

So wrote Baptist minister James Bicheno in his book *The Restoration of the Jews – The Crisis of All Nations*, published in 1800.[27] The world seemed to change on cue when the clock struck the new century, just as it did with 1500. This time, millennial thought was increasingly at work.

The long-brewing Christian vision of the "return" of Jews to Palestine in preparation for the Second Coming of Christ moved from talk to action. Evangelist sects moved to Palestine to await His return, as messianic, imperial, and economic interests converged to finance a common interest: the large-scale surveying of the land. During the preceding three centuries, the simultaneous pull of Protestant messianism and scientific mapmaking seemed a contradiction. Now, they would work together in unison.

The Land of Gilead
THE SEA OF GALILEE
SYRIAN SEA
A PROSPECT OF JERUSALEM
Palestine
The Valley of Elah
The Country of the
THE NEW CITY OF JERUSALEM

FIG. 130: *A new map of the Land of Promise and the holy city of Jerusalem describing the most important events in the Old & New Testaments.* Ultimately based on a 1641 map by Jan van Doetechum that saw two eighteenth-century English adaptations, now expanded with extensive explanatory annotations and fourteen side panels depicting Biblical scenes. Thomas W. Duffield, Philadelphia, 1823. [Norman B. Leventhal Map & Education Center at the Boston Public Library]

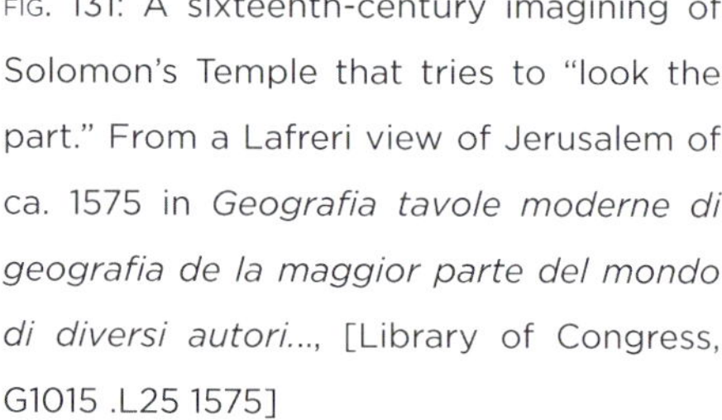

FIG. 131: A sixteenth-century imagining of Solomon's Temple that tries to "look the part." From a Lafreri view of Jerusalem of ca. 1575 in *Geografia tavole moderne di geografia de la maggior parte del mondo di diversi autori...*, [Library of Congress, G1015 .L25 1575]

FIG 132: View of Solomon's Temple from the 1823 map of Palestine in fig. 130, copied from a 1754 map by Robert Sayer, and ultimately from a late 17th-century wooden model commissioned by Hamburg senator Gerhard Schott.

In churches and schools, consumer maps of Palestine proliferated as educational tools for Bible instruction, and were being published in the young United States, where much of the fervor over Palestine was brewing. The encyclopedic evangelist teaching aid in fig. 130 presents Palestine as a Biblical wonderland that is in respects more divorced from reality than its medieval ancestors.

No archaeological trace of Solomon's Temple, said by tradition to have existed between the tenth and sixth centuries BCE, has ever come to light. Throughout the Middle Ages and early Renaissance, maps of Jerusalem and Palestine commonly illustrated the legendary temple in an imaginary but "appropriate" form, among the more detailed of which is that in the sixteenth century view of Jerusalem in fig. 131. In contrast, the massive European baroque palace in the Duffield map (fig. 132) betrays a mindset almost comically removed from the realm of possibility, and presages twentieth-century Zionist references to a vast ancient Hebrew kingdom that covered much of the Levant.

Such an expansive view of Biblical Israel's breadth was championed by the first modern British society devoted to Palestine, the Palestine Association, founded in 1805 by the man who had wrestled the Rosetta Stone from its French discoverers in Egypt, William Richard Hamilton. The short-lived association's most visible fruit was its 1810 publication of the account and map of Ulrich Jasper Seetzen to the Levant. In it, the association states that it considers Palestine to be "all the countries on either side of the river Jordan, inhabited by the Tribes of Israel."

Both sides of the Jordan were indeed being eyed by foreign powers jostling for a share of the

FIG. 133: Eastern Mediterranean, and detail of Palestine, from *Aṭlas, ay majm ʿkh r ṭat rasm al-arḍ*, published in Malta, 1833 and 1835 by the Church Missionary Society Press. The work is the first printed world atlas in Arabic. [Library of Congress, G1019 .A845 1835]

spoils of a declining Ottoman Empire. Jews found themselves pawns in these imperial Levantine projects and Protestant end-of-time theology—the beginning of modern Christian Zionism and its sponsor states as symbiotic, entwined partners.

In November 1840, politically savvy Princess Lieven, wife of the former Russian ambassador to London, received a letter from her equally savvy friend, the wife of the British Foreign Secretary, citing the value of the evangelists to British imperial goals:

> We have on our side the fanatical and religious elements, and you know what a following they have in this country. They are absolutely determined that Jerusalem and the whole of Palestine shall be reserved for the Jews to return to; this is their only longing to restore the Jews.[28]

"They" in each case refers to Christians, not Jews, wanting to "restore the Jews" to Palestine.

In 1841 and 1842, Charles Henry Churchill, an army officer who served as a British consul in Syria, corresponded with Moses Montefiore, President of the Jewish Board of Deputies in London, imploring him to act upon British proposals to gather the Jews and begin their "return." Montefiore was certainly not against Jews going to Palestine (indeed he helped Jews who wanted to go there), but neither he nor the Board of Deputies was interested in Britain's proto-Zionist scheme.

Proponents continued to offer their own variations on the theme. In 1857, one James Pierce sent letters from Jerusalem to the Earl of Clarendon arguing for "an encouragement of Jews at large to inhabit and cultivate Palestine" in context of various political considerations, citing the "considerable agrarian advantages of Jews, as Children of Israel."[29]

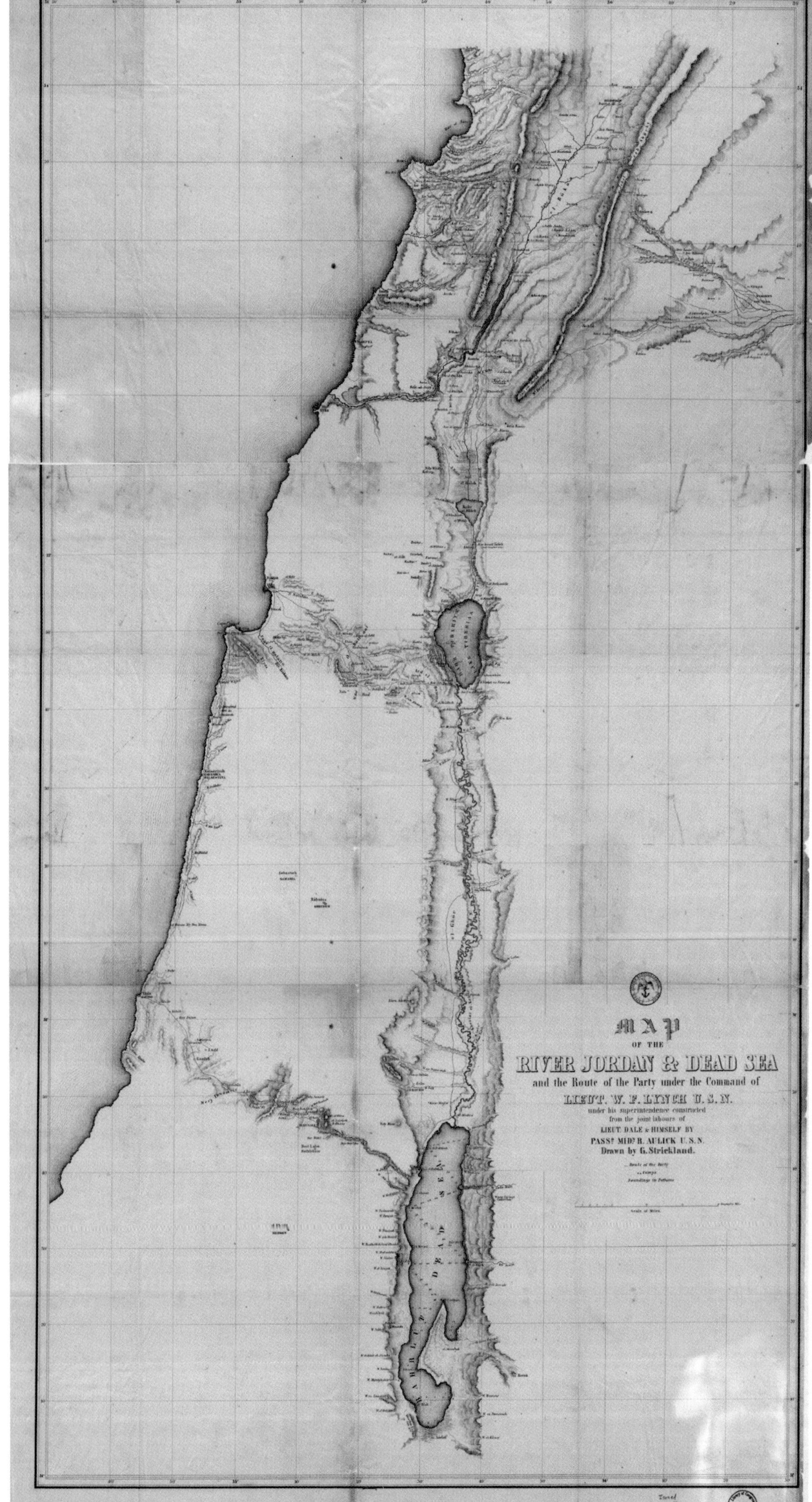

FIG. 134: *Map of the River Jordan & Dead Sea : and the route of the party under the command of Lieut. W.F. Lynch, U.S.N. under his superintendence constructed from the joint labours of Lieut. Dale & himself by Passd. Midn. R. Aulick U.S.N.*, United States Hydrographical Office, lithograph, 1849. [LOC G7512.J6 184- .U5]

Messianic excitement was equally inseparable from American (USA) hunger for influence in the Levant. When in 1847 a two-year project to map the Dead Sea and the Jordan River north to its source was approved by the US secretary of the navy (fig. 134), the expedition's leader, W.F. Lynch, wrote of the need "to ensure the restoration of the Jews to Palestine" in context of being "prepared for the final dismemberment of the Ottoman empire."

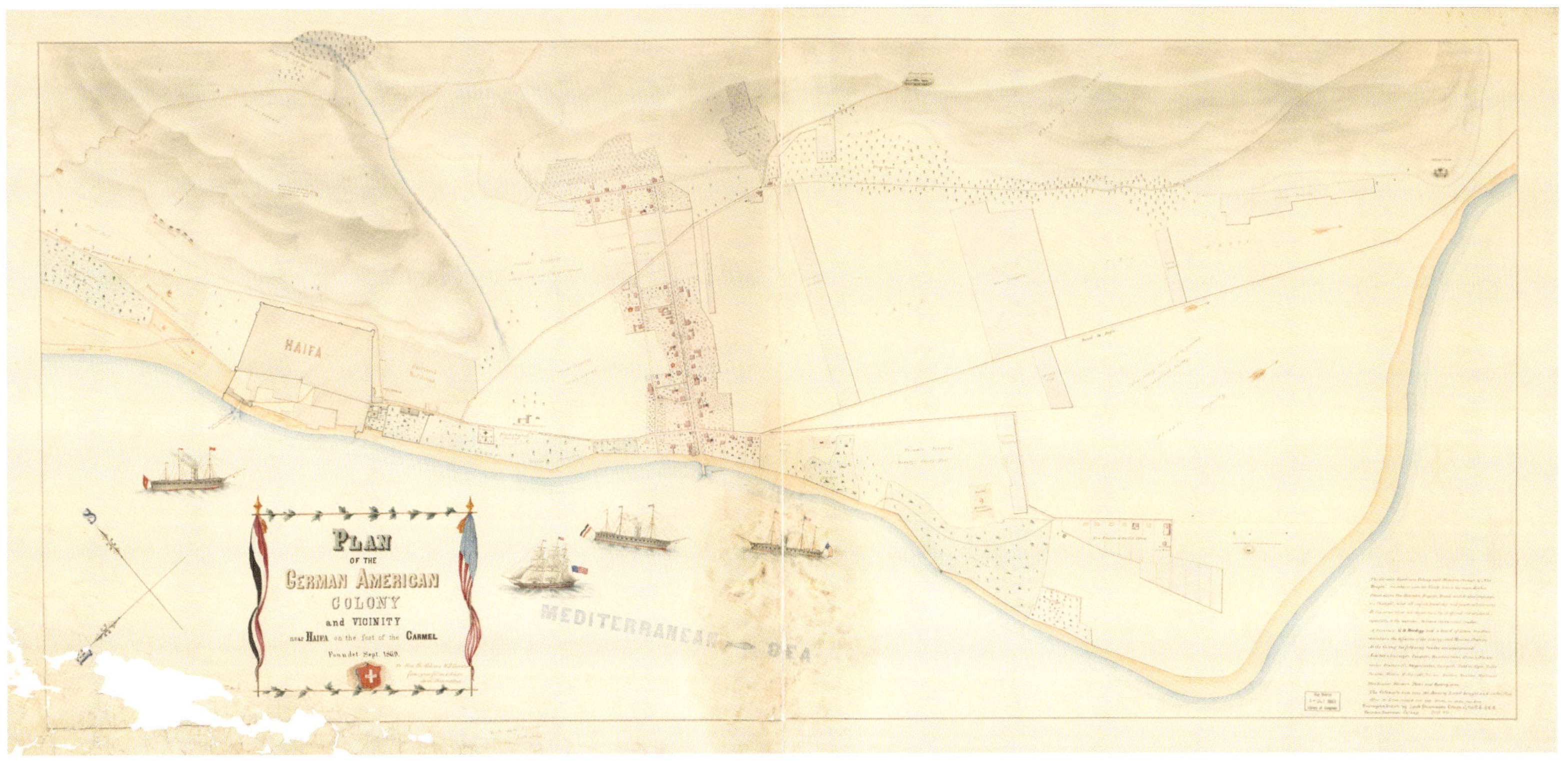

FIG. 135: *Plan of the German American Colony and vicinity near Haifa on the foot of the Carmel foundet Sept. 1869 ...* Manuscript, Jacob Schumacher, Haifa, 1873 [Library of Congress, G7504.H2 1873 .S3]

The Templers, a Lutheran evangelical group, established four colonies in Palestine in anticipation of Christ's arrival, most prominently the Haifa-area German American Colony in 1869, led by architect and engineer Jacob Schumacher. He dedicated his 1873 map of the colony (fig. 135) to the US senator Carl Schurz, perhaps in the hope for US political muscle in dealing with the Ottomans. Among the map's legends is the "castle built by Ibrah. Pasha bombarted [sic] by the english & austrian fleet 1840," a reference to the battle ending Egypt's short-lived designs on Palestine and return to Ottoman rule.

Where and when, according to the Templers, would Christ make his appearance? Jerusalem, the settlers believed, and imminently. The Bohemian botanist Franz Wilhelm Sieber had produced a new plan of the city in 1818, but it was Britain's Ordnance Survey that took the initiative for a truly comprehensive survey, its first project beyond British shores (figs. 136, 137). A six-member team under Charles William Wilson worked for seven and a half months between 1864–5, producing a report that was exhaustive and scientific, within its Biblical constraints. Wilson cites the Scriptures, and even psalms, to "confirm" geographic identity and to guide what they were looking for.

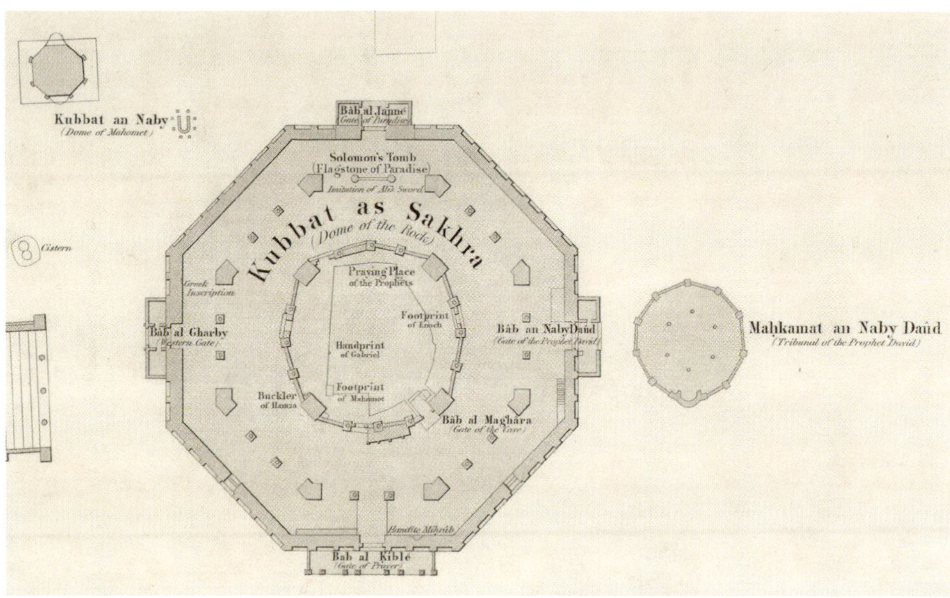

FIG. 136 (above): The Dome of the Rock, with the Dome of the Ascension to its upper left and the Dome of the Chain to the right, detail from the 1865 Ordnance Survey of Jerusalem.

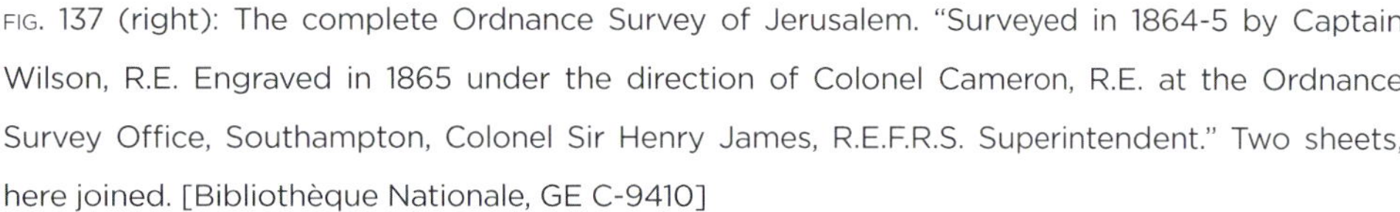

FIG. 137 (right): The complete Ordnance Survey of Jerusalem. "Surveyed in 1864-5 by Captain Wilson, R.E. Engraved in 1865 under the direction of Colonel Cameron, R.E. at the Ordnance Survey Office, Southampton, Colonel Sir Henry James, R.E.F.R.S. Superintendent." Two sheets, here joined. [Bibliothèque Nationale, GE C-9410]

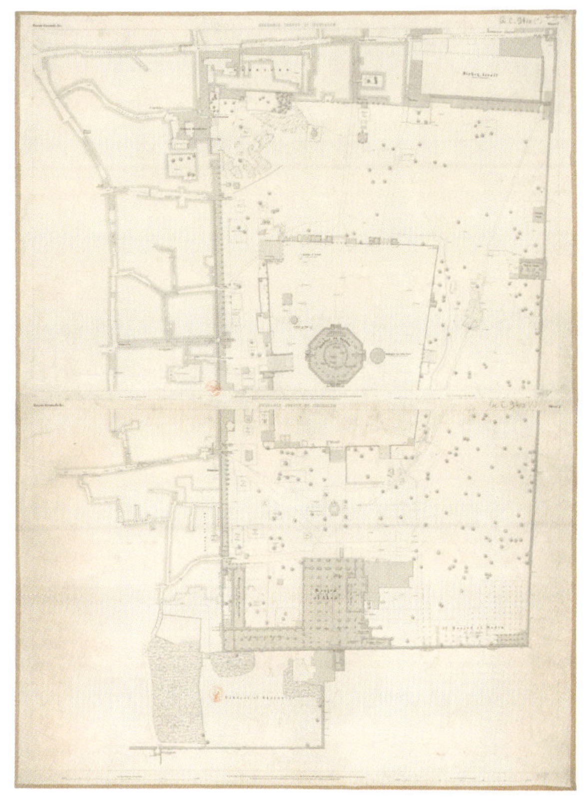

Funding came from the wealthy Baroness Angela Burdett-Coutts, who hoped that aquifers might be discovered that could benefit the city. This hope was not realized: the authors noted several good springs "some little distance from Jerusalem," but of insufficient elevation to transport by conduit. The rich alone, they wrote, could afford to have the water brought to the city.

The Jerusalem survey was the springboard to a full, meticulous survey of Palestine: the Palestine Exploration Fund, the consummate product of nineteenth-century hybrid messianic-imperial mapping of the land. The resulting surveys were extraordinary in their detail—detail intended both to benefit British designs on the land and to prepare for the return of the Messiah. Speaking at a Palestine Exploration Fund meeting in 1875, the Earl of Shaftesbury spoke of the fund's responsibility "to go over every corner" of Palestine and to

> prepare it for the return of its ancient possessors, for I must believe that the time cannot be far off before that great event will come to pass.

He pointed out that former Prime Minister Aberdeen agreed: the Holy Land should "return into the hands of the Israelites." Venturing yet further into the netherworld whose gates they had opened, he exudes confidence that further excavation in Jerusalem will bring them to the very Ark of the Covenant, the chest said to contain the tablets on which are written the commandments handed to Moses by God.[30]

FIG. 138 (left): *Map of Western Palestine from surveys conducted for The Committee Of Palestine Exploration Fund ...* 1881

FIG. 139 (below): Palestine Exploration Fund, grid map correlating separate and composite maps, “Diagram of Sheets to be constructed on a Scale 3/8 of an inch to a mile. / Size of sheets 43.5 miles W. to East by 45 of Latitude.” Manuscript dated June 23, 1884. [The National Archives, MPI 1/197; photograph T. Suárez]

Archaeological excavations were not actually part of the PEF’s mandate, but its surveyors did quite a bit of digging. They expected the distrust they felt from the Ottoman authorities about the excavation—but expressed astonishment that the Palestinians themselves had no interest in helping the British dig up their country. In the expedition’s *Recovery of Jerusalem* (1871), one of the PEF’s cofounders spoke of that project, “so obvious a duty for the English nation to undertake,” versus that “singular union of craft, ignorance, and stupidity which can only be found in Orientals.”

FIG. 140: The Four Kingdoms of the Image, and the Stone Kingdom, Basil Stewart, 1927.

The Dream of Daniel had been influential in Christian proto-Zionists' thinking since Luther. It was also primary evidence for another messianic group, with a big twist: the British Israelites, a group originating in the mid-nineteenth century that believed that British white Protestants, royalty included, are the true descendants of the Lost Tribes of Israel and inheritors of the prophecies. Though a fringe movement, it could only have further emboldened the mainstream British sense of entitlement to the land, and the movement lives on today in the form of Christian nationalism and the Christian Identity movement. Map from T*he Witness of the Great Pyramid. An Exposition concerning the Anglo-Saxon Race, their Identity, History, and Destiny, as revealed by Scripture and the Great Pyramid, with special reference to current events. London: The Covenant Publishing Co.* [Cornell University, P.J. Mode Collection, 1224.01]

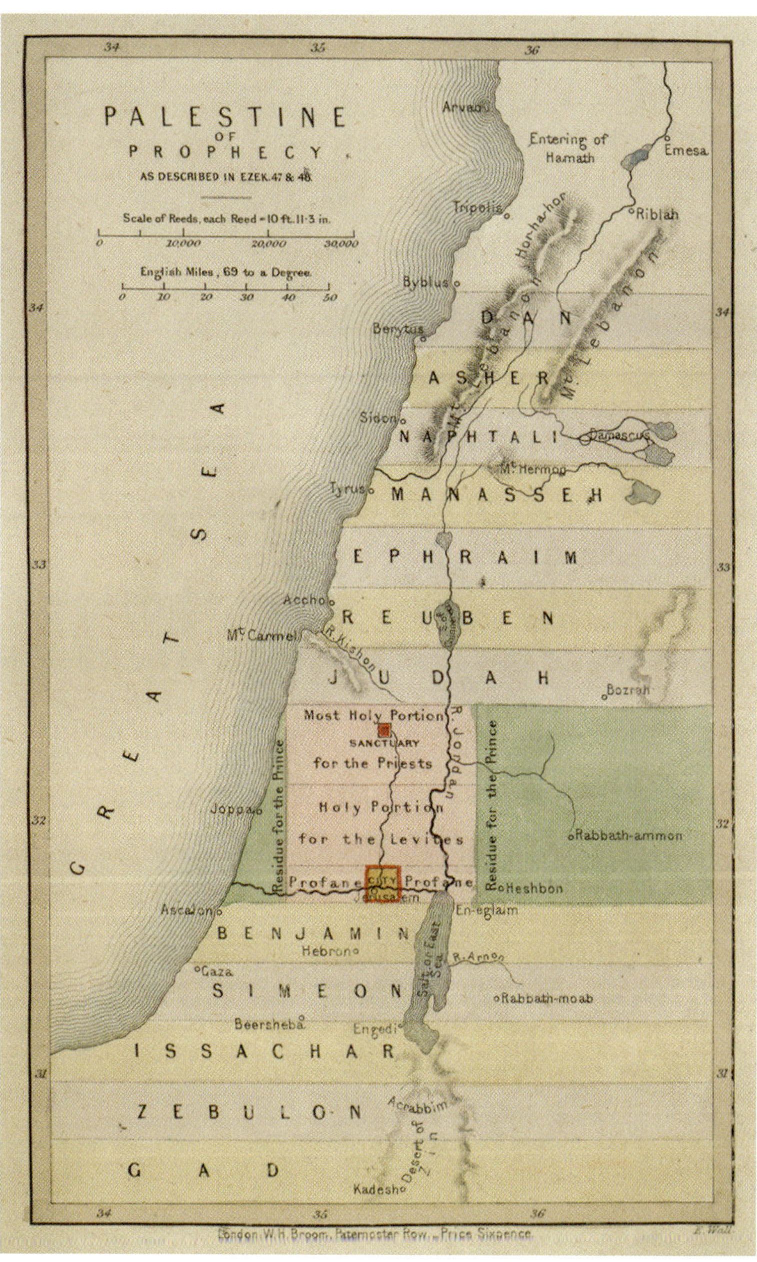

FIG. 141: *Palestine according to the Prophecies,* from a Bible owned by Horatio Spafford and with his extensive annotations, the English version of Bagster's Polyglot Bible, London, 1870s. [Library of Congress, Part I, Box 2, Folder 3: American Colony in Jerusalem, series: Part I: Topical File, 1871-2004]

FIG. 142: Photograph of the home of Anna and Horatio Gates Spafford, Lake View (Chicago), Illinois. Stone & Brooks (Photographer) ca. 1875 [Library of Congress, American Colony in Jerusalem Collection, Part I, Box 1, Folder 3; G1019 .A845 1835]

In the summer of 1881, Horatio Spafford, a US lawyer and former Presbyterian church elder, moved to Palestine with his family as part of a group of thirteen adults and three children anticipating the return of Christ, establishing the American Colony.

Tragedy had preceded the move—first, the Great Fire of Chicago (1871) destroyed his real estate investments, then their four daughters perished in a transatlantic voyage disaster, and one of three children born after the tragedy died of disease. As if searching for meaning, the Spaffords began a messianic sect defined by the conviction that the Second Coming was near. When preaching proved insufficient, they entrusted their hybrid house/church to a friend to pay off accumulated debts and set off for Palestine, establishing the American Colony. The group endured until the 1950s, leaving behind an important early photographic record (such as fig. 129) and the well-known hotel made from its final premises.

Preparations for Christ's arrival were severe; they included celibacy, even for married couples—though as the years passed and the twentieth century arrived with no sign of Christ, such rules were modified according to divine "messages."[31]

In his diary entry of the first of January 1882, Spafford is ever-confident: "Best wheat crop this year for 100 years," he writes exuberantly, as if he actually knows this. The crops are proof that "the time has come ... The blessed truth! The blessed sign!"[32]

His confidence had not ebbed when in December 1885 he wrote to A. Löwry, secretary of the Anglo-Jewish Association:

> I believe the set time to favor Zion ... for the fulfillment of many a glorious promise to literal Israel, has come ... and God is again and finally saying to the Hebrews, Go up and possess the land ... May God raise up the many who shall have an understanding of the times [meaning those] who shall know what Israel ought to do.[33]

Spafford's reference to "literal" Israel encapsulates what will be the linchpin of Christian support for the Zionist project, and the narrative of the Zionist movement itself: that the state self-declared in 1948 under the name *Israel* is the continuation of the realm of that name seemingly created by God in Genesis of the Old Testament. This was the fruition of an idea long-established in Protestant thought. As Sir Henry Finch explained it in 1621, when the Holy Ghost (i.e., God) speaks of Israel and its geographic parts, he

> meaneth not the spiritual Israel … but Israel properly descended out of Jacobs loynes … not a few, singled out here and here, but of the Nation in generall.

Presaging the anti-Jewish bigotry of today's Zionist Christians, he writes that there will be those Jews who, "even then [will not] stoope to Christ" and so be condemned by "the wrath of God."[34]

FIG. 143: Manuscript map of Jerusalem and environs by Horatio Spafford, 1881 or slightly later. [Library of Congress, American Colony in Jerusalem series: Part I: Topical File, 1871–2004]

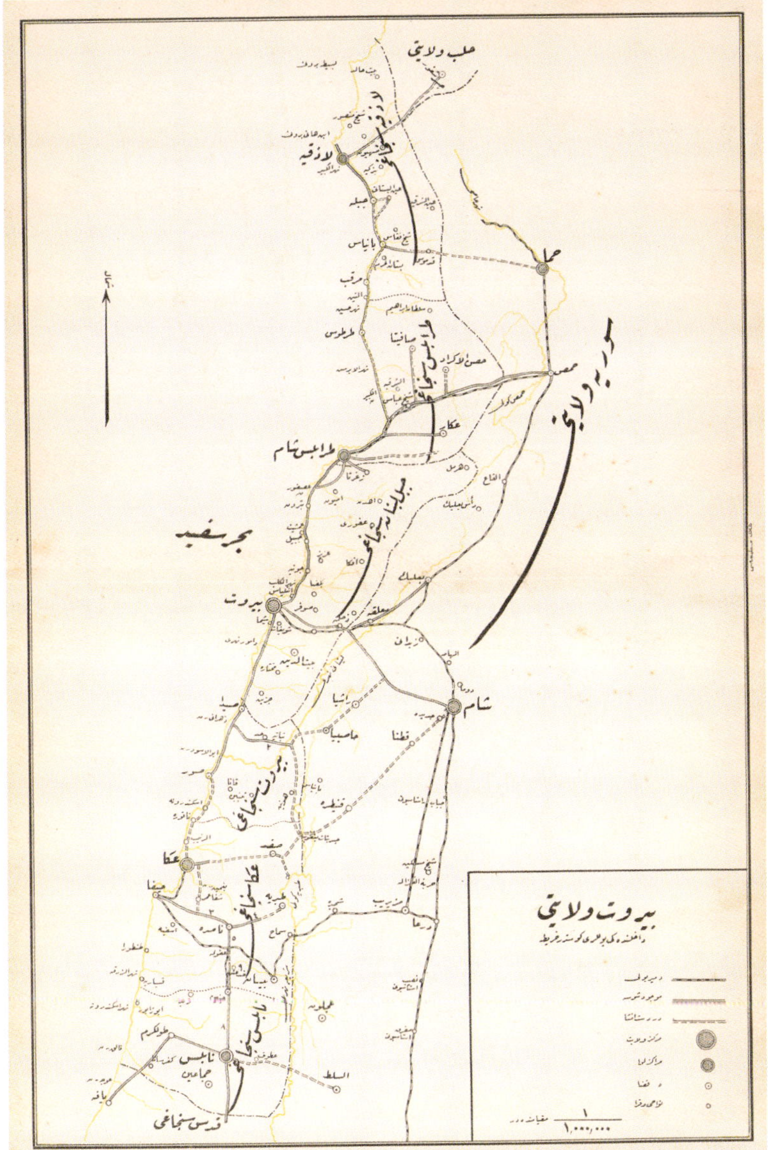

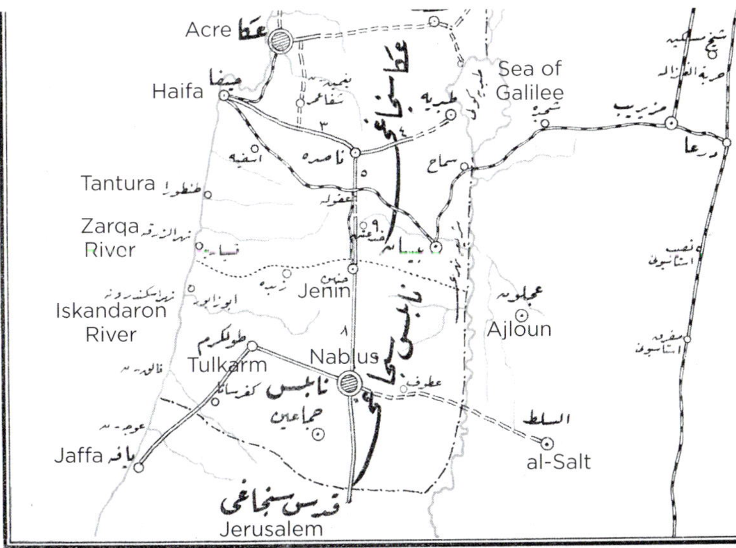

FIG. 144 & key map: *Beirut Province.* Ottoman map of Lebanon and Palestine as far south as Jaffa and Jerusalem, made on the even of the First World War that brought the end of that empire. Interior Ministry for Vilayets, Istanbul, 1913. [David Rumsey Historical Map Collection]

Spafford drew a map of Jerusalem and environs that charts the prophesized future, and specifies verses from the Bible as surveyor directions for the colony's preparations. "The red dotted line," he annotates, "is intended to show about the course of the limits referred to in Jer 31.38-40 & Zech 14.10." Extracts of these verses follow:

> Behold, the days are coming, says the LORD, that the city shall be built for the LORD from the Tower of Hananel to the Corner Gate. / The surveyor's line shall again extend straight forward over the hill Gareb; then it shall turn toward Goath [the last place-name a "hill of death" in the upper left]. / All the land shall be turned into a plain from Geba to Rimmon south of Jerusalem. Jerusalem shall be raised up and inhabited in her place from Benjamin's Gate to the place of the First Gate and the Corner Gate, and from the Tower of Hananel to the king's winepresses.[35]

Spafford's dotted lines mark the "Valley of Dead Bodies," which colony members would all know was a reference to Jer 31:40. They would also know that *Goath* is a hill near Jerusalem cited in Jer 31:39 that determines the future size of the city—a future which for the colonists had all but arrived.

As the Colony was established in 1881, the PEF's large-scale surveys were consolidated into a single map of Palestine (fig. 138). The following year, the first proto-Zionist settlers arrived.

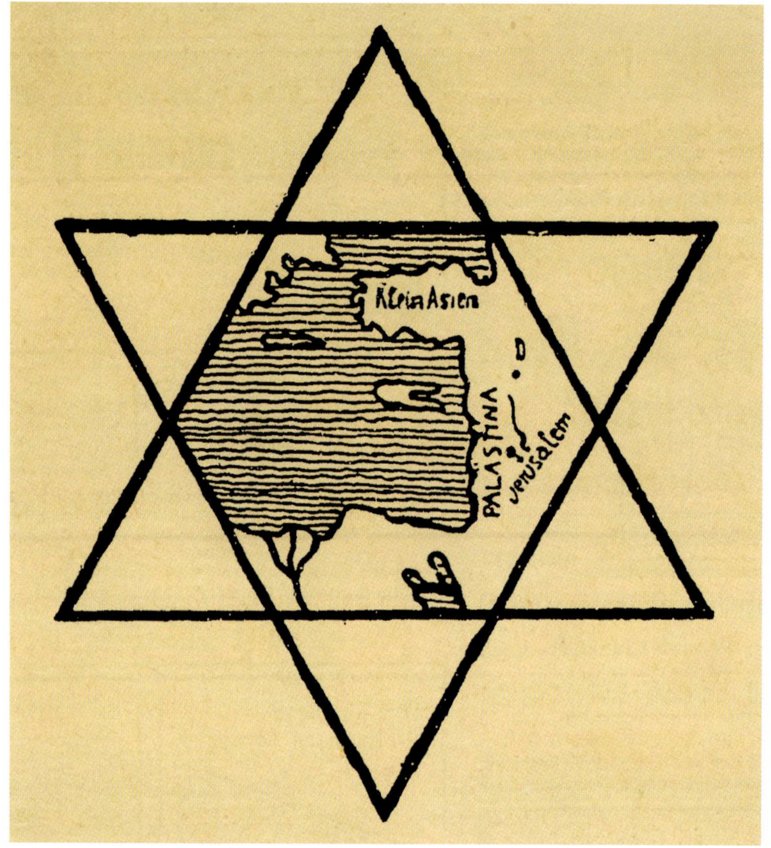

FIG. 145: Star of David with a map of the eastern Mediterranean, on the heading of the weekly *Die Welt,* from June 4, 1897 to December 29, 1905.

FIG. 146: The map post-Herzl, used in *Die Welt's* heading from Jan 5, 1906, to the last edition, Sept 25, 1914. The triangles are now interlaced, as if a nod to the mystical Seal of Solomon.

Zionism was not formalized as a political ideology until Theodor Herzl's 1896 *Der Judenstaat* ("The Jewish State"), a practical manual for establishing colonies. This foundation work of the Zionist movement contains little hint of the messianic mysticism to come, nor the use of Biblical geographic names. The word "Israel" appears once, in context of the role of ministers. Herzl calls the land *Palestine*, and refers to it as "our ever-memorable historic home," but there is no indication that he is spinning his project as the reincarnation of that home. For Herzl, *Palestine* was the magic name that would attract settlers, that "the very name of Palestine would attract our people with a force of marvellous potency." According to those who carried on his project, he was half correct: Palestine was indeed the sole realm that could inspire the necessary fervor—but calling it *Palestine* was a blunder.[36]

The following year brought the First Zionist Congress in Basel, and in Vienna, the founding of Herzl's weekly Zionist newspaper, *Die Welt* ("The World"), which ran until the outbreak of World War I. A map of the eastern Mediterranean, framed within a Star of David and affixed between the heading's *Die* and *Welt*, was the first image to meet readers' eyes (fig. 145). This "Zionist" map by the movement's founder is straightforward and secular: moving clockwise from the upper left, we see southeastern Greece, Crete, Turkey (*KleinAsien*), Cyprus, the Levant, Jordan River, Dead Sea, and on the bottom,

FIG. 147: East-oriented "Map of Palestine from Israel to Egypt" in Hebrew and Russian, by Avigdor ben Mordekhai Malkov, 1899. The fat peninsula on the lower right is Arabia, the Persian Gulf above, Red Sea below. From there, the straight diagonal line is the Suez Canal, which had opened in November 1869. The map stretches northward (to the upper left) to Sidon on the coast and Mount Hermon in the interior. [NYPL catalog ID (B-number): b23178445; breaks in the folding map here minimized in the image]

the Red Sea and Nile Delta. The entire southern Levant is *Palastina*, with Jerusalem and Damascus marked (the latter simply with a "D").

The map continued to form the centerpiece of this principal organ of the Zionist movement through to the end of 1905, surviving Herzl by a year and a half. But with the first issue of 1906, it was replaced with a simplified map that bore no place-names and served simply as the backdrop for the bold "W" of the title's *Welt* (fig. 146). As we will see, Herzl's "Palestine" map had become a liability.

Herzl's movement did not get off to an auspicious start. Early settlements floundered and survived only with the constant infusion of foreign capital. Europe's Jews in general seemed uninterested, preferring emancipation and equality to a new ghetto in a foreign land. Many Jews and non-Jews condemned Zionism as simply a new form of anti-Jewish racism, and indeed Herzl so loathed religious Jews that his diatribes against them could easily be mistaken for Nazi propaganda. Thus Zionism would have likely died with Herzl due to its advocates' insurmountable marketing problem—had messianic Christianity not spent the previous four centuries solving it for them.

Whether consciously or intuitively, Herzl's successors seized on the free marketing advice. Protestant evangelists were impatiently awaiting precisely what Zionism offered. In his preface to a 1904 edition of *Der Judenstaat*, the Zionist activist Jacob de Haas speaks openly about Herzl's failure to understand how to sell his project. Herzl, he says, based his state on the needs of the oppressed, and envisioned it someplace "over there," which was the "cloudy word" Palestine, a word "sufficient to condemn it in the eyes of most Western Jews." To rise above these "violent natal sufferings," Zionism was now to be based not on the oppressed, but instead on "a bundle of emotions wrapped in the praying shawl of the Jew; and these, when spread out, make up a flag which can only float in the breezes of Zion"—that is, Israel. At publication, Herzl had just died.

Those who carried the torch after Herzl repurposed his 1896 product in two-millennia-old messianic packaging. By the end of World War I and the Balfour Declaration (November 1917), Zionism had indelibly reinvented itself. Christian millennialists were ready customers.

"Are we not witnessing," US Rep. Albert Rossdale testified in 1922 in support of Zionist colonization in Palestine, "the truth of the words of the prophets of the return of Israel, the assurance of whose restoration gleams through the whole vista of prophecy?"[37] The repackaging of Zionism and the place-name *Israel* served both to secure Western messianic support and to lure Jewish settlers.[38]

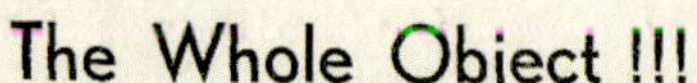

The Whole Object !!!

« The Whole object of His Britannic Majesty's Government is that both Arabs and Jews should be able to live together in peace and amity...... »

« From Colonial Secretary's speech » broadcasted

الغـــاية كلها!!!

« ان كل غاية حكومة جلالته هي ان يتمكن العرب واليهود من العيش معا بسلام ومحبة في فلسطين ... »

(من خطاب وزير المستعمرات المذاع بالراديو)

Vol. XX No 90 - 3261

« السنة العشرون »

العدد ٩٠ - ٣٢٨١

فلسطين

FALASTIN

Jaffa Saturday 27 June 1936

سياسة القهر والشدة ونتائجها

The Whole Object !!!

الغـــاية كلها!!!

هجرة العرب المجاورين الى فلسطين

FIG 148, 149: Political cartoon-map mocking William Ormsby-Gore, Under-Secretary of State for the Colonies, from the Palestinian newspaper *Falastin,* June 27, 1936. "The Whole Object!!! «The Whole Object of His Britannic Majesty's Government is that both Arabs and Jews should live together in peace and amity......» (from Colonial Secretary's speech broadcasted)." The prominence of Jaffa reflected ongoing tensions between the British and the people of that city. Two days after the cartoon's publication, the British blew up part of the ancient city on the orders of Ormsby-Gore.

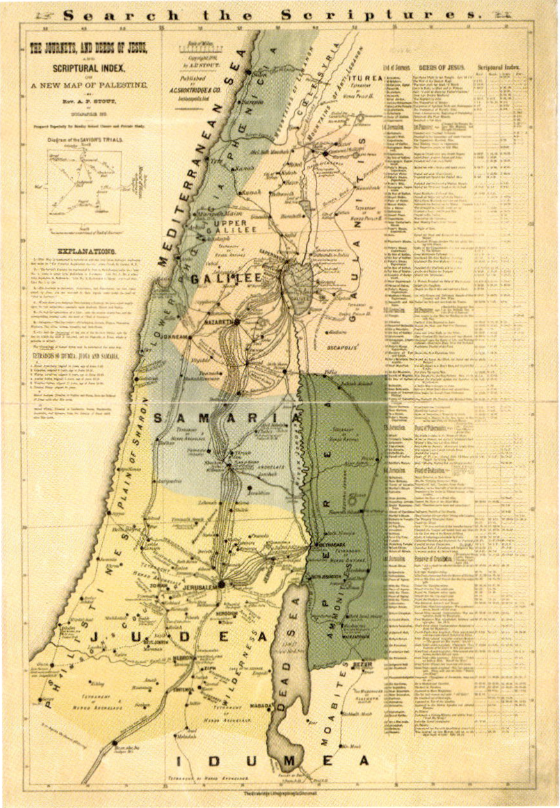

FIG. 150: *The journeys, and deeds of Jesus, and scriptoral index on a new map of Palestine.* Andrew Pearce Stout, based largely on the Palestine Exploration Fund surveys. Cincinnati, the Strobridge Lithographing Co., 1881. [Library of Congress, 2009579464]

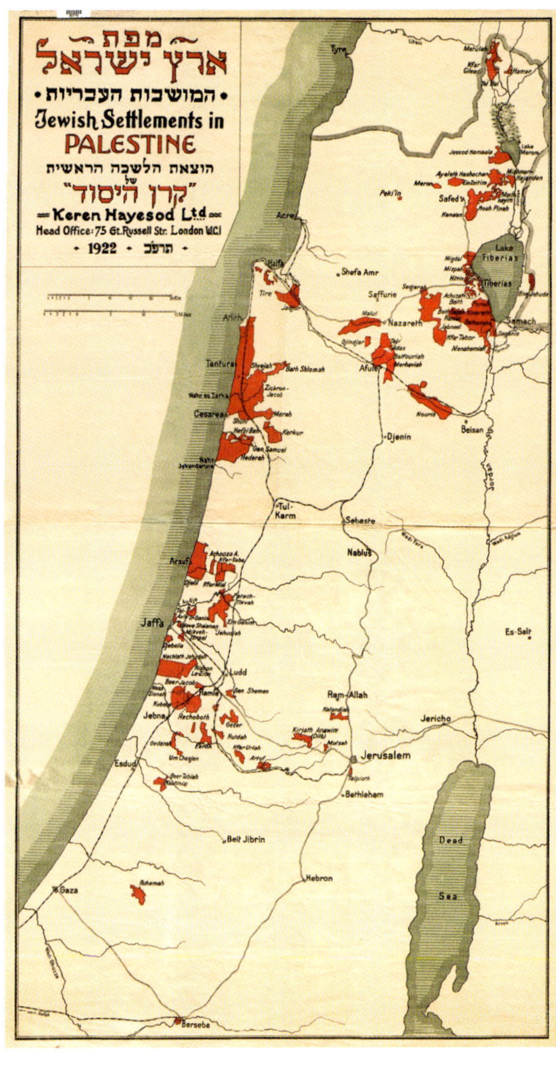

FIG. 151: Jewish settlements in Palestine, map by the Karen Hayesod, established at the World Zionist Congress in London in 1920 as a fund-raiser for Zionist settlement. London, 1922. [Bibliothèque National, ark:/12148/btv1b10104158b]

By marketing it under the brand name *Israel*, the Zionists' "product" was the sacred realm venerated in Christian masses, spirituals, and in some of the most profound works of Western art—a place-name originating in Genesis and seemingly created by God, one that touches a chord deep within its sponsor states' collective cultural subconscious and against which unkind words are a sacrilege. Christian messianism + sacred nomenclature fused to form a magic shield around the project, a magic shield without which the Israeli state's entire arsenal would be impotent.

Old Testament place-names became "proof" of modern Zionist ownership of the land. In June 1947, Menachem Begin, future Israeli prime minister but at the time the wanted leader of the terror gang Irgun, used the argument to threaten members of UNSCOP, the UN body then deciding Palestine's future. "Is it not absurd to turn the Hills of Judea, Samaria, and the Galilee over to non-Hebrew ownership?" he pushed selected committee members, who had been secreted to his hideout circumlocuitously and blindfolded. "Do not the names themselves bear evidence to whom they rightfully belong?" The circular-reasoning was to reinforce his threats of world-wide terror should the UN not give all of Palestine to the Zionists—threats that the UN knew represented mainstream Zionism.[39]

FIG. 152: Irgun emblem, a rifle over a map of "Erez Israel." The map shows Israel as perceived in its grandest Biblical context, which includes Jordan and part of Lebanon and Egypt.

The vertical line to the left of the rifle is the Jordan River, with the Sea of Galilee and Dead Sea shown. Historic Palestine—the land to the left of that line—is the blue and brown areas of the Partition map on the next page.

The rifle symbolizes what the emblem says in English and French: that the taking of the entire land by force of arms is "the sole solution." From an Irgun leaflet, *The Jewish Struggle*, London, January, 1946. [Photograph T Suárez]

THE BRIEF, FRAUGHT LIFE OF THE PARTITION MAP: AN AUTOPSY

Five months later, in November 1947, the UN ripped up the map of whole Palestine and proposed a map of chopped-up Palestine in its place: the 1947 UN Partition plan (fig. 153) which—ostensibly—divided historic Palestine, the region from the Jordan River to the Mediterranean Sea, between a "Jewish" and an "Arab" state, plus a small international zone comprising Jerusalem and Bethlehem. The map was christened on November 29 with the UN's passage of Resolution 181, and was to go into effect six and a half months later, with the end of the British Mandate. To say that the map was a failure would be misleading. Rather, it was never intended to succeed—or, perhaps more accurate to say that it succeeded brilliantly in what it was actually designed to accomplish.

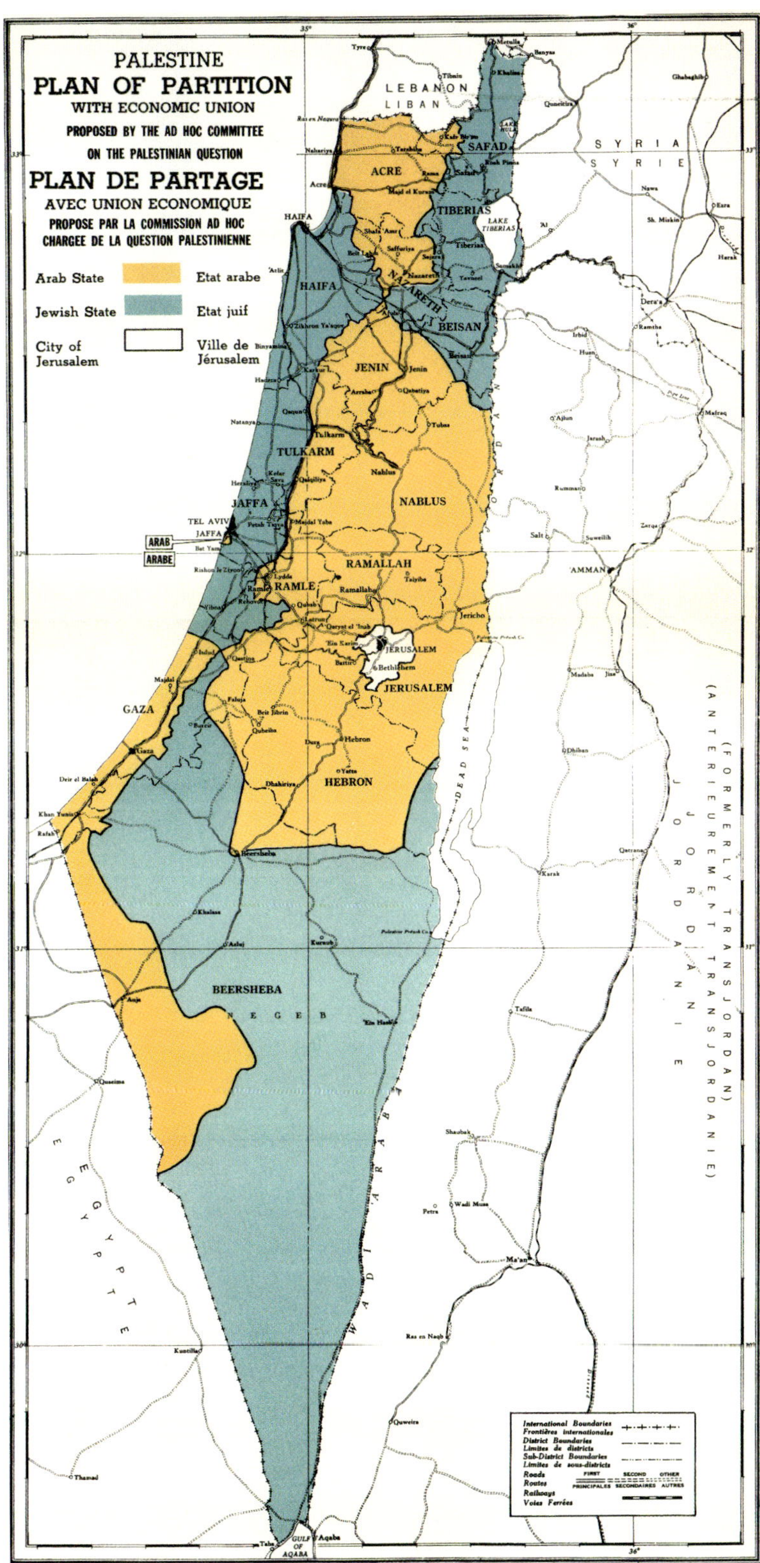

FIG. 153: The UN Partition of 1947, UNGA Resolution 181, Annex "A," partitioned river-to-sea between a "Jewish" and "Arab" state as recommended in UNGA Resolution 181: the blue, Zionist, the brown, Palestinian. The white area near the middle was to be an international zone encompassing Jerusalem and Bethlehem. [source: UN Document symbol: 103.1 (b)], scan of a 1956 printing]

To understand the map, we need first to briefly backtrack three decades. In 1917, among the Zionists' key selling points for British support was their claim to be surrogate empire builders. A modest Zionist presence in Palestine, the sales pitch went, would help Britain add the coveted jewel to its collection. As the years passed, this however did not play out as advertised. By the 1940s, the Zionists, having sufficiently established themselves, instead waged a terror campaign to oust the British, such that by 1947 the British were anxious to evacuate (their word). That "evacuation" is what Partition was about.

Getting all of Palestine at a minimum, and depopulating it of non-Jews, had always been the Zionists' singular goal, from the "moderates" of the Jewish Agency who argued their case at the UN, to the acknowledged terror gangs, principally the Irgun and Lehi.[40] They differed only in tactic. The terror gangs were ideologically driven; they demanded the entire land (in its wide Biblical definition) outright as their God-given property, as illustrated in the Irgun emblem in fig. 152 and the cartoon in fig. 154. The Jewish Agency also invoked the Bible as its "deed" to the land, but was pragmatic. It recognized the risk that the UN might be forced to propose a single democratic state if pushed to grant all the land. The surer strategy was to get recognized Zionist sovereignty on part of the land and then, armed with the mantle of statehood, take over and ethnically cleanse the rest by force. Partition was a chess move, a means to a different end.

FIG. 154: Zionist anti-Partition cartoon. Juxtaposed between Nazi death camps and an angel reasserting God's promise of "Eretz Israel" to "the children of Israel," British Foreign Secretary Ernest Bevin (left) and Prime Minister Clement Attlee use scissors in allegorical partitioning of their "Map of Palestine." Palestine is here much of the Middle East, the parameters cited in the cartoon's title, thus dramatically overstating the Zionist "loss" of land. (The Jordan River is the line closer to Bevin, with the Dead Sea at its end.) The cartoon is from *The Jewish Struggle,* a newspaper supporting the terror gangs Irgun and Lehi, and opposing the Jewish Agency's pragmatic flirtation with Partition. [London, August 1946, The National Archives (UK), HO 45/25586, photograph T Suárez]

"Moderate" Chaim Weizmann, who would become Israel's first president, described the tactic to Benito Mussolini during his 1934 meeting with the fascist dictator. Statehood on any part of the land, he explained, was the "Archimedean fulcrum"—with its leverage, they would conquer the rest. David Ben-Gurion, who would become the state's first prime minister, proposed it three years later, after the Peel Commission produced the first formal plan for Partition. He refined the strategy by 1941, writing that it would be "an irreparable mistake" to *suggest* Partition; instead, statehood should be extracted from the *offer* of Partition—precisely as events played out in November 1947. Once the state is secured, he wrote, it would then be enlarged by force to the Jordan River at least, and into Transjordan if possible.[41]

During 1947, as the UN publicly claimed to be weighing the fate of Palestine, Partition was already assumed to be the answer, *and* it was assumed to be a fraud. As the British Colonial Office put it in February that year, Partition was for the Zionists merely a "temporary expedient."[42] US-UK documents state outright at the time that there will be no Palestinian state, and even speak of "giving" tidbits of the spoils to the surrounding countries to buy their acquiescence. What was the motivation? Why, when November came, did the UN approve it, knowing it was a scam? British documents record the reason: the certainty of heightened Zionist terror if they did not, terror that had already reached Britain and Europe. By granting the Jewish Agency what it wanted, Britain could walk away from the catastrophe it had created, and the UN could claim to have acted. The Palestinians would be left as the terrorism's sole victims.

But the pretend Partition still had to be mapped—and for the fledgling UN's esteem, it mattered *how* it was mapped. The British, again, recorded the thinking: the UN drew the Partition line to give more than half of Palestine to the Zionists, far in excess of their settlements' population, in the theory that doing so would bide the world body a bit of time before Israel's armies expanded beyond and pronounced the map dead. In effect, the UN placed the Partition where it estimated Israel would reach after its first expansionist war. Even this cynicism, however, proved naive. The Jewish Agency began defying the map's artificially large boundaries immediately after the UN vote, snuffing out the map's last breath within two weeks. In mid-December 1947, still six months before the map was supposed to take effect—and, should it matter, six months before the "Arab armies" entered the scene—the British already confirm its death with the simple epitaph: "It does not appear that Arab Palestine will be an entity."

The Zionists were elated at the passage of Partition because they understood the map's inner meaning. In the words of British High Commissioner Cunningham as he observed the jubilation firsthand, the ecstatic crowds viewed Partition simply as "a preliminary step to a Jewish state in the fullest extent of its historical bounds."[43]

The Partition map's death strategy for all-important Jaffa was particularly cynical. As a key ancient hub of Palestinian life, commerce, and culture, the UN could not have overtly "given" the city to the Zionists, and so after some deliberation, it was decided to map Jaffa as an isolated "Arab" speck, defenseless and barely visible within the

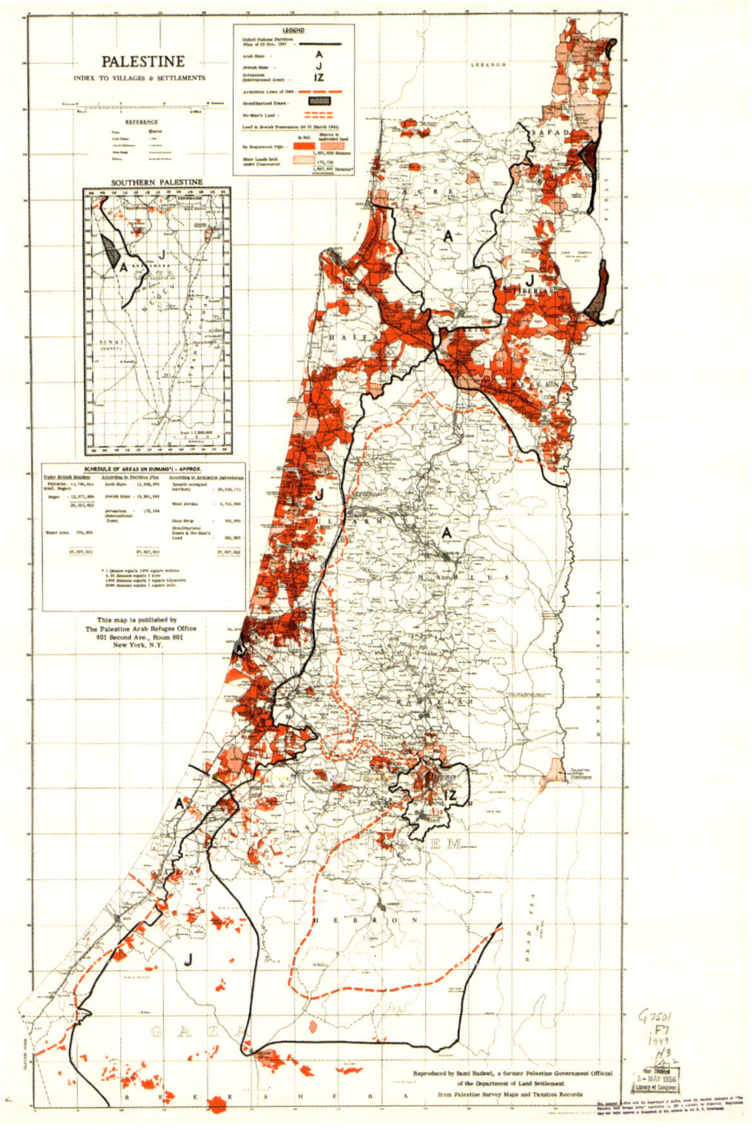

FIG. 155: Sami Hadawi was an authority on the land and population in Palestine during the British Mandate. After he and his family were ethnically cleansed from Jerusalem in 1948, he devoted himself to documenting the human displacement as well as the Zionists' theft of Palestinian property. In this map, he records the legal state of the land in the aftermath of the 1948 expulsion. Sami Hadawi, Palestine Arab Refugee Office, Palestine Refugee Office (New York), c1949 [Library of Congress, G7501.F7 1949 .H3 TIL]

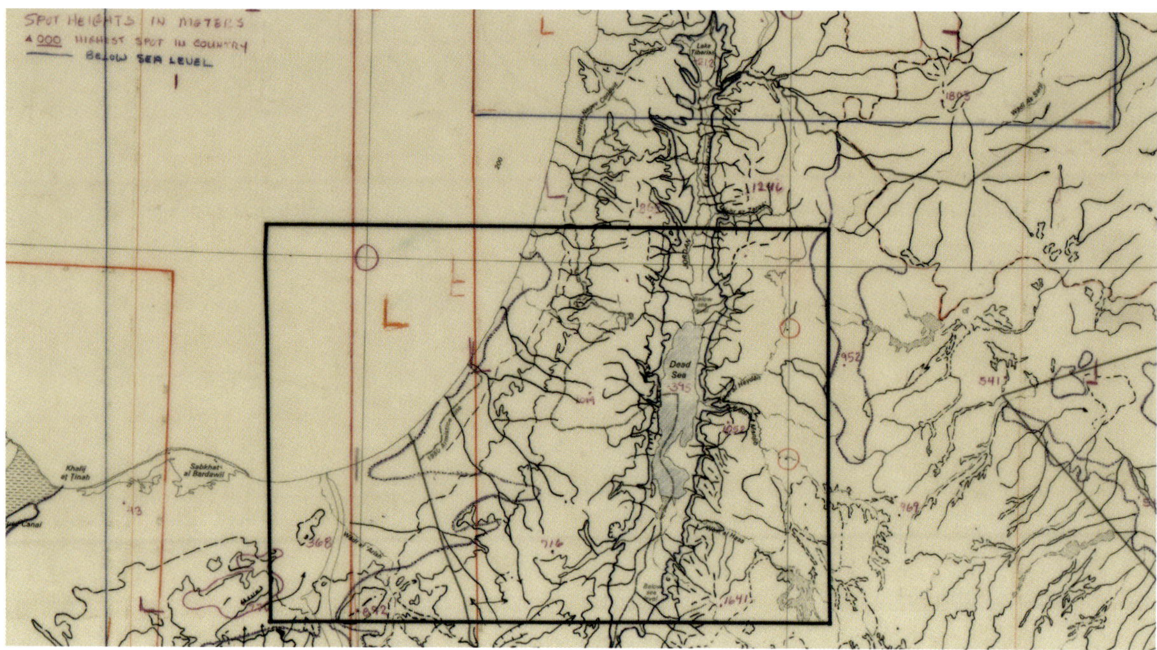

FIG. 156: Detail from a map of the eastern Mediterranean by USA's Central Intelligence Agency's terrain specialists using Swiss "ridge and valley" techniques. United States, Central Intelligence Agency, 1958(?) [Library of Congress, G3201.C2 coll .C6]

Zionist side. This enabled the iconic Palestinian city to be overrun and depopulated in the first days of 1948, swallowed whole with barely a perceptible change to the common cartographic image of the land. The Partition map simply "disappeared" it.[44]

A further gear in the Partition map's erasure of Palestine was its use of the common (but illogical) terminology "Arab state" versus "Jewish state." Jews are a religious and cultural group, whereas Arabs are a linguistic group that included many Jews. But "Arab" had become code for non-Jews, making it easier for them to be "othered" into the surrounding "Arab" countries, while "Jewish state" not only smoothed the ethnic cleansing of non-Jews from it, but formalized Israel's exploitation of Jews as a human shield. With the article *the* added as an integral part of the name, the term "the Jewish state" made ethnicity + nation-state synonymous in order to define criticism of that state as anti-Jewish racism ("antisemitism"). This tribal-geographic-ethnic construct is unique; no analogy exists to any other nation-state with an official or implicit religious or ethnic association.

The modern nation-state, the idea itself—now blending into the old geographic term "country"—had become the measure of all things. Armed with the magic geopolitical term "country," Zionist terror became Israeli military actions, and Palestinians taken hostage became "prisoners." Denied the magic term, Palestinians' self-defense was "terrorism" and attacking Israeli soldiers taken prisoner were "hostages." The systematic blocking of a Palestinian state had to do with more than just stealing land: in our modern geo-political mindset, it had to do with stealing Palestinian personhood.

Such was the industrial scale of Israel's depopulation of non-Jewish villages in 1948 that it soon had no more Biblical place-names for new settlements, and so new ones were created from Talmudic names, from Zionist heroes, and historical references. As but one example, after the Israeli state exterminated the Palestinian village of al-Dawayima in October 1948, it invented the name *Amatzia* for the settlement built on its ruins, after King Amaziah of Judah, who reigned in the eighth century BCE. At the time of its destruction in 1948, al-Dawayima was a town of about 3,800 people; Amazia's today is roughly 200.[45]

FIG. 157: The beginning of "O come, O come, Emmanuel" (*Veni, veni, Emmanuel*), a Christian hymn with origins in monastic life of the 8th or 9th century. [here, John Mason Neale translation, in *Hymns Ancient and Modern*, 1861]

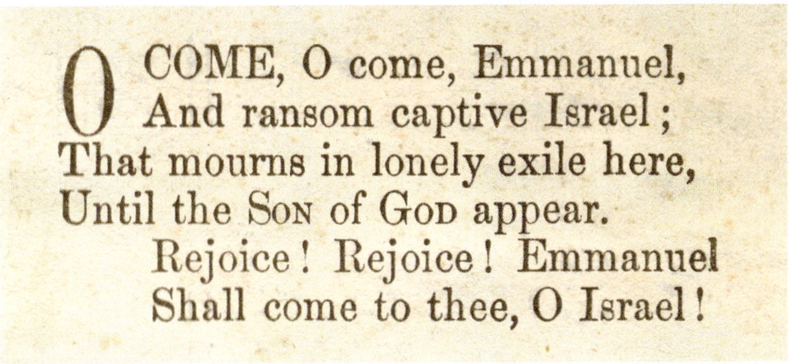

O COME, O come, Emmanuel,
And ransom captive Israel;
That mourns in lonely exile here,
Until the SON of GOD appear.
Rejoice! Rejoice! Emmanuel
Shall come to thee, O Israel!

THE PLACE NAME *ISRAEL*

Winston Churchill offers a striking example of the extraordinary military power of the sound *Israel* over the Western psyche. When in the first days of January 1949, the new Israeli state shot down five British planes sent to observe its aggression in the Sinai, killing two British pilots, Churchill not only defended Israel, but branded the UK's foreign secretary as "antisemitic" for condemning the attacks—bizarre behavior explained only by Churchill's belief that "Israel" is *Israel*. "I seem to have heard of it in bygone days," he quipped in defense of Israel's attacks.[46]

The mystique of the place-name *Israel* in the Western psyche enables Israeli leaders and their Western partners to paint its adversaries in apocalyptic or oracular light—a fight between good and evil, between light and darkness, between civilization and barbarism in US and Israeli political talk. Gazan victims of genocide are made into the Amalek, a Biblical people that God commanded Israel to exterminate outright, every man, woman, child, infant, cattle, sheep, camel, and donkey. Lest that be insufficient, the Palestinians became Biblical monsters: "Is the Israel-Hamas war the war of Gog and Magog?" as a June 2024 headline in the *Jerusalem Post* read.[47]

The place-name *Israel* continues to power the psychosis to which even stewards of the US's most prestigious academic institutions cower. "Are you familiar with Genesis 12:3?" a US congressman asked the president of Columbia University in 2024 in a formal hearing called to address anti-genocide campus activity. "Well, it's pretty clear." God, he explained, told Abraham that "If you bless Israel, I will bless you. If you curse Israel, I will curse you'." Unless she stops campus activity critical of Israel, he warned, her university will "be cursed by God, of the Bible"—to which the Columbia president assured him that she did not want this to happen. The following day, she authorized the New York Police Department to conduct mass arrests of the demonstrators—in fear for her job, not in fear of curses. Similarly, US legislation requiring citizens' anti-boycott loyalty oaths to Israel is supported by the same nomenclature-powered end-of-time fundamentalism—the need for "the Jewish people" to "go back to their homeland ... before Christ returns," as one US lawmaker explained it.[48]

With the power of Biblical nomenclature, the Israeli state became the prophesized Third Temple, and Levantine archeological sites throughout the region became the state's history. Israel's Biblical wardrobe expanded as needed to incorporate its battles, its enemies, its conquests, its challenges, its tragedies, its victories. Emotive labels make its crimes unassailable, through to the genocidal "Operation Gideon's Chariots" against Gaza as this book goes to print in 2025, from the Biblical story of Israel's destruction of the Midianites.

AFTER PARTITION: TWO STILL-BORN MAPS

As Israel's militias seized ever more Palestinian land during the summer of 1948, a revised Partition map was drawn by the UN mediator, Folke Bernadotte. His map proved fatal: Along with his insistence that the refugees return home and that borders be enforced, Bernadotte's map was why the Israeli state assassinated him on September 17, just as it was to be published.[49] The map's offense was not so much its proposed borders, as Israel could simply ignore these as it did the old, but its maintenance of Jerusalem as an international zone. Israel knew it could continue to displace the Palestinians with impunity, but voiding the map's Jerusalem would mean waging war against the "international community."

With Bernadotte and his map dead, Israel continued its seizure of Palestinian land and Jerusalem until, at the end of 1948, the UN mapped ceasefire lines to halt the fighting (fig. 158). Lest it leave any room for interpretation, this Armistice map made explicit that its line was not a new de facto border, as more than half the land the UN had given to the Palestinians lay on the Israeli side. But instead of retreating, Israel went further: it not only quickly settled the Palestinian land it occupied between Partition and the Armistice, but also took Mt. Scopus, which lay on the Palestinian side of the Armistice.

The map went through two transformations at the behest of Israeli expansion. First, its line began morphing into precisely what it is not—a provisional border "giving" Israel the additional stolen land—and after the 1967 war it became known as the "1967 borders." Next, to begin annexing the land beyond that "border," in October and November of 1967 Israel passed then-secret rulings that its maps would not mark the line at all.[50] Thus one map that would seem to be rudimentary for our subject does not exist: a map of Israel's borders. Since the state was founded, it has refused to declare any.

The use of maps as a military weapon continues as digital mapping centralizes control of geographic information. Tested by the author in Israel-Palestine in 2019, Google, the public's dominant source of maps, professed complete ignorance of indigenous Palestinian cities in the West Bank but was eager to help if the destination was any Israeli settlement in it.

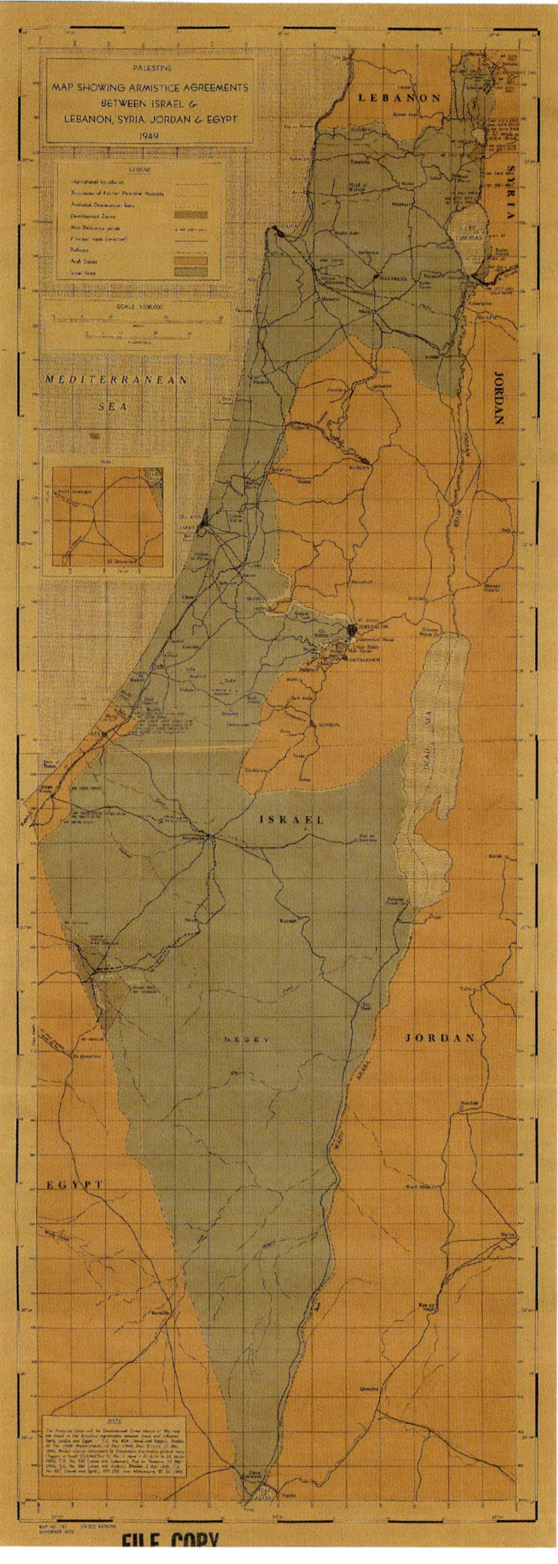

FIG 158: United Nations map showing Armistice Agreements between Israel and Lebanon, Syria, Jordan, and Egypt, 1949. [New York, UN, Nov. 1955]

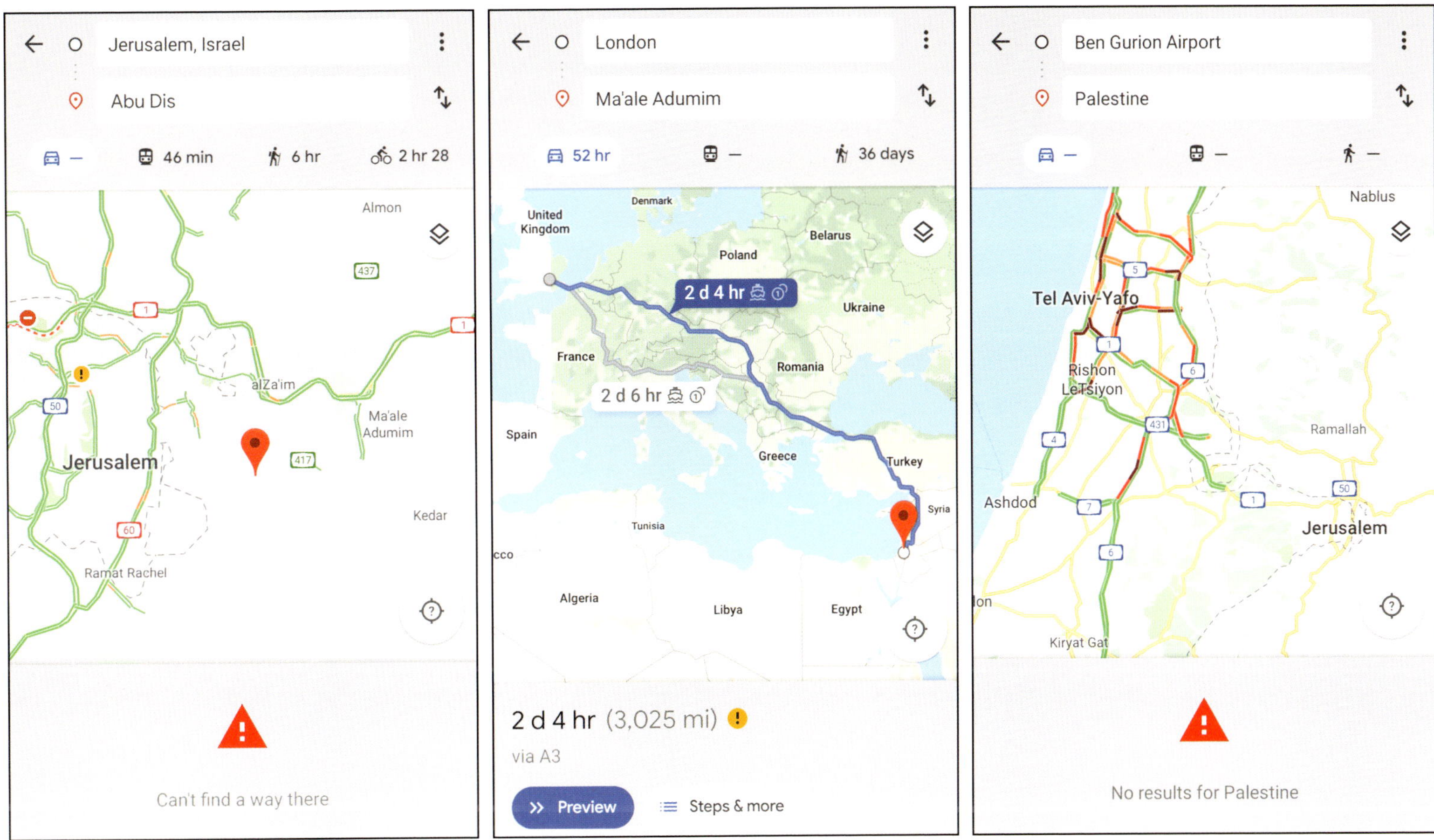

FIG. 159: Screen-grabs of GoogleMaps on an Android phone, 2019. To be mapped is to exist: "No results for Palestine" (3rd map). [T. Suárez]

Google "can't find a way" to go from Jerusalem to Abu Dis (fig. 159), a village so close that part of it is orphaned into Jerusalem by Israel's apartheid wall, but instantly showed the route to the Israeli settlement of Ma'ale Adumim, which encroaches upon Abu Dis—indeed it quickly complied when asked for driving directions to that settlement from London. Nor could Google figure out how to get from Bethlehem to Hebron, the largest city in the West Bank, twenty-two kilometers away on Route 60, but to any of the Hebron-area Israeli settlements, yes. To Jericho, a city of about 21,000 people that has been continuously inhabited for millennia, Google feigned ignorance, but from the same spot it took barely a moment to give driving directions to Israel's Jericho-area Beit Ha'Arava outpost of about 450 settlers.[51]

GoogleMaps' "disappearing" of Palestine is structurally akin to the geographic psychology we saw in the previous chapter, in which people's right to live in their own homes on their own land is not intrinsic, but dependent on the concordance of selected nomenclature and ethnic labels. Why does the entirety of river-to-sea belong to the Israeli state (implicitly, cleansed of non-Jews)? Why are there no "occupied territories"? As the *Jerusalem Post* explains in oft-heard fashion, it is because of the Romans' use of a geographic name two thousand years ago: "the Romans renamed the entire region Syria-Palestina … so as to erase its Jewish roots."[52]

What is extraordinary about this argument for ethnic cleansing is not its "facts" (the name *Palestine* pre-dates the Romans), nor even the implicit anti-Jewish insinuation that Jews cannot cohabit the same land with other people. Rather, its importance is that we are geographically hard-wired to accept that the premise matters: that the ancient origins of a place-name has the power to grant or deny personhood today, to justify the expulsion of anyone to whom that geographic name is or is not attached.

The ghettoization of river-to-sea continues to be fueled by nomenclature and the bantustanization of non-Jews. There is East Jerusalem, treated as part of the state for Jews but part of the West Bank for non-Jews. There is the West Bank, an invented designation to accomodate Israel's 1948 land grab and the blocking of Palestinian sovereignty, itself chopped up into semi-bantustans on behalf of Israeli settlers. And there is Gaza, the bantustan "strip" sealing off those within it from the rest of humanity, as if designated by Israel as the nether realm of a separate race.

Israel treats river-to-sea, and in particular Jerusalem, as a virtual Biblical theme park, a Holy Land tourist map come to life. Any state rich in archaeological remains will flaunt them to bring in tourist money, but Israel's principal purpose is distinct: it is to reinforce the ethno-geographic message that *we are that country you praise and sing about in church. These ancient ruins are ours, and we alone are their people.* "Biblical" archaeological sites east of the Jordan serve to cast the state's conquest of historic Palestine as simply a fraction of what it is owed.

A complete map of the river to the sea would show not just what is there, but also what is missing—millions of people who belong on the map but are interned in surrounding countries because they are not Jewish.[53] A complete map would mark stolen property—homes whose actual owners are locked in camps elsewhere because they are not Jewish. A complete map would show what is there but not visible—aquifers diverted along Israel's pseudo-racial methodology, the whereabouts of the tens of thousands of people kidnapped by the Israeli state, pollution in Gaza's coastal waters by Israel's destruction of its infrastructure, the limits imposed by Israel on Gazan fishermen in their own waters.

Images of ornate sixteenth through eighteenth century "maps of the Holy Land" (in quotes because it is a genre with its own cultural references) grew in popularity in recent decades in the form of lavishly illustrated books, calendars, reproductions, wall hangings, and other merchandising, as well as the sale of the original engravings or woodcuts to collectors. The genre, itself blameless, is exploited to reinforce the deep-rooted mysticism associating the state with the realm in the holy books. Many survive in sufficient numbers that they are commonly traded, and the act of ownership of an original centuries-old map of "Israel" furthers that emotional investment.

A map that, in contrast, does reflect the soul of the Israeli state is one of Gaza that the Israeli military air-dropped over the "strip" in 2009 (fig. 160). Arabic text accompanying the map orders the people in Gaza never to approach within a thousand feet of Israel's heavily militarized "fence," at risk of death. As that forbidden land is the furthest inland, it is Gaza's most fertile.

Who are the recipients of this map, and what happens to them if they disobey it?

Many of the people thrown off their land by Zionist militias in 1948 were shoved into Gaza. Those who tried to go home were either shot dead on sight or captured, often tortured, some then sent on a death march into the desert. Over the decades, Israel conducted various massacres against the population it kept trapped, killing thousands, and increasingly controlled their lives' every aspect. Until October 7 2023, it was a slow-motion genocide calculated to avoid headlines, a genocide fed by Israel's utter terror of Palestinian humanity and Palestinian achievement.

In 2018, people in Gaza disobeyed the map that

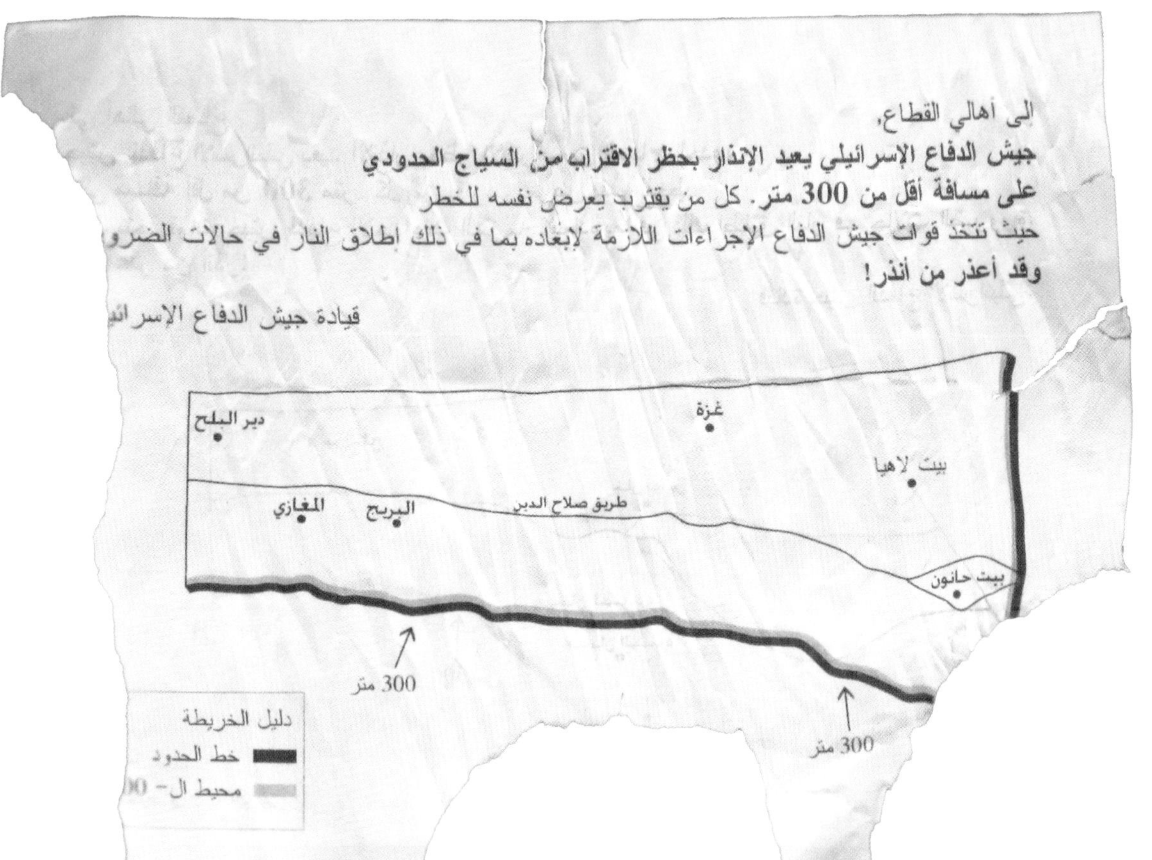

FIG 160: A map air-dropped by the Israeli Air Force over Gaza, ordering its people not to approach within 300 meters of the Israeli barrier, else measures such as "live ammunition" will be used: "Forewarned is forearmed." Gaza's most fertile fishing grounds are also deadly for Palestinians. [photo: T. Suárez, Gaza, 2009]

had fallen from the heavens. Many staged a purely symbolic "March of Return" into the forbidden area in an attempt to bring their desperation to the world's attention. Israeli snipers shot dead two hundred, including medical workers rushing to help the injured, and crippled hundreds more. Since Israeli violence is self-vindicating—the more the state's violence, the more proof that it is defending itself—it successfully spun the atrocity to the receptive West as the thwarting of a Palestinian attack.

And so, the map tells two stories. There is the story it tells those who made it: the map assures them that the people they have locked up in Gaza are so dangerous that "the Jewish state" cannot risk any of them even approaching the militarized barrier of their near-impenetrable camp. But there is also the story the map wants to tell everyone else: that its mapping of Gaza is metaphor. It is actually a map of the soul of Zionism and the Israeli state.

The genocide in progress as this book goes to print is genocide in its truest sense: its goal is not just the erasure of a people, but the erasure of their memory. A step beyond other genocides, Zionism's requires that the Palestinians never existed, not merely that they no longer exist. Maps and nomenclature are a key weapon in this erasure: to be mapped is to *be*; and to be cleansed from the map is never to have been.

Understanding Palestine in its myriad cartographic dimensions, physical and conceptual, is essential to understanding how we got to where we are. As with all history, examining the history of maps is not just for posterity; it is primarily to help us navigate the present and tack toward a better future. The mapping of Palestine is a mirror of ourselves—it has much to tell us.

WORKS CONSULTED

Adler, Marcus Nathan, *The Itinerary of Benjamin of Tudela: Critical Text, Translation and Commentary* [New York: Phillip Feldheim, Inc., 1907].

Arculfus, *The Pilgrimage of Arculfus in the Holy Land (about the year A.D. 670), Translated and Annotated by the Rev. James Rose MacPherson, B.D.* [Palestine Pilgrims' Text Society, London 1895].

Audeh, Ida, and Kate Rouhana, "The Unusual Origins of an Iconic East Jerusalem Hotel," dated July 1, 2024, accessed from jerusalemstory.com, August 2024.

Bacon, Roger, *The Opus Majus of Roger Bacon*, translation John Henry Bridges, Henry Frowde, Oxford, 1897.

Bartlett, John R. (Editor), *Burchard of Mount Sion, O.P.: Descriptio Terrae Sanctae* (Oxford Medieval Texts) 2019.

Bicheno, James, *The Restoration of the Jews – The Crisis of All Nations*, London, 1800 (copy examined 2nd edition, 1807).

Breydenbach, *Bernhard von Breydenbach and his Journey to the Holy Land 1483–4*, a bibliography compiled by Hugh Wm. Davies, J. & J. Leighton Mdccccxi (1911).

Thomas Brightman, The Revelation of Saint John, Illustrated with Analysis and Scholions... Wherein the restoring of the Jewes, and their calling to the faith of Christ... (1644)

Brown, Wesley, *The World Image Expressed in the Rudimentum Novitiorum*, Philip Lee Phillips Society Occasional Paper Series, No. 3, Library of Congress, 2000.

Casola, Pietro /Mary Margaret Newett (editor), *Pilgrimage to Jerusalem in the year 1494* [Manchester University, 1907].

Cohen, Saul B., and Nurit Kliot, "Israel's Place-Names as Reflection of Continuity and Change in Nation-Building," in *Names A Journal of Onomastics*, Vol 29, 1981, p227-248

Conder, Claude Reignier, *The Latin Kingdom of Jerusalem, 1099 to 1291 A.D.*, Committee of the Palestine Exploration Fund, 1897.

Eusebius, *The Onomasticon of Eusebius Pamphili compared with the version of Jerome and annotated by C. Umhau Wolf*, 1971.

Giles, Lionel, "Translations from the Chinese World Map of Father Ricci," Lionel Giles, *The Geographical Journal*, Vol. 52, No. 6 (December 1918), p. 367–385.

Harding, Gerald, "The Cairn of Hani," *Annual of the Department of Antiquities of Jordan*, vol. II, 1953.

Hoskin, Philippa, "Matthew Paris' flawed prediction of the end of the world," Corpus Christi College (Cambridge) [n.d.].

Karamustafa, Ahmet T., "Military, Administrative, and Scholarly Maps and Plans," HOC, Islamic Cartography, p. 209, in *The History of Cartography*, J. B. Harley and David Woodward (ewds), The University of Chicago Press, 1987+.

Kobler, Franz, "Sir Henry Finch (1558–1625) and the first English advocates of the restoration of the Jews to Palestine," in *Transactions* (Jewish Historical Society of England), Vol. 16 (1945–1951), pp. 101–120.

Lampert-Weissig, Lisa, The Shape of the End: Zombies and the End Times, Revenant Journal, pp. 16–43.

— "The Wandering Jew as Relic in Matthew Paris's Chronica majora, in her Instrument of Memory," University of Michigan Press, 2024.

Levy-Rubin, Milka, "The Rediscovery of the Uppsala Map of Crusader Jerusalem," *Deutscher verein zur Erforschung Palästinas*, Bd. 111, H. 2 (1995), pp. 162–167.

Lewis, Suzanne, *The Art of Matthew Paris in the Chronica Majora* [Univ. of California, 1987].

Mandeville, *The Travels of Sir John Mandeville / The version of the Cotton Manuscript in modern spelling*. London Macmillan and Co. Limited New York: The Macmillan Company, 1900.

Lynch, W. F., *Narrative of the United States' Expedition to the River Jordan and the Dead Sea by W. F. Lynch, U.S.N., Commander of the Expedition*, Philadelphia, 1849 [also the Richard Bentley London edition consulted].

Notitia Dignitatum (Register of Dignitaries), ca. 400, History Department of Fordham University (NY), 2024.

Palestine Exploration Fund. Articles of Association. 1879. The National Archives (UK), BT 22/23/6.

Paweł Filipczak, "An introduction to the Byzantine administration in Syro-Palestine on the eve of the Arab conquest." *Byzantina Lodziensia XXVI*, Wydawnictwo Uniwersytetu Łódzkiego, 2015.

Powers, Tom, *Jerusalem's American Colony and Its Photographic Legacy*, 2009.

Rapoport, Yossef, *Islamic Maps* [Bodleian Library, 2019].

Regina S. Sharif, *Non-Jewish Zionism: Its Roots in Western History*, Zed Books, 1983.

Ruth Kark, "The Lands of the Sultan Newly Discovered Ottoman Cadastral Maps in Palestine," in: Tolias, G. and Loupis, D. (eds), *Mediterranean Cartographies*, Athens: Institute for Neohellenic Research INR/NHRF 2004, pp. 197–222.

Sela, Rona, "Scouting Palestinian Territory, 1940–1948: Haganah Village Files, Aerial Photos, and Surveys," *Jerusalem Quarterly 52*, p. 38–50.

Seetzen, M, *A Brief Account of the Countries adjoining the Lake of Tiberias, the Jordan, and the Dead Sea. by M. Seetzen* ... Palestine Association of London, 1810.

Sizer, Stephen, "Christian Zionism: Its History, Theology and Politics," AAARGH, 2005

Vreté, Mayir, "The Restoration of the Jews in English Protestant Thought 1790-1840," *Middle Eastern Studies*, Jan 1972, Vol. 8, No. 1 (January 1972), pp. 3–50

Webster, Charles, *The Foreign Policy of Palmerston 1830-1841: Britain, the Liberal Movement and the Eastern Question*. Vol. 2, p. 761. (1951/1969)

Wilson, Charles William, *Ordnance Survey of Jerusalem, under the direction of Colonel Sir Henry James*, London: Her Majesty's Treasury, 1865.
— *The Recovery of Jerusalem. A Narrative of Exploration and Discovery in the City and the Holy Land. By Capt. Wilson, R. E., Capt. Warren, R. E., etc., with an introduction by Arthur Penrhyn Stanley, D. D., Dean of Westminster* ... 1871.

ENDNOTES

1 My thanks to Dr. Ghada Karmi, to whom I had turned for advice on the terminology. She had already faced this issue in her writing about the history of medicine, when many physicians were not Arabs, but practiced a common form of medicine called "Arabic medicine."

2 Translation from Gerald Harding, "The Cairn of Hani," *Annual of the Department of Antiquities of Jordan*, vol. II, 1953.

3 The Peutinger map is known by the meaningful-sounding Tabula Peutingeriana—but Peutinger was nothing more than a sixteenth-century owner of what is alleged to have been stolen property, and *tabula* (map) is often mistranslated, leaving us with the convoluted "Peutinger table." Efforts to change the name have failed to overcome inertia.

4 O. A. W. Dilke, "Cartography in the Byzantine Empire," p265 in Vol. 1, Harley /Woodward *History of Cartography*, states that "The Madaba map was clearly intended to instruct the faithful."

5 The UN Security Council ordered Israel to end its seizure of East Jerusalem with several Resolutions spanning 1968 to 2016: 252, 267, 271, 298, 465, 476, 478, 2334. For the Madaba map and Israeli excavation in East Jerusalem, "For the First Time the Main Road of Jerusalem, from 1,500 Years Ago, was Exposed," Israel Antiquities Authority, Feb 11 2010, reported in many popular news stories.

6 Latin and Arabic mapmaking, typically referred to as "European" and "Islamic"—see Introduction.

7 P.D.A. Harvey, in *Medieval Maps of the Holy Land*, p. 33-4, argues that this new Red Sea is an erotic forgery arranged by the nineteenth-century mathematician (and apparent thief and fraudster) Guglielmo Libri. The claim is that the new Red Sea is phallic (this explaining the lower bulge), and that Libri sought to sell it as a rare, early monastic pornographic joke for substantially more money to a private collector. This writer questions the very premise that a knowledgeable nineteenth-century fraudster might reasonably have expected that faking such a "joke" would net him a profit—rather, indeed, than risking a hefty loss. (The map was sold posthumously by his son to the Biblioteca Medicea Laurenziana, with no record of the issue.) In correspondence with the author, the Biblioteca Medicea Laurenziana took no position on the question.

8 The most detailed evaluation of the erasures is in Harvey, *Medieval Maps of the Holy Land*, p. 40–59.

9 Quoted with minor editing.

10 Harvey, *op. cit.*, p. 94, dates the "interior" map in the Archivio di Stato di Firenze at ca. 1300, which as an estimate is nominally the same as the earliest known Sanudo-Vesconte map two decades later. The later Bodleian copy is used here because it is much clearer. This map is sometimes erroneously associated with William Wey, who visited Palestine briefly in 1458.

11 Knowledge of Atlantic islands came from Portuguese exploits westward in the fifteenth century, supplemented by myth; also, extracts of the twelfth-century text of al-Idrīsī have been interpreted as suggesting Arabic contact with unspecified Atlantic islands, and may in turn have influenced Latin charts.

12 The Barcelona merchant was Domenech Pujol; See HOC, "Cartography in Medieval Europe and the Mediterranean," p. 437.

13 For al-Sharīf al-Idrīsī's background, I defer to Yossef Rapoport, *Islamic Maps*, rather than most sources placing him as a native of Ceuta and a prolific traveler (and whose ultimate work as a geographer never quite made sense chronologically).

14 Quoted from Rapoport, slightly condensed. Regarding the weight of the disc, it was said to be 400 *ratls* of 112 dirhams each (dirham = 3 grams).

15 Some lettering appears to be missing on this copy, e.g., "sy" is visible and surely should be syria. The Bodleian's copy, Tanner 190, shows no evidence of loss and has only that single word syria in the northern Levant.

16 The reader is probably aware that there is much controversy in academic circles regarding the veracity of Polo's travels. This author is more persuaded by his defenders than detractors, but the question is irrelevant to our topic, which is concerned solely with the effects of his account.

17 Translation, *The International La Sfera Challenge*.

18 The use of two registers offered some advantage beyond color: it freed the printer from the logistical problems of place-names and geography occupying the same or close space, and so a Basel printer used the process for a monochromatic map of the world in 1532. (Authorship unknown, but Sebastian Münster, cited in Chapter 4, is possible.) In 1513, the publisher of Martin Waldseemüller's edition of Ptolemy used a single-page map Lorraine to attempt a more sophisticated tri-color block printing, in which place-names were red, and wash color was added to mountains and emblems. But these early attempts were not followed up, in part because the woodblock medium was losing favor to copperplate engraving, for which the device of multiple registers was not suitable. True color map printing had to wait until the nineteenth century.

19 Sylvanus, 1511; Walseemüller, 1513 /20; Lorenz Fries, 1522 /25 /35 /41.

20 Two previous *isolarios* (island books), neither touching on Palestine, were in Italian, by Bartolommeo da li Sonetti (1485) and Benedetto Bordone (1528).

21 From Martin Luther, *On the Jews and Their Lies* (1543), translation Martin H. Bertram, AAARGH, 2009

22 The Walters Art Gallery dates the map as 1500–1600. Based on the world map in the same atlas, this author places the map much closer to 1600.

23 There is little evidence of Ottoman organized cadastral mapping of Palestine, but the possibility that such maps lay out of reach in Israeli archives has been raised. See Ahmet T. Karamustafa (re: written records), and Ruth Kark (re: maps), *op cit*.

24 Quoted from a 1941 facsimile of the original copy in the California State library.

25 Brightman, *op. cit.*, Ch XVI, p173.

26 The "Palestinian" Myth - A view from the Arab Perspective, Dr Harry Mandlebaum, *The Jewish Chronicle*, April 1, 2010; Whose land is this?, Jeffrey Levine, The *Times of Israel*, November 9 2023.

27 James Bicheno*, op cit.*, p. 79.

28 Quoted from Charles Webster, *The Foreign Policy of Palmerston 1830–1841: Britain, the Liberal Movement and the Eastern Question*, vol 2, p. 761. (1951/1969)

29 Manuscript in TNA, FO 226/120.

30 Palestine Exploration Fund, *Quarterly Statement for 1875*, London, p115-7

31 Library of Congress, "American Colony in Jerusalem, 1870 to 2006". Good family news is also cited as a "sign."

32 Library of Congress, Part I, Box 1, Folder 16: American Colony in Jerusalem. Quote marks in the original have been removed.

33 From a typewritten copy, in which not all of the original was legible to the copyist. Library of Congress, Part I, Box 2, Folder 7: American Colony in Jerusalem series: Part I: Topical File, 1871-2004.

34 Sir Henry Finch, *The World's Great Restauration, or Calling of the Jews, and with them of all Nations and Kingdoms of the Earth to the Faith of Christ* (1621), p. 2, 6.

35 New King James Version

36 *A Jewish State*, 3rd edition, NY, 1917, p.12.

37 Congressional record, 1922 House of Representatives, June 30, 1922B, National Home in Palestine for the Jewish People, cont. Pages 9809–9820.

38 For example, in 1941 at a secret meeting of (mainly) Zionist leaders, a non-Zionist participant, Robert Waley Cohen, proposed that only a neutral geographic name like "Palestine" would be inclusive of all citizens if that was truly the nature of the state being proposed. This was dismissed by Ben-Gurion, et al., on the grounds that they needed a Jewish name like Israel or Judea in order to attract enough settlers. TNA, FO 371/45355.

39 Jewish Legion, *Report of the Conference between Representatives of the United Nations Special Committee on Palestine and the Commander and Two Other Representatives of the Irgun Zvai Leumi*. (London: Published by the Jewish Legion, November, 1947) [Copied examined: TNA, KV 5/39]

40 That the Zionists, including the "moderates," were unwaveringly determined to sieze and ethnically cleanse Palestine since at least the immediate post-WWI period is incontrovertable, but beyond the remit of this book. The reader is directed to, e.g., Ilan Pappé's seminal *Ethnic Cleansing of Palestine*, or this author's *Palestine Hijacked*.

41 Chaim Weizmann to Benito Mussolini, Rome, February 17, 1934; Ben-Gurion, his 1937 letter to his son Amos; Regarding 1941, his "Outline of Zionist Policy" (see Suárez, *Palestine Hijacked*, page 256.

42 TNA, KV2 2251, "The I.Z.L. and the Jewish Agency." For a detailed account of the Partition, with citations, see Suárez, *Palestine Hijacked*, chapter 6.

43 TNA, FCO 141/14284, No. 295, 12th December, 1947, among others.

44 This was so successful that the multipart "disappearing Palestine" maps promoted by Palestinian advocacy groups today typically forget Jaffa on their Partition segment, unwittingly hiding this key Israeli depopulation of non-Jews.

45 1945 statistics, al-Dawayima had a population of 3,710; Amatzia in 2022 was 203 (Israel Central Bureau of Statistics)

46 TNA, FO 800/811, "Prime Minister's Personal Minute,"

M512-52, October 19, 1951.

47 The source of this particular Good vs. Evil quote, typical of many, is Mike Johnson, Speaker of the House of Representatives, "US evangelicals drive Republican support for Israel," BBC News, November 15 2023. Gog and Magog, *Jerusalem Post* staff, June 16, 2024.

48 Statement of Minouche Shafik, President, Columbia University, before the Committee on Education and the Workforce, US House of Representatives, April 17, 2024 (exchange is with Rep. Rick Allen, R-Ga). For boycott, Alan Leveritt, "We're a Small Arkansas Newspaper. Why Is the State Making Us Sign a Pledge About Israel?," *New York Times*, Nov. 22, 2021. The anti-BDS loyalty quote is by Senator Bart Hester of Arkansas.

49 Bernadotte's murder is usually attributed to Lehi ("Stern Gang"), but this is incorrect. While Lehi assassins did indeed pull the trigger, they were working for the Israeli state under Ben-Gurion, not Lehi. See Suárez, *Palestine Hijacked*, 289-96.

50 "Erasure of the Green Line," in Akevot, Institute for Israeli-Palestinian Conflict Research.

51 According to the National Library of Israel, the 2021 population of Ha'Arava was 451.

52 Lee Bender, "'Occupied' Territories?: Hebrew Origins of Palestinian Arab Towns in Judea-Samaria," *Jerusalem Post*, Jan 18 2017.

53 See Suárez, "Palestinians remain holed up in internment, not 'refugee,' camps," *Middle East Monitor*, Aug 2, 2023.

54 Israeli maps also block Gaza fishermen from Gaza's most fertile fishing grounds.

Following its expanded occupation and ethnic cleansing of Palestine after the 1967 war, Israel banned any expression of Palestinian identity, including the colors of the Palestinian flag as metaphor—for example, a watermelon (Military Order 101, August 1967). Ten years' imprisonment was the penalty if caught. The forbidden metaphor-fruit reemerged in response to anti-Palestinian crackdowns of the post-October 2023 world, including, most defiantly, as a map of river-to-sea, the rind the Jordan River and eastern frontier. In response, in 2025 the New York Police Department labeled the image of the watermelon in this context a "symbol of hate." [image T Suárez]

ABOUT THE AUTHOR

Thomas Suárez possesses a rare combination of expertise for this book's cross-disciplinary demands. He authored three previous books on the history of cartography, chapters in academic volumes, curated an exhibit of early maps at the Federal Reserve in Washington, DC, and designed the La Jolla Map Museum. His *Early Mapping of Southeast Asia* (1999), widely considered the standard work on the subject, was among the evidence used by the Philippine government at the UN in 2013 in its successful challenge to Chinese maritime aggression (Annex 528); and in 2007, it was Suárez who contacted Scotland Yard and correctly identified cartographic treasures stolen from the National Library of Spain, leading to their return and the arrest of the thief.

His books on Zionist-era Palestine have been praised by such icons as Ilan Pappé and Noam Chomsky. In Palestine, he taught violin at the Jerusalem branch of Palestine's National Conservatory of Music, but was then blocked by Israel from teaching violin in Gaza. He was however a firsthand observer to the aftermath of Israel's "Cast Lead" attacks on Gaza of Dec 2008 to Jan '09.

Israel's Origins and Evolution

Israel in Biblical Times

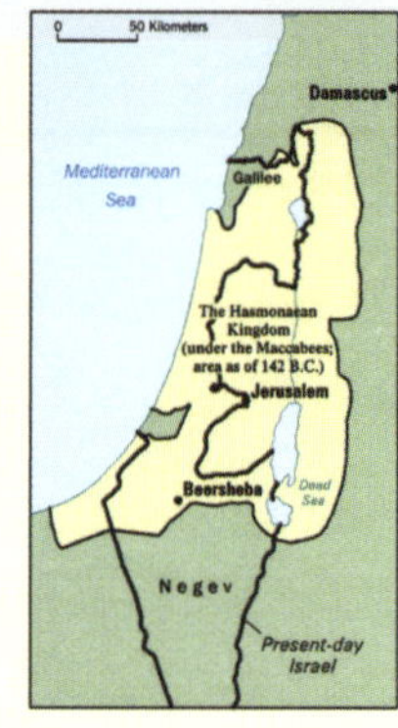

The difficult boundary, territorial, and resource problems associated with the presence of an Israeli state surrounded by Arab peoples can be understood only in the context of the long history of the Jewish people. In that history, a united, independent Israel has existed during only a few relatively short periods. Biblical writings indicate that King David first united the Jewish tribes around 1000 B.C.; his influence probably extended from the Gulf of Aqaba to the Euphrates but did not include Philistia—the vicinity of the present-day Gaza Strip. Following the death of his son Solomon some 70 years later, the kingdom split into two weaker states: Israel, conquered by Assyria in 722 B.C.; and Judah, conquered by Babylon in 586 B.C.

After a series of foreign rulers, Jews again experienced approximately a century of self-rule under the Maccabees between 166 B.C. and 63 B.C. Although the bounds of this kingdom extended into what is now western Jordan, they did not encompass parts of the Negev and Galilee that are now Israeli territory. The Roman conquest ended Jewish autonomy, and, after several Jewish revolts, Rome expelled many Jews from their homeland, which the Romans called Palestine. Most of the world's Jewish population remained outside Palestine for the next 18 centuries.

Palestine (British Mandate) 1920-48

Although Jews kept alive the hope of returning to Palestine, the concept of a Jewish state there did not crystallize until the founding of the World Zionist Organization in 1897. Subsequently, immigration by European Jews accelerated, and—after the Balfour Declaration of 1917 extended British encouragement to Zionist aspirations—Jews increasingly settled in Palestine, which the League of Nations mandated to Britain in 1920.

Palestine (UN Partition Plan) 1947

Jewish settlement during the mandate years aroused Arab resentment and led to frequent strife. The 1947 United Nations partition plan—which would have created a Jewish state, an Arab state, and a UN-administered Jerusalem—sought to resolve this conflict, but the surrounding Arab countries opposed the plan and invaded Israel immediately after it proclaimed its independence in May 1948.

Israel 1949-67

By the end of the 1948-49 war, the Israelis held more land than the UN plan had prescribed for them. About 750,000 Palestinians—some 80 percent of the Palestinians who lived in what became Israeli territory—fled or were pushed out by advancing Israeli forces to surrounding Arab countries. Jordan occupied the West Bank, which it later annexed—an act recognized only by Britain and Pakistan—and Egypt occupied and administered the Gaza Strip. Jerusalem had become a divided city: Israelis held the western, Jewish-inhabited part and Jordanians the eastern portion, including the religiously significant Old City. Israel unilaterally proclaimed West Jerusalem its capital in 1950, a move still unrecognized by most of the international community.

Israel and Occupied Territories Since June 1967

In the aftermath of the 1967 war, the Israelis occupied the West Bank, the Gaza Strip, the western portion of Syria's Al Qunaytirah Province (the Golan Heights), and Egypt's Sinai Peninsula. The Israelis reaffirmed their control of these territories during the 1973 war. In late June 1967, Israel unilaterally incorporated some 67 square kilometers of West Bank land within the city bounds of Jerusalem and in 1980 proclaimed a united Jerusalem as its capital—a move that amounted to de facto annexation. In 1981 Israel also unilaterally annexed the Golan Heights. The international community has not recognized these declarations. Israel returned the Sinai to Egypt as part of the Camp David accords; and in September 1993, Israel and the PLO—after formal mutual recognition—signed a Declaration of Principles eventually extending limited self-rule to Palestinians in the West Bank and Gaza Strip.

730773 1-94

The Gaza Strip & West Bank
~A Map Folio

Central Intelligence Agency

Directorate of Intelligence

1994: The Israeli state's creation myth is used by the US Central Intelligence Agency to explain the "conflict" to its staff and government officials

As the USA's principal foreign intelligence and counterintelligence organization, the Central Intelligence Agency (CIA) seeks out hard data and strict analysis—yet for Israel, it adopted that state's "narrative." In this map progression "prepared for the use of US Government officials," the CIA explicitly connects today's Israeli state to the Biblical King David three thousand years ago. It invokes the Zionist narrative that Jews—referring to them with the pejorative tribal connotation—"kept alive the hope of returning to Palestine," and frames their problem in terms of being "surrounded by Arab peoples." Palestine is by its very nature presented as the home of this construct of "the Jews"; but for Palestinians, their opposition to being ethnically cleansed from their own homes is dismissed as a matter of emotion rather than the most rudimentary human rights: it is framed as "Arab resentment." The preeminent US intelligence-gathering body even flubs the UN Partition Plan in Israel's favor (third map from the right): it marks Jaffa as Israeli, when it lay on the Palestinian side of Partition. [Library of Congress, G2239.6 .U5 1994]